MORE
THAN SEX

MORE
THAN SEX

REINVENTING THE
BLACK MALE IMAGE

George Edmond Smith, M.D., M.Ed.

Foreword by
Gwendolyn Goldsby Grant, Ed.D., M.A.

KENSINGTON BOOKS
http://www.kensingtonbooks.com

KENSINGTON BOOKS are published by

Kensington Publishing Corp.
850 Third Avenue
New York, NY 10022

Library of Congress Card Catalogue Number: 99-63483
ISBN 1-57566-498-4

First Printing: January, 2000
10 9 8 7 6 5 4 3 2 1

Printed in the United States of America

To my partner in life, Brenda, who has been with me every step of the way. Her contributions to the writing of this book are appreciated more than she knows. It is because of her genuine unconditional love for me, unending support, and effort that I was able to complete this task—one that, at various times, seemed to be quite overwhelming and insurmountable.

Contents

Acknowledgments

Special thanks to:

Mark DeHaven
James Wadley
Regina Rexroat
Barbara Lowenstein
Carla Fine
Karen Thomas
Dennis G. Smith
Gary W. Smith
T. Gilbert Ford
Daniel Evans
Arthur Lewis
Helen Morrison
Jackie Blake
Diane Albritten
Elba Gonzales

Additional special thanks to:

My family, for without them this story would never have been told,
and to my sister who passed away before the book's completion.

Foreword

D r. Smith has joined the ranks of physicians, therapists, counselors and psychologists who dare to forge a new frontier in the
field of psychology, which means opening up our own lives as professionals to fashion a dynamic healing model that includes the mind,
body and spirit connections. As African Americans, we share a common motherland and history and a collective (Ujima) spiritual–
psychological counteraction to life's challenges that has been our
strength in ages past, and can become our model for future healing
of the African American family.

I call George Edmond Smith, M.D., the "daring doctor:" bold, un-
afraid, focused, on a mission and filled with the healing spirit of our
ancestors. The "medicine man" for our villages, towns and cities. Not
only medicine for the mind, but medicine for the spirit.

Spiritual decline is part of the sexual demise taking place in our
communities. Confusing the physical act of sexual intercourse with
the spiritual manifestation of love is at the core of our sexual descent.
Sexual myths have become self-fulfilling prophecies in the black
community.

High divorce rates, rampant sexually transmitted diseases and a
high percentage of black children growing up without fathers is a

good indication that the false notion about black male sexual superiority is just that—a false notion. To measure one's self-worth in physical or sexual terms is to live up to standards created by others.

That is exactly what slavery conditioned us to believe: that sex and reproduction defined our primitive impulses; and, tragically, some of us are caught in the psychological chains of that slave mentality today. Dr. Smith breaks into these myths and exorcises our historical demons for us, giving us new insights.

Images of the black male have been historically distorted. Brothers have been programmed to believe that the sexual focus is the basis for manhood. Early in the book the author corrects this misconception and advises black males not to define themselves through their sexuality alone. Only immature men focus on the immediate gratification of sexual conquest.

A sex-focused life limits aspirations and self-worth. The sexual element, the author contends, has driven black men for centuries and must be replaced with a more positive, intellectual demeanor. I believe man means mind, not penis. A male infant has a penis, but he is not yet a "man." Phallic-focused men are limited in their definition of manhood and limited in success appropriations.

In my book *The Best Kind of Loving*, and as an *Essence* magazine advice columnist for over seventeen years, I have continually advised black women to find and love themselves before they look for a man. Love self first is also the theme of this book. As a psychologist, I know that love of self is a defense against immoral and violent behavior toward others.

The author agrees that friendship–companion idea should precede becoming lovers. I also believe friendship is fundamental to lasting relationships. The book makes the case, in no uncertain terms, that if you truly love yourself then you will be attracted to the loving traits of another person who possesses the same attributes. What we are advertising internally becomes what we attract externally. Here is the crux of the matter: *What you believe is what you receive.*

Research studies reveal that males tend to be visually oriented. This "surface" approach to relationships has caused many unhealthy alliances to end in divorce or single parenthood. Dr. Smith provides four phases of relationships so that brothers will not burrow themselves down into one facet of the relationship, which is usually the sex and infatuation phase.

Dominant, abusive fathers sometimes set the life pattern for young black males. The author's own father dominated the household and the challenge to overcome this crippling mind-set was part of his motivation to write this book. He challenges himself and the reader to discover "the softer side" of manhood and not to consider it unmanly or feminine. Without including the softer side of manhood, men develop poorly integrated personalities: forever limited by macho mania, which is an unhealthy lifestyle.

Hopefully, *More Than Sex* will dispel the myth that if you want to hide something from a brother, put it in a book. Once the word hits the grapevine (black communication system) about this self-inventory approach to healing our relationships that Dr. Smith has designed, helping "good lovers become great lovers and good fathers become great fathers," the race to the bookstore will turn into a stampede. That's a prediction.

Equal empowerment for males and females is the theme of this book and should become the theme song for the new millennium, helping to build strong relationships throughout the world, not only in the black community. Unconditional supportive love is the means by which we create working relationships, minus trivial fault finding and offensive name calling, that is a common occurrence in many relationships. Healthy self-image prevents these kinds of abusive exchanges, which is sometimes the precursor to domestic violence. And without a doubt, "all black men are dogs" and "all black women hoochies" clichés should be banished from our vocabularies.

Aside from the case studies in the book, which are insightful, motivating, educational and informative, the author describes the story of a young African American father and his three young children, whom he had brought to the author's office for a medical checkup. The parental scene was poignant and soul stirring. This particular father was cuddling the baby while his toddlers were playing at his feet. The beautiful imagery was so powerful in the doctor's waiting room that staff and physicians alike were captured in its glow and enraptured in that male-parenting moment.

Dr. Smith's purpose in writing this book is to preserve that paternal portrait and make it reality in the black community. His academic goal is to provide data and raise community consciousness; his spiritual–moral goal is to restore the strength of black families. That, in my mind, is a noble mission.

The mythic African American phoenix rising from the ashes of slavery is part of our black heritage, and Dr. Smith knows instinctively that we have the potential to rise up for the "second reconstruction" and rediscover what I call our "blackprints for healing." Similar to architects and engineers who need a blueprint to guide them in building a new structure, the black community needs *More Than Sex* for a better architectural design that will minimize sexual preoccupation and help to lower high divorce rates in our communities.

A majority of black children are being raised without fathers in this country. The book upholds the idea that the number one priority for black men is raising black children with a healthy sense of self-worth and self-esteem. Although the author did not have a strong father–son bond himself, he compensated for that loss with strong male models from the community.

He firmly believes that mentoring black children, especially males, is the job of every adult; and, in some cases, positive peer counseling can also be effective. Smith believes that if each black man would take responsibility for the future of just two black children, situations would begin to improve in the black community.

Sex has become the life center for many black men and the threat of impotency unbearable. What Dr. Smith found is that the introduction of Viagra as a medical remedy for impotency has also opened up the dialogue about sexual issues for some black men. The black man on "booty call" is challenged in this book and is replaced with a more reasonable view of manhood: one that is less sexual and more self-appreciative and family oriented.

The player and multiple partners attitude has only produced medical problems for the black community. For example, federal statistics project that by the year 2000, African Americans, while only 13 percent of the population, will account for 50 percent of all AIDS cases. According to the Centers for Disease Control, the rate of sexually transmitted diseases is still not under control in the black community. The Balm in Gilead, a New York-based national organization involving black churches in the fight against HIV/AIDS, is proof positive that religion has a role to play in human sexuality education also.

One study in the book emphasizes the fact that black males play a major role in the dynamics of relationships. This is particularly true of the sexual exchange. Black and Hispanic men become the focus of a sex education study that included a straightforward male responsibility for venereal disease and birth control approach. A year and a half later the results of the study determined that by placing the primary focus on educating black and Hispanic males, teen pregnancy rates dropped significantly. These findings makes this book an important contribution to the research literature on the subject of black male sexual responsibility.

Most of the sex education for pregnancy and disease prevention has been directed toward young black females. Education and intervention must also be directed toward brothers who have irresponsible sexual encounters on a regular basis. Sex education must also include teaching morals and values, along with scientific data. The author drives home the need for sex education in our schools. We must begin to view the subject of sex as just another health subject on the long list with chest X rays, blood tests, eye examinations, dental hygiene, etc. We have allowed the politics of sex to destroy the commonsense approach to the subject.

Irresponsible sex and sexually transmitted diseases are closely allied. This is also related to the idea that nothing bad can happen to me belief that some young people seem to have, what the author describes as the "indestructible syndrome." All of the sexual research data have proven this to be a very dangerous youthful fantasy. The author's medical training is helpful in eliminating false beliefs about STDs and directing the reader toward more responsible sexual conduct.

The subject of sex must be purged of taboos and old wives tales. Our Victorian attitudes only perpetuate the pornographic, forbidden fruit aphrodisiacs for young men. Everyone knows that which is forbidden has the most appeal. What is made clear in the book is that sexual prowess is not a sign of manly strength and that stimulated male genitalia should not take precedence over intelligent decision-making. In other words, *not using your erection to determine your direction.* I have continually said that all sexual decisions should be made on your feet when you are fully clothed.

African American sexual history carries with it a series of plantation abuses and resultant stereotypes that have followed us to the dawn of the new millennium. Healing this sexually aberrant saga is the task of every black household. Finding books, lecture series, support groups, a therapist, certified sex counselors is a must if we intend to master the monstrous task of dispelling the sexual myths and stereotypes that prevent us from establishing healthy, lasting relationships. Our very existence is at stake here.

Exposing this sexual pathology is extremely urgent for the black man. Sexual aggression in men is associated with crime, the exploitation of women and children, bad scripts for boys, the breakdown of families and overconfident sexual posturing that masks insecurities and anxieties that are born of false personas in black men. All of this operates on both conscious and subconscious levels, and is therefore a lifetime task. Reading the book will become one of our beginning steps in the right direction.

More Than Sex sets a sexual truth standard for black men, and I was always taught that in truth there is freedom. The medical–psychological intervention style the author uses is particularly valuable for brothers because they are sometimes reluctant to seek medical or psychological assistance for any problem below the waist or above the shoulders.

Black male medical histories are replete with hypertension, high blood pressure, diabetes, prostate difficulties and other complications that can disrupt sexual functioning. Because of the give-me-sex-or-give-me-death mind-set of some men, any breakdown in health status that leads to sexual dysfunction will lead to defeatist attitudes among black men. The book inspires hope and healthier ways of expressing our sexuality.

Community research, through his medical practice, helped the author discover that black men who have a sexually superior attitude are headed down the path to failure, despair and poor health. Dr. Smith also conducted surveys and focus group discussions designed to identify unhealthy sexual beliefs among black men. What the author found was those men who did try to live up to the "sexual giant" image fell into a pattern of "emotional distancing" from their partners and never developed a capacity for any kind of intimacy: sexual, psychological or spiritual. Conclusion: Unexamined sexual stereotypes for black men become self-fulfilling prophecies and recycled behavior.

This weakened self-fulfilling state of mind leads some brothers to believe that if they are not having sex, they're not having a relationship. I call that poor penis politics. And for me, it is politically incorrect and a sad state of affairs for the black family.

Men must be taught that the major sexual organ is the brain and how we manage our thought processes determines life's outcomes. The author reminds the reader that anger and lust are located in the same brain locations. It is no wonder that some men associate sex with strength, power, control and violence. Some men have been known to obtain erections in fits of rage and/or violence. This volatile brain connection becomes very evident in cases of rape.

The *Change Your Brain, Change Your Life* book is a breakthrough program for conquering anxiety and impulsiveness written by Daniel G. Amen, M.D. It is part of the new frontier of medical psychology that will help to undo the damage of negative conditioning through the kinds of cognitive exercises Dr. Smith outlines in his book. Brain power is superior to penis politics.

Sex is our total sense of self, not just an anatomical location. Sexuality represents one small segment of the total human communication system. It is just a singular entity there are so many other facets to what Dr. Smith calls the programming of the "personality pie." Different slices of the same psychological pastry: the mental, spiritual, physical, emotional and sexual portions. Each slice or segment should share its own unique influence on the total composite of one's behavior, according to Smith's theory. All of this represents a well-integrated personality. And one must work to develop each segment with the same effort.

One of the main purposes of this book is to help black men develop all segments of their personalities equally. In his medical practice, Dr. Smith found that many black men who have poorly integrated personalities spend much of their effort developing their physical and sexual identities. That eventually means some men look for women that add to parts of the "pie" they do not possess. But the author warns that what really happens is the man's personality stays unbalanced throughout the course of his life and leaves him feeling empty and unfulfilled personally.

A book that integrates the scientific with the practical regarding the sensitive issue of human sexuality is welcome literature in the black community. The black sexual experience, as a matter of historical record, has been deliberately distorted and stereotyped. Consequently, out sexual issues have been systematically ignored in major sexual research arenas, which is part and parcel of the whole issue of denial regarding the peculiar institution of slavery in this country.

Psychological baggage of any kind disrupts access to the truth and really promotes denial. By including his own pathology regarding his relationships with women, Dr. Smith avoids this defensive reaction called denial and convinces the reader that healing is not only possible, it is paramount for black family survival.

Sex plays a part in the breakdown of communication between black men and women. Female respondents in survey results always cite lack of communication as one of the major problem areas in relationships with black men. As result, we become lost in a sea of mistrust, based on poor communication. The author's sex survey unravels the intricacies of black male sexuality.

We need what I call Dr. Smith's *truth serum* to get rid of the blaming, accusations and always wanting to be right or win the argument. Diagnosis: *Macho sex and fault-finding equals painful relationships.* This requires *bypass surgery:* Bypassing negative confrontation and embracing freedom of expression and unconditional love.

The author offers noncombative and a no-fault-finding approach that works. It involves getting in touch with our own feelings first in order to improve communication with others. We could all benefit from a personal feelings inventory. Reaching inside of ourselves for answers to communication problems we may discover family patterns that occurred in our childhood that have been recycled in our own lives.

It is important to remember that most of our struggles are within ourselves and no one can do the repair work for us. The beautiful message in this book is that each person must take full responsibility for creating his own outcome. Blame and fault-finding are passé and unproductive.

What one learns in this book is how to be an active listener, express back what your partner has said and stop saving up hurt and hostility for ammunition for the next fight. Winning arguments and keeping score is a minus, and admitting when you are wrong is a plus. I call this *magic mathematics* for working relationships, which always includes healthy discussion without a "scorecard." Men and women need to know that admitting you have been unfair is not weak or soft, it demonstrates nobility of character and a willingness to compromise. It's part of bypass surgery recovery behavior.

Learning how to be a sensitive human being begins early in life. Therefore, we must get rid of gender bias that teaches nurturance for girls and tough-it-out for boys. Because of his broken childhood, the author is very forceful when he warns parents that boys are children, not little men. Boys must be *taught* affection. How else can they learn the *rules of intimacy?*

Readers have a homework assignment to be more affectionate toward young male children: touching, hugging, kissing and cuddling them in nonsexual ways. Teaching good touch-bad touch early helps to prevent childhood sexual abuses. Adult males cannot model intimate behaviors they have never learned.

Studies show that men in general define their masculinity in sexual terms first, unless they have been taught from early childhood to appreciate the emotional benefits of nonsexual affectionate gestures. The earlier black males learn that an erection is not an emergency that he must act upon, the sooner he becomes a candidate for the loving father and companion that is needed to build black families.

The importance of positive sexual male models is addressed in these pages because it is one of the ways to help younger black men develop healthy sexual identities. Sexual identity is more psychological than physical, that is why it is so important for black women raising children in single parent households to provide stable male models for their young male offspring. Don't allow television, negative peer influence and other media to reinforce negative black sexual stereotypes that will cripple the black male child's psyche and self-esteem and make him a one-dimensional man who is phallic-fixated.

There is great hunger in the African American community for an honest and practical treatment of the subject of human sexuality and relationships. I believe sexual confidence comes with knowing that there is a connection between spirituality and sexuality. Otherwise, we will forever be doomed to play out the negative sexual stereo-types that seem to hound us no matter what we achieve. The Supreme Court Justice Clarence Thomas and law professor Anita Hill sexual harassment debate is a good case in point.

What I treasure about the book is that sex is removed from be-tween our legs to a more reliable location between our ears. Sexual-ity then becomes a composite of the emotional, spiritual and the physical makeup of us all. The author makes that perfectly clear to the reader, bypassing, as it were, the black male's stud-kicking com-edy of errors, hopefully, not to be repeated in the future.

The reader discovers the wholistic definition of human sexuality in this volume. Brothers are released from penis size fixations, perfor-mance anxieties, sexual myths and finally they can develop healthy egos that are the forerunners of working relationships and the emo-tional building blocks for strong black families. *More Than Sex* is truly the brother-healing, family-saving book that we have been wait-ing for.

Trust me, black men and women who read this book will be able to say, "I'm saved." Saved from societal myths about their sexuality and stereotypes that stymie the black man's inherent *style* or *savoir-faire*. And I'm here to tell you, black men do have a *"polished sure-ness"* that needs cultivation. I've been married to a stylish black man for over a quarter of a century myself.

—Gwendolyn Goldsby Grant, Ed.D., M.A.
Psychologist, Certified Sex Counselor, Advice Columnist
for *Essence* magazine, Inspirational Orator and Author of
The Best Kind of Loving

INTRODUCTION

The American *ideal* . . . of sexuality appears to be rooted in the American ideal of masculinity. This idea has created . . . good guys and bad guys, punks and studs, tough guys and softies, butch and faggot, black and white. It is an ideal so paralytically infantile that it is virtually forbidden—as an unpatriotic act— that the American boy evolve into the complexity of manhood.
— James Baldwin

Sexuality is a powerful force that profoundly affects not only our daily lives, but the very definition of who we are as people: how we feel about ourselves, how we love others, and, perhaps most important, how we pass these feelings on to future generations. The term *sexuality* encompasses a multitude of beliefs, attitudes, and behaviors that exist in all of us. Sexuality is, therefore, much more than sexual intercourse.

While the subject of sexuality generates intense interest in this country, almost nothing statistically is known or written about the sexuality of African American men. What information is available tends to rely on myths and stereotypes, boxing black males into destructive patterns of emotions and behaviors and, in turn, ultimately blocking the potential for truly fulfilling intimate relationships.

By definition, sexuality includes self-image, body image, gender role, values, and cultural experiences. In its complete definition, sexuality must also include the impact of communication and intimacy and not just the process of coupling and reproduction, or more broadly, that which is commonly referred to simply as "sex." The study of male sexuality dissects how men feel, think, and behave sexually; probing into black male sexuality is the primary focus of this book.

Even though many factors of sexual attitudes and behaviors of all men may vary, what is constant is the heavy influence of income levels, and perhaps even geographic location. Is it then possible that black males in the southern part of the United States differ in their sexual attitudes from those in the north? Most likely, attempts to answer this question produce varied opinions from those who strive to stratify black male diversity. However, it is my belief that African American males share a common trait that defines who they are— their sexuality.

Intimacy, an essential foundation for loving relationships, seems to be prevented by African American males' inhibitions in feelings, attitudes, and sexual expression. My role as a black male physician treating other black males daily in a very personal setting allows me access to firsthand accounts by men who are fearful, unfaithful, promiscuous, angry, and otherwise unhappy in their relationships. Their subsequent behavioral patterns have repeatedly blocked the opportunity for intimate and loving relationships.

During my graduate studies in psychology, I learned interviewing methods from a prodigious clinical psychologist named Arnold A. Lazarus. Not only is he respected and renowned for his psychology work, Dr. Lazarus has a unique ability to encourage patients to open up and disclose inner secrets in ways that other doctors find exceedingly difficult. One day when I asked how he was able to do this, he replied, "I first open up to the patient." I liked his simple reply so much that I have patterned my clinical practice after Dr. Lazarus. I opened up first to the men and sometimes spent hours sharing my own stories about relationships and my attitudes toward sex.

One explanation for black males maintaining this unsatisfying pattern is the historic portrayal of negative stereotyping. Literary accounts of the black male as a "hung dragon" were originally crafted by white men to frighten white women during slavery. Today little has changed. For example, black males continue to be portrayed by the media as animalistic and sexually charged beings. Movies with titles like *Booty Call* and *How to Be a Player* have done little to erase this attitudinal image of black males and sex.

That black males still buy into this myth is cause for great concern. Many believe that they are "head and shoulders" above other male ethnic groups in terms of physical endowments and "sexual power." Although difficult to accept, it remains that many black males accept this notion and totally embrace the myth. Some black males feel that without our sexual power we bring nothing to a relationship. This point is highlighted in the case of "Troubled Mr. J."

Mr. J is a fifty-seven-year-old patient in my primary care practice whom I have treated over many years for diabetes and high blood pressure. He is a proper man who had a strong religious upbringing. Managing his health was frequently difficult due to poor compliance to my treatment plan. Over the years he steadily gained weight and did not take his insulin as directed.

When Mr. J's first wife died in a car accident, he vowed not to re-marry until he found Ms. Right. That opportunity came five years later, when he met his second wife singing in the choir at church. Although it was love at first sight, his apprehension about marrying again was not without emotional barriers. Mr. J, unbeknownst to his new bride, was suffering from impotency and felt inadequate and fearful as a result.

Because of intense religious commitment, he had remained celibate after his first wife's death. However, increasingly anxious over his sexuality, he postponed his second wedding so many times his future bride, now terribly annoyed, threatened to leave him. Not surprisingly, Mr. J became very depressed.

Noticing his lack of enthusiasm for his upcoming marriage, I suggested during an office visit that he and I discuss it. Only then did he reveal his dilemma. He reported that throughout the courtship with his fiancée, he had grown more and more affectionate with her, kissing and embracing more often. However, because of his fear that something more sexually intimate would happen, he had begun to behave somewhat coldly, creating emotional distance. He confided, "You know Doc, I have not had an erection in years." He went on sadly, "How can I be in a relationship if I can't perform sexually? I'm not even a *real* man." Mr. J, simply put, was decidedly afraid. I was greatly troubled for this man, as he was defining his worth only in physical, sexual terms. Equally troubling was my failure to explore his sexual history sooner. Fortunately, following proper treatment for impotence as well as personal counseling, all ended well for Mr. J; unfortunately, this is not always the case.

There are many black men who rely on their sexual power in an attempt to pursue, conquer, and control women. Even though Mr. J's obstacles were fear and embarrassment, he truly believed that his impotent sexual performance was directly linked to not being a "real man." Many black men similarly define their relationships in terms of how they perform sexually. The expectation that an erectile state adequately measures how well they form and sustain relationships is remarkable, as this quite clearly is not the case.

Based on statistics regarding the high divorce rate among African Americans, the message that black males are sending each other (physical sex equals top relationship priority) is in profound conflict with black women's needs. When the foundation of any relationship is based solely on physical sex, little room exists for nonphysical intimacy to grow. Boundary lines are crossed prematurely; divorce rates soar. The false notion of black men being sexually superior leads many down the path of failed or unhappy relationships and, consequently, into confusion and despair.

Because many black men focus only on the "sex" aspect of sexuality, the African American family is deteriorating at a phenomenal rate. As a community researcher, I frequently conduct educational initiatives to address health care issues in the African American community. These research efforts include conducting surveys and focus group discussions designed to identify attitudes and behaviors of blacks on various topics. As part of the research process in preparation for this book I conducted many focus-group sessions involving black males, discussing attitudes and feelings about their sexuality and relationships.

Information resulting from those frank, round-table discussions appears intermittently throughout this book. There was, however, one consistent answer to a question that bears reporting at this point. From a group of fifteen black males aged eighteen to fifty-nine, with widely varied socioeconomic backgrounds, the question "What is the most important part of a relationship?" consistently resulted in the answer "sex." One man summarized thusly: "If I could not have sex, then it would not be a relationship. I'm sure my woman would leave me."

From this example, the conclusion that African American males have been misled about what it takes to sustain a relationship is apparent. This misinformation, along with these men's self-descriptive perceived images of being "sexual giants," suggests that some may even feel that they lack the essential elements needed to provide true, long-lasting love for their mates unless sexual performance is present *and* a major focus in their relationship.

Joseph L. White and Thomas A. Parham suggest in their book, *The Psychology of Blacks: An Afro-American Perspective*, that the essential elements of a good relationship should be built on bonds of sharing, nurturing, tenderness, and a strong appreciation for each other. They argue that these essentials would provide the necessary foundation for coping with and enduring strong social and economic stressors. Conversely, fear of commitment and an inability to sustain lasting love relationships create disappointment in some black men, resulting in a reflexive "emotional distancing" from their mates. These negative feelings serve to inhibit black men from nonphysical intimacy with the people in their lives.

One patient of mine who had experienced several failed relationships flatly refused to be a part of the dating scene for fear of rejection. It felt safer for him to read adult magazines, drink alcohol, and masturbate rather than to approach women in an attempt to develop a long-term intimate relationship. I met this patient during his last year of life. He died at forty-four, from alcoholic cirrhosis of the liver, alone in this world.

The bottom line is that failing relationships mirror insecurities and self-worth. Black males who have failed to sustain loving relationships must come to the realization that physical sex does not measure our status as men. Often we seek love through immature methods of game-playing or deception in futile efforts to escape true emotional, nonphysical intimacy with our partners. By doing this, we fail to grasp the true meaning of love.

Love, in its purest form, cannot be sexual control of oneself or another. Any such narrow view of sexuality results in inappropriate acts. Consequently, failed relationships fuel feelings of inadequacy that

negatively contribute to the black male psyche. The black man's sexuality must be much more than sex. It must include a sense of self,
body image, perception of success, and social conduct. Sexuality can
be healthy or unhealthy, and it determines our ability to enter into
loving relationships or even sustaining a family.

Sexual misconceptions prevent us from communicating intimately
with our mates. The phrase "Real men don't cry" has allowed black
men, disastrously, to hide behind true inner emotions in relationships. The consequences of squelching emotion create an unreality
with regard to feelings essential for honest personal interactions.
Black men who do not touch on their inner emotions or examine the
sexual misconceptions set before them will not master the behavioral
development necessary to interact with others in healthy ways. We
must come to terms with our pathological approach to love.

Changing one's attitude toward relationships is difficult, especially
when most black men are reluctant to talk about their true feelings
with someone or to seek professional help. My goal for this book is to
promote open and frank discussions about the sexual misconceptions
that prevent us from communicating with our mates and subsequently cause us to be out of touch with the feelings necessary for
honest interaction. Addressing sexuality among all African Americans can enhance the sexual expression of black men so that it can be
nurtured into the deepest intimacy levels with their partners. Hopefully, this book will promote awareness and increase knowledge with
respect to sexuality in the African American population, as well as
offer solutions for problem relationships.

This book is not written for, nor influenced by, other referenced
studies addressing the sexuality of black men. Rather, while familiar-
izing myself with other studies, I deemed it crucial to explore this
topic with free-floating spontaneity, complementing my professional
insight as a physician. Not many individuals outside of our African
American ethnic group have approached and questioned us about
our innermost feelings. It stands to reason that some black men, and
even a few women, might feel betrayed—or might even deny—the
presented data. Yet the fact remains that we black males have kept
most of our inner thoughts to ourselves; we have become great ac-
tors on the stage of life at a great price.

Telling my story about black love and sexuality—writing this book—became a source of healing and psychic relief for me. A cathartic experience has allowed me to place responsibility with myself for not sustaining long-lasting partnerships in my own past. The focus is now on me, not on the female I too frequently blamed. You, as the reader, may or may not identify with my personal story in this introduction; however, chances are you know someone who is, or has been, in situations such as those I talk about. This understanding has taken many years of self-reflection and honest discussion with others. By opening up and seeking advice from those who were wiser than I in the ways of love and intimacy, I have been able to modify my approach to relating to my mate and have experienced intimacy at levels deeper than I ever thought possible. This is my hope for you.

Information in this book generates ideas never publicly discussed by those who have researched in-depth attitudes and behaviors of black men and women. It is my belief that if black males dump their emotional baggage and defense mechanisms, a smoother transition can be made in moving toward healthier relationships not controlled by the act of sex. Black men, while trying to receive recognition as heads of their households, have had difficulty fulfilling this goal. Because of a perceived discriminatory practice of an oppressive culture, self-images of black males have suffered.

It is exceedingly difficult to shake off a label of "trifling" and worthlessness when unable to provide the essentials for one's family. Black men have the highest unemployment rates; most are aware that when compared to the rest of society, they also die sooner as well. The higher mortality rate is the consequence of inappropriate social behaviors and a host of disease entities, such as AIDS and cancer of the prostate. Drugs, alcohol, and mental illness incapacitate many more. As a result of these facts, black men have repressed their feelings of fear and have grown hostile toward the system.

Inner rage and resentment has escalated and, unfortunately, the release valve has tended to open while interacting with our mates. Anger cannot safely be directed toward the real enemy because fighting the system means defeat. Black males who are not in touch with these feelings are unable to share hidden fears with their mates, instead continuing in an unhealthy manner within their relationships. The hidden rage that black men carry may take on many forms. Quite often fear is masked with a facade of masculinity while "trying to be a real man."

The psyche is vulnerable and often weakened by the stamina it takes to erect and maintain this emotional wall around one's self. Sapped of energy, some men will give up on relationships and seek comfort through the use of drugs and other risky, unsafe behaviors. Perhaps this is a subconscious act of punishment for dishonesty in loving partnerships, or perhaps it is simply an escape from confronting their real feelings about themselves.

An example of this process is a black male patient of mine who came in for the treatment of sexually transmitted diseases several times over a two-year period. He was a professional man, well aware of my concern for his situation and safety. During a conference he revealed that his wife had just received a promotion and was now earning more money than he. Surreptitiously I was shocked because I never even knew he was married. He had not revealed in his health history or in any other personal information that he had a family. This patient confided that his marriage was falling apart and he was finding it difficult to talk to his wife because their discussions would escalate into outright arguments. In a pensive tone, he told me that he would get so mad he would leave his home, pick up a prostitute, and take drugs or drink until he was sick and miserable.

So why was this intelligent, professional black man abusing himself, particularly during a period when he was feeling elevated rage? My suspicion was twofold: that he viewed his sexuality negatively and, as a result of inner rage coupled with an inability to communicate, he chose the outlet of physical sex and self-destruction. Verbally unable to communicate his disdain to his wife, his anger and dissatisfaction were directed in a sexual way toward another female.

In testimony, during a subsequent conference with me and with the patient's permission, his wife cried when I told her the real reason for her husband's outbursts. She said that if only he could have told her his fears she would have loved him even more and they could have tried to work the problem out together. This man could have shared his feelings—he was intimidated by her new job and status—with his wife; instead he had picked fights with her. Openness could have led to the formation of an emotionally deep and loving partnership.

Interactions of social forces, along with biological factors, are capable of shaping the black man's self-image. The image of one's self is influenced throughout life by the ability to fulfill roles deemed by society as proper for one's gender. Black men need not follow the stereotypical roles that "men work, women cook and have kids." This can and must be replaced by "black men should love, and in an equal fashion, walk alongside black women." While this is a role that has not been completely realized, it remains a highly rewarding and achievable goal.

In summary, sexuality is the main ingredient within the black man's repertoire of self. Many black men traditionally bring unhealthy attitudes and behaviors to relationships guided by physical sex. Life events and social myths force us to live up to the standards others create; the stress of meeting societal expectations can be extreme. Part of sexual health is dependent upon mental health: Stress, resentment, guilt, and anxiety are all factors that inhibit the development and maintenance of loving relationships. In turn, sexuality has the potential to be healthy or unhealthy, much like the physiological processes of the human body.

Through my work as a family physician, psychologist, researcher, and educator, I have realized that my personal experience of sexuality and intimacy seems almost universal for black men. Our collective history and our individual experiences conspire, all too often, to create in us a fragmented, distorted, or incomplete sense of what it means to be a man. This, in turn, has an immense impact on African American women and children.

I was fifteen years old when my father died in Trenton State Prison, having been convicted for armed robbery. He had abandoned the family much earlier, leaving me in the care of my mother. Even when he had lived with us, though, my father did not provide the kind of role model I needed as a young boy. Instead of the strong, brave man I wanted to look up to, my father was an unpredictable, abusive alcoholic and drug addict. And instead of teaching me to be proud of being a black man, he taught me that I should be wary and ashamed.

I did manage to find more positive male role models as I grew older. As a national track star and a gifted student, I was fortunate to have supportive and encouraging male coaches, mentors, and teachers. When I began my pilgrimage toward romance and the pursuit of family, however, I realized with great disappointment that I could not make relationships survive beyond sexual intimacy. For many years, I cast blame on my mates for these unsuccessful experiences. Like many African American men, I justified my failures by claiming that black women were too domineering, sexually hung up and demanding, and competing with me for power in the relationship. I scoffed at remarks that labeled me chauvinistic, undependable, emotionally distant, and abusive. When all else failed, I fell back on the dependable declaration that "she was not the one for me."

It was after years of experience and self-reflection that I began to accept the significant negative role that I played in these failed relationships. I could no longer ignore remarks made by my partner stating that I was chauvinistic, emotionally distant, and abusive. Clinging to immature emotions and a false belief that my physical, sexual self would be enough to sustain my mate's happiness kept me from reaching deep levels of emotional intimacy with my mate. This distorted view of what I had to offer as a man prevented the emotional closeness necessary for a relationship to flourish into true companionship.

I could never comfortably discuss my inner feelings of fear and insecurity without feeling vulnerable or defeated. At that time, being in a relationship was, to me, a competitive game of love and I refused to be the emotional loser. Nevertheless, in the end I was always the one who lost. This style of thinking originated early in my childhood with the endless emotional combat between my mother and me. If I talked back to her she would smack me on the mouth with an open hand. I often felt abused and angry. We never bonded and I hated the feeling of powerlessness she bred in me. I suppressed my emotions and became callous and cynical. With no father in the household and being the oldest child, I was forced to become "a man." My resentful and angry attitude later surfaced in my close relationships with others, especially if I perceived characteristics similar to those my mother possessed.

My childhood interactions with my mother taught me how to relate to women, but not in a healthy way.

Early experiences caused me to shield my inner fears and fueled my need to always be in control, particularly in relationships where emotional closeness and love made me feel weak and vulnerable. Practicing as a family doctor and psychologist, I have come to realize that my experiences are common to many black men. In my office, I sometimes witness a single mother aggressively disciplining her male child. While I understand that measured discipline is necessary, I still wonder how the child will grow and develop emotionally, or if he will have a healthy sense of self. And, equally important, will he be able to love freely in his relationships without having to always be the one in control?

In medical school, I completed a month's rotation in psychiatry at a state penitentiary. Many of the men I interviewed were black males, some of them murderers and rapists. A common theme in all of their histories revealed that they all perceived the absence of love in their lives as children. Their mother/son relationships had not been good, and abuse had generally been present. Other common factors included the impact of the lack of a father figure in early childhood, with which I could readily identify.

Unremarkably, they had all had many failed emotional relationships. All were angry, and had been most of their lives. They openly admitted to hating the system and also harboring fear of it. These black men exercised their time and energy toward living a life trying to outsmart the "system" and, to get around it, they participated in crime. Abuse was rampant throughout their lives and directed toward their various mates.

The common explanation for this abuse was their perception that their manhood was being challenged. Not uncommonly, these incarcerated black men share distinct feelings with those who do not choose to participate in a life of crime. Showing weakness and a submissive side would imply equally that the incarcerated men would cease to exist or risk being overtaken by another person. Physical and emotional force, then, meant "maintain control."

This book explores how many black men come from similar disadvantaged families and share similar experiences as mine. It does not preclude the fact that there are black men who have been raised with all of the advantages of a loving home but nevertheless enter adulthood abusing and controlling others as well. Again, sexual stereotypes generate and perpetuate this type of behavior and poor sense of self.

Maturing into adolescence and early adulthood, I was equipped only with ideals about how relationships and families should be formed and sustained. Education helped me to form these ideals but not how to apply them, as they were not concrete in my mind. After all, I had experienced no real frame of reference. However, I bought into them even though I feared my ineptness at achieving love and happiness.

Armed with all the facts I needed to develop a relationship, I entered into each with abandon because I did not know how to actually implement one. Fear handicapped me emotionally because I did not know what was expected and therefore, as do many black men, I substituted sex for love. Early on, I sought women with weak and gullible natures, and soft, compliant ways that yielded to manipulation. I tenaciously sought this kind of nature as a substitute for my mother, whose emotional armor had never allowed me to enter into and embrace her hidden softness. This, in turn, erroneously allowed me to believe I was preventing hurt. Necessarily, this book includes some issues faced by black women as well, particularly in how they relate to black men in relationships. As a result of stereotyping, some black women harbor resentment toward their mates and black men in general, resulting in negative circular relationship behaviors. Some of my black female patients say they are sick and tired of the treatment they receive from black men; the macho, cool, aloof, and abusive image has become less and less tolerable to women.

Some black women nevertheless have allowed themselves to become emotionally exhausted, obese, and unhealthy as a defensive response to their failed relationships with black men. Black women are often the target of the black man's unhealthy approach toward relationships and become deprived of emotionally expressing themselves intimately with their partners. Some choose to relinquish their attempts to have their men love them, in return for simple security that lacks intimacy.

Other black women, many of them younger, tell me in my office, "I'll show him. He can't get over on me." These women respond to black men by mirroring behaviors, engaging in risky sexual practices and/or becoming emotionally withdrawn just like their male counterparts. Besides being unproductive to the relationship, this practice contributes to the breakdown of families and limits the hope of ever entering into truly loving and intimate partnerships.

When preparing to write this book, I talked with many black women who expressed similar concerns. Their feelings reflected desires to be protected and cherished by their men, to be free to express themselves and their feelings openly without fear of being brushed off. While society has influenced many to believe that black men are not to be trusted, especially with respect to sexual fidelity, these black women desperately wanted to be able to trust their mates. Some felt forced into infidelity to "protect themselves" emotionally against inevitable pain of their man's repeated affairs. This rift creates an impossible situation. A great number of black women state they have become resigned to sharing their man with other women, and on the surface this might seem to present a workable solution to the very certain shortage in proportion of black males to black females. However, as this behavior will never foster positive, lasting, and fulfilling relationships, nor provide exemplary role models for children, workable solutions to the discrepancy are possible and must be explored.

My colleagues and I have attempted to address issues that are indigenous to the black community. The contributors are doctors and researchers who have collected facts directly from African Americans, and the stories and accounts are true. Black men have articulated their truths, discussed how they felt, and were able to think through their real feelings about their relationships and personal lives with others like themselves. A great deal is revealed about why black men conduct themselves the way they do in relationships. Throughout the process of writing this book, we have established a clearer understanding of the black man's obstacle with intimacy and the dynamics of his resulting failed relationships. Not all black men behave badly or have a distorted view of their sexuality and relationships, and certainly not all have had to raise themselves from the pathological dust of their beginnings as did I. For those black men and women who share and identify with what is written in this book, perhaps the healing can begin. I hope that your reading will be enjoyable, informative, and even cathartic, as it was for me to write.

Chapter 1

AFRICAN AMERICAN HISTORY AND THE SENSE OF SELF

It is a peculiar sensation, this double-consciousness, and this sense of always looking at one's self through the eyes of others, of measuring one's soul by the tape of a world that looks on in amused contempt and pity.
—W. E. B. DuBois, *The Souls of Black Folk*

As much as all Americans, black and white, seem at times to want to forget that not so very long ago this country held a large portion of its people in bondage, the emotional scars of slavery are still with us. Whether we know it or not, to some extent we black men measure ourselves with the plantation owner's "tape."

The focus of this chapter is to explore the African American male's focus on the physical aspects of sexuality and its roots in our historical heritage. As slaves, black men were literally valued for their bodies in age, size, strength, and endurance. As free men in today's society, we continue to be valued and to value ourselves for much the same attributes. For example, black athletes, some of the most prominent role models in our community, continue to be admired and paid for their size, strength, and agility. The slaveholder's shackles no longer bind us, but we are still constrained by the narrow vision of our own worth.

The plantation view of black male sexuality is evident in American attitudes, beliefs, and myths. The sexual prowess of African American males is still exaggerated by black and white Americans alike. In an article entitled "Sexual Stereotyping of Black Males in Interracial

Sex," G. L. Davis and H. J. Cross report that the black man is widely believed to have sexual intercourse at an early age, with many partners, and, frequently, with little or no intimacy. The same article indicates that African American males are perceived to be genitally focused.

There is a deep-rooted insecurity in African American men as a result of sexual stereotyping. If all that black men have to offer is the ability to physically satisfy a woman, then doesn't it stand to reason that we would have to keep satisfying women sexually to prove that we have something to offer? If you take away a man's swagger, macho posturing, and practiced come-ons, what you have left is a man wanting love, acceptance, and intimacy. These emotions become difficult to express and men become terrified of rejection.

Needing an outlet for their emotions, black men have a tendency to exercise their feelings of fear and rejection by using size and strength as a safety net. The expression of our emotions becomes stifled by our need to prove our masculinity. These behavioral patterns have been passed on to each generation as a result of the historical enslavement and oppression of the black man and his family, and are evident especially in the very young.

I frequently conduct educational forums for children in the Philadelphia school system and my message is simple and consistent: Study hard and you, too, can achieve. Usually I close my discussions by asking the children to vote for the person or profession that they would want to become or belong to as an adult. Most of the children vote for athletes who are big and strong. Although occasionally a hand will raise for the choice of becoming a doctor, this is genuinely a rare occurrence. I find that male black children collectively feel as though strength and size will ensure their achievement in life.

Certainly the media lags in reinforcement of blacks striving for intellectual achievement and spiritual fulfillment. Historically, television, newspaper reports, and other types of media, including the Internet, have bolstered negative images of blacks. Admittedly there have been rare occurrences throughout history that have been a positive force, but they were simply not presented frequently enough to counteract the negative stereotyping. The flare of the civil rights movement of the sixties and the image of Dr. Martin Luther King, Jr.

as a positive role model was cut short by the black leader's death. That fateful day impeded the momentum necessary for building positive self-images among blacks. Sadness replaced hope, and anger replaced cooperation, only fueling the fire of the black man's need to prove himself as strong and worthy.

Because white society has so emphatically attempted to shame and enfeeble black males, the idea of reclaiming one's manhood assumes prominence. As noted filmmaker Marlon Riggs documented in his movie, *Black Is . . . Black Ain't*, several women who claim "Black is beautiful" really mean black men are beautiful, and Riggs described how the Black Power movement too often equated blackness with masculinity, relegating women to the margins or treating them as sex objects.

Most people feel that the days of slavery no longer exist and that in order for blacks to move forward and achieve, dwelling on the past must stop. However, it is necessary to reflect on the past so that black men can understand why we react the way we do, particularly with our mates. Although progress has been made, actions of black men indicate that a physical, sexual mentality still exists and is utilized as the foundation for long-term relationships.

Ironically, it is precisely this immature view of sexuality that prevents black men from entering into and maintaining satisfying, nurturing relationships. African American men and women have become alienated from each other, in large part because they do not know what the other really needs and wants. During one of my focus groups, a young black professional woman shared her disdain, musing that "The problem is that we, as women, want closeness, better communication, and real love. All they [black men] want is sex."

The high rate of divorce and the large number of single-mother households in our community are alarming indicators of the poor health status of the African American family. African American history, combined with the black man's social conditioning throughout the years, has profoundly affected the negativity of the black man's sexuality and his role in shaping a positive image of black societal role models for this country. This plantation mentality with respect to sexuality is evident in many black men's beliefs and actions. By all accounts, the sexuality of black men is still exaggerated by Americans in general. Black men slough off, defend, and even deny collective remarks that include stereotypes and myths. Like a prophecy fulfilled in which he has no individual control, the black man ends up behaving in ways that only reinforce myths and negative media images—a catch-22.

The few articles and books written about the sexuality of blacks from a historical perspective often portray black men as having sexual intercourse often, and starting at an early age. Nor are black women spared this stereotyping, characterized as promiscuous, oversexed temptresses, or as overweight and sexually inhibited mammies. These stereotypes have done a great deal of damage to black men and women, and have served as one of the origins of the disorganization of the black family structure from the time of slavery until today.

Because of frequent slave trading, the pre–Civil War black family was constantly changing and expanding. White slave holders held no regard for the black family unit and the constant uprooting of slaves proved maintaining a cohesive family quite difficult. Black women and men were deemed "objects" and their purpose was only to serve the whims and needs of the white slave owners. Slaves who exercised their minds or wanted to read and write were targeted as a threat to the security of the white plantation owners and thus were often killed or sold.

This sentiment, albeit slowly changing, persists today among some people in the white community. One example, reflected in federal government programs, is the diverting of monies away from black communities and families into other programs such as political campaigns. Other federal study initiatives that have shown blacks how little they are valued as a people are demonstrated in the Tuskegee experiment (conducted from 1932–1972), which used blacks as guinea pigs to study the long-term effects of untreated syphilis. Any positive change has come slowly.

Myths about the black man's sexuality began to surface during the time of slavery. For a black man who was enslaved, everything, including pride, was stripped from his being until all he had left that was potent and powerful was his physical, sexual self. Of course, there were instances in which the slaves empowered themselves by being proud of the number of bales of cotton they could produce and lift. However, this was not true freedom of achievement. The act of sex assisted the enslaved black man in maintaining his masculinity and gave him the freedom to prove his power while in bondage to the white man.

The stereotyping of black men was used by white male slave owners as a scare tactic to keep white women from sleeping with the black slaves. It is important to understand those early verbal messages, myths, and stereotypes were historically not discussed in secrecy among the white plantation owners. Designed to scare white women into avoiding the black male slaves at all costs, the comments by white slave masters about black men being sexual "studs" and having "gigantic penises" only served to reinforce the black man's image of his sexual self, as he listened in silence, unable to respond. Imagine yourself as a slave for a moment, deprived of everything and hanging on to a thread of dignity as the white plantation owner talked about how you, a black man, were "hung like a horse" or had a gigantic sexual organ. It would seem that one's personality, in such a state of despair, would hold on to every seemingly positive statement that he could, regardless of accuracy.

Black stereotypes flowed from white fears and attitudes toward African Americans. Earlier mythical images of black men as "harmless, playful eunuchs," which justified slavery, were eventually replaced by threatening, highly sexualized images that limited black men's expression of the full range of their selves.

One myth I recall while growing up was the uniqueness attached to white women. They were "pretty," according to public scrutiny, and black women were not. White women seemed to be the epitome of sexuality personified, and black women were devoid of this image. The media, educational system, and other blacks drilled this notion into me constantly. As a child, the prohibition of black men to be associated romantically with white women only perpetuated my desire to experience the white "forbidden fruit." Since I could not have one of these "perfect women," it seemed as though I was not a "perfect" man. Anger grew, and I began to feel less than worthy.

The civil rights movement in America did much to erase this system of brainwashing but the residual notion of good and bad in the minds of black men still lingers. Not surprisingly, the black male's historic fixation with the white woman, along with other false beliefs and myths that were created by white society, ultimately impaired the black man's psyche and personality.

Richard Wright once said that, "if blacks were to survive, they would have to be schooled in the ways of the white world." Throughout history, black women were often compared to white women. The black woman's thick lips, coarse hair, and sexual uptightness were always denounced or overemphasized. In the 1940s, Wright stated that "white women were perceived as the Immaculate Conception of our civilization."

There were rarely black images on television, in the media, or even in pornography. The sexuality of blacks was never talked about openly unless it was in the crime section of newspapers. If a black image was seen on television, it was always in a negative light, often portraying blacks as studs or pimps, never as businessmen or doctors. It wasn't until the early eighties, when Bill Cosby played Dr. Heathcliff Huxtable on *The Cosby Show*, that a black man was portrayed as a successful, educated man married to a black woman of the same stature.

A patient of mine was recently released from jail and had to follow up with me for treatment of his high blood pressure. Mr. S was a handsome thirty-five-year-old man, whose movie-star looks had begun to tarnish and fade from the many years of late-night partying, a poor diet, and alcohol abuse. However, he still saw himself as a player and as God's gift to women. After completing fifteen months of incarceration, Mr. S had returned to his old tricks. He had been convicted of domestic violence toward his girlfriend, a white woman. After treating his blood pressure problem for several months and gaining his confidence, I began to gain insight into his personality and his attitudes about his sexuality.

Much of Mr. S's life and interests centered on his bedroom performance. In addition to his white girlfriend, there was also a black female whom he saw on a regular basis. He was sexually involved with both women and most of his time was spent juggling time between the two. Over the course of many months of seeing him at my clinic, I had the opportunity to meet both women. Other than their common love for this man, their personalities, economic status, and appearance were diametrically opposed to one another. Ms. T was a black professional who was attractive, well groomed, and physically fit. She was obviously an intellectual with a high level of education. On the other hand, Ms. C was an obese waitress who often appeared disheveled, spoke with a great deal of "hip-hop" street slang, and had several teeth missing when she smiled.

Prior to my meeting both women separately, Mr. S one day boasted proudly to me, "Yeah, I got a white woman!" For reasons unknown to me, he revealed that for many years he felt powerful and "like a real man" with his white girlfriend. Additionally, he treated his black female friend with little respect—like an object. He told me that she made him feel dumb and inadequate. As odd as it may seem, somehow she would tolerate his abuse, perhaps hoping that one day he would change his ways.

The only time Mr. S physically abused his white girlfriend was the day he went to jail. She called the police after he punched her in the face, and broke her nose. Apparently he had returned after a job interview, having been turned away for lack of qualifications. She had set up the interview with a white male friend. The specifics of that interview were never openly spoken about to me; however, Mr. S did inform me that he felt disrespected and that the white interviewer had not treated him like a "real man." Angered and enraged, he had taken his feelings out on his white girlfriend.

I could write another book on the psychosocial dynamics of Mr. S's story, but one thing is certain: he had been influenced by the "plantation" mentality. Being a "stud" preoccupied his identity and his sense of being a man. Sex was his object of power, not a true love for either woman. He had also bought into the myth that he would be a real man if he conquered a white woman. When the system said "no," his sense of self and sexuality, which included his attitudes and beliefs, came crashing down around him.

The impact of historically generated myths and stereotyping in the minds of black men cannot be underestimated. Black men are indoctrinated early by their parents and peers, and often adopt these subliminal messages without even realizing it.

In another case, Mr. P did not come from the ghetto, nor did he have a dysfunctional family. In fact, he had a good relationship with his mother. However, as he grew up and became a scholar and athlete, he still saw women as only sexual objects and often, colloquially speaking, "thought with his penis." He frowned upon interracial dating because of his parents' influences upon him; they had been active in the civil rights movement. Yet despite his upbringing and a clear understanding of rights for blacks, he always chose women with fair skin, and Caucasoid features.

Mr. P had been influenced by the power of the "plantation" mentality, which has caused countless black men to incorrectly perceive that there will be more rewards and acceptance for being with someone who is less threatening or not as "dark and mysterious." The movie *School Daze,* by Spike Lee, works from this theme of blacks often separating themselves and forming biases for one another based on the lightness or darkness of one's skin color.

During the early 1900s, blacks who were well off both socially and financially were light-skinned. Those who were not so well off had noticeably darker skin tones. Ever since the first African arrived in Jamestown, Virginia, in 1619—in chains—Americans of African descent have been subject to efforts to erase or separate their differences and, in so doing, their humanity. Black people used to call other blacks who valued light skin over dark skin "color-struck." Today, a preference for light skin, called "colorism," still exists in American society.

As in history, kinky or curly hair is characterized as "bad" hair that is unmanageable. Straight hair is found more desirable among some African Americans. Darker skin, wide noses, thick lips, and fuller curves are often viewed as abnormal and not sexually appealing, according to the white-dominated media. In American culture, blacks constantly see images and hear messages from the days of slavery that are not reflective of the truth about African Americans. Some of these fabrications: the black man's penis is larger than those of other ethnic groups and he is a "king of sexual prowess," coarse hair texture is unattractive, and black women are promiscuous and indiscreet.

Enlightening you, the reader, with the truth about who we are as sexual beings will undo centuries of mental chains and shackles that have hindered us from becoming more than what we have been perceived. By disrupting the cycle of the plantation mentality, we will move into loving and intimately satisfying long-term relationships that are truly fulfilling.

If it is love that is sought in the hearts of others, then first let the seeds of love be deeply planted in the heart of the one who seeks it.

—The Author

Chapter 2

SEX, IMAGE, AND STATUS

Eventually, the truth pushes itself up through the sands of deception—so that men can know them . . .

—An American Indian proverb

Not long ago, a man whose family are patients of mine came in for a routine physical. At thirty-six, this handsome black man is a true success by all accounts. He has a college degree in business and a great job. His wife is a teacher and they have two well-behaved, bright young children. During his physical, this successful black man squirmed uncomfortably when I casually asked him about his family. He paused for a moment and then said, "You know, Dr. Smith, I just came back from visiting a fraternity brother down in Miami, and I really feel like I am missing out on the good life. My friend has a Lamborghini, girls in thong bikinis by his pool, and all of these famous ball players coming around. I really don't think I want to be married anymore. Family is nice, but I want some thrills and some action."

Within just one week of visiting a friend whom he had not seen in several years, this man's sense of his own success—the foundation of a loving relationship and a happy family—was undermined. Rubbing elbows with professional athletes and models had not only failed to grant him sincere satisfaction, it had tapped into a destructive need many African American men hold fast: to maintain the sexual image of "stud."

Sex, image, and success are inextricably interwoven for most black males. It is by looking through his sexual window that the black man often sees his world; his image is defined through his sexuality and his success as a man often depends on how he views his sexual self. The African American man tends to feel that in order to survive and succeed in a world constructing obstacles as fast as he can overcome them, he must depend on his sexual image. His successes are too often defined by how he performs sexually or by how many women he has bedded.

The Reverend Jesse Jackson has recognized that "the burden of being black is that you have to be superior just to be equal. But the glory of that, once you achieve, you have achieved indeed." Black men must not allow their sexuality to stand in the way of pursuing real success. The perception of sex as the defining factor for the black man's image has distorted our sense of self. Men like Dennis Rodman, who sports garish rainbow-colored hair and a pierced body, and Tupac Shakur, whose gangsta rap cost him his life, are too often regarded as successful role models. This creates a mockery of who the black male truly is and what he can accomplish.

In history, the black culture used both war and song as methods of survival. Tribes were constantly confronted by other groups wrestling for land boundaries; rights of settlement were regularly challenged by outsiders thirsting for more power. Consequently, the biggest and most athletic societies typically became the overthrowers and everyone else, the overthrown. In essence, he who wielded the strongest power and possessed the most money, ruled.

Song became an integral part of historic culture as it celebrated these often vigorous victories of war. During times of peace, song contributed greatly to the African culture's entertainment prior to slavery in America. Later in black history, song eased the brutal pains of slavery.

Athleticism and song, then, have been indispensable since the beginning. Both most likely will continue as such through generation upon generation, contributing to the speculation of why many people, especially black youth, are so intrigued today by super athletes and rap stars. Black culture tends to glorify African Americans who transcend the plight of oppression and excel in a predominantly Caucasian world, especially those doing it in large numbers. While the same is applicable to successful black scholars who have overcome lives of poverty, their numbers unfortunately are few. Athletes and rap stars steadily increase in popularity as central role models for our youth.

Certainly not to diminish the successes of African American athletes or music stars, a question nevertheless begs to be asked: Why do our children look up to basketball players and rap stars specifically? Certainly social order is partly responsible for blocking opportunities for young black men to achieve other avenues of self-expression, but what is the main draw toward rapping and sports?

When I was a young black boy, society defined for me what it deemed I could achieve. The value I placed on what I was to become centered on what others told me and showed me. Many times the message was that by being physically big and strong, I would find life easier by pursuing sports and playing the game to win, as opposed to learning good work ethics and developing my intellect. Friends who were social and could sing or play instruments were nevertheless pressured to pursue entertainment for their "out" and self-expression.

In the 1960s, black people didn't complain much because they were happy to see brothers making it. (Anyway, if we did complain, we were often persecuted for stepping out of bounds.) Back then, many of the black men who did make it out of the ghetto started out as good role models. Yet as time passed, something began to happen with some who had achieved fame. Drugs became cool; perhaps the money and stress of being a spokesperson for the black race created too heavy of a burden. Whatever the reason, many ceased being good strong role models.

Standards for African Americans shifted as black athletes and musicians made more and more money for their mostly white promoters and agents. When a famous black man did something unseemly or detrimental, it was often smoothed over in deference to the money factor. Our black youth increasingly idolized athletes and rap celebrities, their behaviors changing to mimic those of the "star."

Today, when sex and drugs have become commonplace, interwoven into the lifestyles of many athletes and entertainers, it is ever more imperative that we reach out to young black men. Emphasizing the solid foundation of doing well in school first and chasing the dream of sports or rap later is our greatest hope to stop the negative cycle. Too many times young black men find themselves accepting the attitude that it's okay to do drugs or to practice indiscrimate sex, setting themselves up for disasters.

Why does this repeatedly happen? Why dye their hair green, for that matter, like Dennis Rodman's signature hair? One could argue that it is the rebel in teenagers that stimulates doing the same things they see successful athletes or musicians doing. Certainly exercising independence need not be a negative thing; in fact, it is a natural part of the growth process. However, if the emulation of the rebellious athlete or "gangsta" rap star involves drugs or other aberrant behavior as a result of a strong need to fit into a group and/or to mask insecurities, then it becomes frighteningly detrimental for that black child's future.

The needs of our young black men are successfully met when they begin to negatively rebel and there is a positive black man or woman in their path to guide the way. Pain, loneliness, and isolation are frequently masked as rebellion. Sex and/or drugs often feel like the cure-all, with a casual attitude toward sexual behavior itself often acting like a drug. Unless their foundations are solid, young black men also buy into societal proscriptions, further distorting their senses of self. As this distortion begins at a very early age, the importance of black men and women's awareness, their discouragement of false lures and their encouragement of a solid future, cannot be overemphasized.

The act of sex itself, basically instinctual and a primitive act designed for procreation, in reality has absolutely nothing to do with the black man's image or his success. The advertising industry, however, likes to promote a different sentiment. Acutely aware that incorporating sexual innuendo into print ads and commercials causes sales to skyrocket, the business world makes considerable money with little concern for how its advertising tactics, in the moral sense, affect humanity. Its primary concern is imbuing a "feeling" into the person who will then buy the products it touts. Unaware purchasers

complete the cycle, hoping to be more appealing to others by enhancing their image, looks, or personality.

Advertisements directed toward black men lead them to believe
that if they use a specific cologne or wear a certain garment, they,
too, will attract the type of woman pictured in the ad. Although very
few of those women (models) exist in average societal circles, the
suggestion remains that if the black man buys the advertised products, visually pleasing light- or white-skinned women will surely lean
on his arm. No matter what values or concepts of love he might have,
he is encouraged to be viewed as cool and successful in this mythical
manner.

The enigma that the African American male must solve is, Why
must he define himself through his sexuality? Must a black man confirm his manliness by how many beautiful women he has? More importantly, why is another person's perception so important to a black
man's image? A perceptive observation is offered by the Reverend
Jesse Jackson: "achievement of an education and obtaining knowledge would most define a black man's image and earn him well-
deserved respect, and not the 'stud' label that he so often misguidedly
seeks."

Andre Agassi, the professional tennis player, has contended that
"image is everything." But just how important is image, really? By
definition, image is represented as the "character that is projected to
the public." Ezra Pound, United States poet and critic, more
poignantly placed image into a category of constant flux. He argued
that "image is more than an idea—it is a vortex or cluster of fused
ideas and is endowed with energy." To black males, "fused ideas" are
projected as sexual energy; arguably, both Agassi's and Pound's
provocative comments may, in fact, prove more true than not. The
black man's image is in constant motion, changing shape to suit its
wearer and dependent upon others for that change.

People of all ethnic groups have a personality component that
makes them wish to adapt and conform to the conditions of their environment. Sigmund Freud, an Austrian physician and the founder
of psychoanalysis, named this need to comply the id. Freud suggested
that the id allows people to conform to and benefit from established
social laws. The women-should-wear-dresses-and-men-should-wear-

pants mentality, therefore, allows individuals to perceive themselves as nonthreatening, likable, and part of the fixed social order according to the norms of society.

Patterns of behavior do change and are dependent upon the image that the black man embraces, one that can interfere with the honest and true image of himself. These realizations proved true time and again in focus groups I have conducted, the foundation for the images that shape the black man's sense of self. As black men, particularly those younger than thirty, appear to have a vital need for approval from others outside their immediate family circles. Two particular focus groups are of interest here.

With colleagues, I conducted groups concentrated on image and success, and their interrelation. The first, Group A, was comprised of nine black men aged seventeen to thirty and the second, Group B, included twelve black men aged thirty-one to fifty-five. Identical questions were posed to both groups, resulting in differing responses, perhaps with age as the influential factor. For example, when asked what made them feel successful, Group A responded, "How others perceive me." Yet there was one common thread across both groups: neither discussed love as a priority.

The younger men felt that owning a nice car, wearing designer labels, and being invited to the "best" parties, along with having the money to uphold this lifestyle, were most important. The older Group B felt that having a good job, a nice home, a woman and even children to take care of, along with having enough money to support the people in his life, were of most importance. Both groups ranked having love in their lives and feeling love for another person at the bottom of their list of important needs for success. The older men felt it important to be perceived as responsible by others in their profession and neighbors as being successful. In order for them to feel like "real men," others must recognize them as being well-off financially. And able to take care of their family.

However, the older men did not rank how others saw them materially of primary importance, as did the younger group. Having a strong relationship with a woman ranked high on the list of those in Group B, but Group A did not report the same feelings; rather, while having a relationship with a woman was important, it was not crucial for the relationship to be a strong one. More important was that the woman on one's arm be beautiful, to project a successful image. Love was not a dominant factor in either group's equation and there was no primary value placed on love in any group member's life.

Groups A and B were obviously very different in many facets of their approaches to relationships. It can be argued that many of these vast differences relate directly to the men's level of emotional maturity. Typically, it is only through experience that sophistication is realized.

A look at my own past relationships might aid in exemplifying this argument. More times than I now care to admit women told me that I was very immature. Interestingly, this remark always confused me because in my own mind I was "cool" and grown up. I always concluded that when women said I was immature, they must be joking and teasing the way I always did with them.

As a boy I taunted my sisters, and as I grew into a man I broadened this pattern to include other women. Perhaps subconsciously I believed that the joking kept me on the offense and women on the defense. In any case, early in my youth I had read somewhere that women liked witty, humorous men. As time passed, I came to understand that I was not called immature because of my wisecracking manner, but because of the way I approached a relationship as a whole.

Unfortunately, I had always entered into a relationship for what I could personally obtain from it, or for what being with a woman could do for me. I was unable to focus on the beauty of a relationship or the joy it could bring. In early years, much as a baby cries out for immediate attention, I would seek immediate gratification for my needs and wants, even if they were inappropriate. Acting out simply became a way of life. Eventually I gained understanding that my immature behavior stemmed from unrealistic notions of what a relationship was supposed to be. I was idealistic, not realistic; age and experience helped turn this mind-set around.

Upon emotionally maturing, I came to appreciate the many wonderful unconditional qualities of a true relationship. As I grew more comfortable in a long-term, loving relationship, the beauty of my mate's face began to take second place to the beauty of her mind and spirit.

When I conducted the focus group, I saw from the beginning that there were common traits in Group A, that did not exist in Group B. The younger men congregated together, joking with one another and apparently trying to be more aloof than the next guy. The older men were quite comfortable sitting or standing alone while they waited for the group to start. Chitchatting with me or reading to pass the time seemed to be more common with the older men. While this chitchat by the older men can perhaps be attributed to nervousness, similar behaviors are observable upon visiting the coffee shop next door to my office. In either case, there is evidence to suggest that the older men are more comfortable with who they are and therefore do not need to congregate to expel nervousness. While both groups thought sexual prowess to be their main contribution to a relationship, it seems that the older men understood that a relationship itself was more important than exercising individuality. This is probably due to their maturity and experience levels.

As often as possible, I make time in my practice to share personal experiences with young male patients. Some understand the importance of maturity and unity within a relationship and some shrug it off as if I were speaking in a foreign language. Frustratingly, the vast majority seem destined to make many of the same mistakes I made and may therefore never have the opportunity to know the splendor of a shared relationship. Sometimes it seems that a readiness factor exists within the black man's psyche that must ripen before he is ready to mature emotionally and to see all women realistically—as companions and not play toys. Certainly experience—other than sexual—is the key to maturity. Regarding all women for who they are and not what they can do for a black man is the first step toward realizing emotional maturity. It takes practice to shift the focus, but it can be done!

Group A also reported that their actions were motivated by what they saw on billboards, in magazines, at the movies, through music, and heard from friends than was the older Group B. The older group did not feel that the media played any part in their motivation to act upon their decision making in life. Their colleagues and neighbors, were the determinants of their self-image. Both groups felt being successful meant being perceived as emotionally, physically, and financially strong. Ironically, both groups defined a man as a strong person who can take care of himself and is able to make his own decisions without the help of others.

The two focus groups in this example reveal some important findings. First of all, there may be a difference in how younger black males and older black males think. Values also appear to differ from young to old, most likely due to experience. However, in both groups, the black men deemed physical sexuality as an integral part of their success as men. While this perception may hold true for all ethnic groups, for black men it has grown to problematic significance.

One specific event that exemplifies this impression occurred while I was practicing medicine in Philadelphia during the summer of 1998. Annually, during the month of July, black sororities and fraternities gather in Philadelphia's infamous Fairmont Park to celebrate the Greek Week festival. Included during the traditional celebration are concerts, lectures, and the sale of college paraphernalia, the proceeds going to charities benefiting blacks. Although the charities did benefit, the event was marred by several alarming situations: some included law enforcement officials imposing order, creating an atmosphere of apprehension centered on black men exercising their manhood and sexuality. The media subsequently reported how some black men had committed sexual offenses, including rape, against young black women at the festival, behaving in a manner that perpetuates the black male myth and negative stereotypes.

During the heavy media coverage of the incidents, a term—previously unknown to me—was used to describe the behavior of clusters of black men assaulting black women. "Whirling," as explained by a member of the media, is collective predatory behavior of groups of young black men, and was first coined in Atlanta, Georgia, at another large social event. Simply put, a group of black men emerges from a crowd and encircles an unsuspecting young black woman, much as a lion might trap a vulnerable antelope. Rendering her helpless, the men close the circle around the woman; grabbing, probing, punching, and often raping their prey, they tear away her clothing as she screams for help. Bystanders are either unable to see what is happening because of the large group of men encircling the woman, or unable to assist due to the sheer number of men involved. Muffled cries for help from the victims often go unheard. Remarkable as it may seem, when the groups of black males are finished, they fade back into the crowd as if nothing had happened, leaving the victim brutally traumatized.

At least a dozen incidents of whirling occurred during the Greek Festival in Philadelphia. As the news unfolded, it became evident that the groups of black men who committed these acts of sexual violence were so large, there was no way to identify each and every one. Additionally, according to local police, many of the terrible acts of whirling were perpetrated not by students but by local gangs or thugs operating on the perception that their manhood stems from a sexual, conquering nature.

Sadly, instead of using the opportunity of a highly publicized event to redefine who black men are as a people, the incidents promoted the negative stereotypical image of the black man using his sexuality to overpower a woman in an attempt to prove his manhood. The media coverage, however negative, validated his behavior, making him feel like an important man.

These incidents provide insight into how black men reason and how their attitudes and collective sense of individual sexuality come into play when they try to uphold images of themselves based primarily on physical and sexual conquest. Black men have forgotten their individuality and have melted into the acceptance of an image that does nothing but destroy the public's perception of the African American male. With sadness and trepidation I pose this question: How can black men allow their behaviors and sense of self to confirm to the rest of the world that, yes, we are primitive thinkers and an animalistic people who are bent on sexual conquest and the torture of our black women? How could a black man justify this to himself while calmly saying, "Yes, I participated in an act of sexual violence, but everyone else was doing it too . . . and, I really do respect women." The truth, the bottom line, is that sex, image, and success are all interwoven with the end result determined by the individual, who is just that—an individual.

It is not uncommon for my office to be besieged by troubled mothers expressing the need for guidance regarding their young sons' negative attitudes. Their behaviors often indicate that a life of crime is imminent, motivated by the desire for designer labels and high-dollar automobiles. In other instances, frantic wives will complain of their husband's misuse of the household budget to impulsively buy cars and clothes that put him "in with the boys."

W. E. B. DuBois, a prodigious educator and famous civil rights leader, summarized thoughtfully, "An American, a Negro—two souls, two thoughts, two unreconciled strivings; two warring ideals in one dark body, whose dogged strength alone keeps it from being torn asunder." The strength that DuBois was referring to had nothing to do with physical prowess. On the contrary, it relates to perseverance, tenacity, and the longing to become more than our predecessors. As an American, the black man has at his fingertips all of the tools necessary to succeed in life even without those designer clothes and that new car.

Although many black men continue to go around in circles making the same mistakes, paradoxically they continue to expect different results from the same actions. The black man falls continuously into the stereotypical traps when defining who we are. He becomes one of "the boys" so that he is accepted. His distorted thinking is ultimately focused on sexual conquest in an attempt to prove to his friends that he is a "real man." This is precisely how the myth of the black man as a sexual predator perpetuates itself.

Recently, two sexual scandals in the United States armed forces exemplify and reinforce this myth in a very public way. It is a classic example of the myth reinventing itself and fulfilling the prophecy, thereby reinforcing the negative image of the black male. One scandal was caused by drill instructors who were charged with raping subordinates under their command. These drill instructors were black men and the tense situation created chaos and notoriety for the Army. A similar case involving a white commander, barely made a ripple in the news media.

This public image of black males as sexual predators becomes big news and creates a domino effect, gaining momentum from a prejudiced, unforgiving, and relentless media. The fact that the black family still exists, flourishing with love, has become but vague echoes in the minds of many. While some black males continue to work in earnest to adopt the media-defined sexual ways of life, black families, mates, and public images continue to suffer.

It is significant at this point to mention a few words about image with respect to black women. Dynamics differ somewhat among black women and men, especially when referring to how women think, feel, and behave. One might argue that black women are smarter than their male counterparts when it comes to both reactive and proactive behavior, due in part to a lesser impact by negative stereotypical myths. Many African American women have a tendency to choose those images most conducive to positive results, lessening negativity in their lives. As a whole, black women tend to react to stereotypical myths with indifference and a "silent strength" that keep them from being negatively labeled and, unlike black men, these women speak out and stand up for themselves when faced with negative images.

From the days of slavery, black women were attuned to the stereotypes placed upon them by white slave owners. Knowing that their role was predefined, they did everything within their power to keep oppression from affecting their everyday lives and to keep their families together. These remarkable women sacrificed much of themselves in the struggle to care for those they held most dear. They had a strong sense of self and an awareness of what was required to achieve and to maintain a sense of unity during the days of the slave trade. Outside influences not applicable to the yearning for her family's freedom meant very little to the early American black woman, her strength emerging as the cornerstone for the black family unit in a time of unmerciful slavery. As the black woman overcame abundant obstacles, her personality and inner strength grew and became more secure. This will to survive that has been passed on through generations is in strong evidence today.

It was not until the turn of the century that the black woman began to take notice of how she was being perceived by other ethnic groups, namely the dominant white society. Black women endured the posturing of white women in the media, who proclaimed that the epitome of beauty and sexuality was the blue-eyed, curvaceous blonde. As discussed in the chapter on history, black women were labeled by the media such as print ads, newspaper articles, etc., as having thick lips, kinky hair, a bad attitude, and other negative attributes.

Although there were many great black women such as Mary McLeod Bethune, Sojourner Truth, and Harriet Tubman, it was not until the civil rights movement of the sixties that black women's voices were really heard, openly professing what they were truly about as women. Even though stereotypes existed, black women used their great strength to reveal themselves, and united in large numbers.

Black women benefited significantly during this period of social change for blacks. They were able to catapult themselves to a level of pride and accomplishment both positive and easily accepted by society. Black women latched on to historical black female role models, molding themselves in the positive images of their black sisters. These role models were the scholars, poets, and businesswomen who began the journey of redefining all black women. One of the most inspiring African American women of our time, the poet Maya Angelou, has stated, "There is a kind of strength that is almost frightening in black women. It's as if a steel rod runs right through the head down to the feet," which demonstrates the intensity of the black woman's struggle to define herself in a dominant white society.

Even though trends keep redefining who is deemed beautiful, black women still come up short. Although many black women have made it to the interiors of magazines, few have found their way to the coveted front covers. Sparse numbers of black women grace the runways of the fashion industry. The only places black women are continually honored for their beauty are on the covers of black-owned magazines and within black-owned media. This both frustrates and angers black women as the majority of images still reflect the white female with straight hair and fair skin as the epitome of beauty. Hopefully, as time passes, society will become more aware that beauty is not defined by skin color, but by the genuineness of the image portrayed. Black women deserve to be recognized for their beauty and own their place in the world, that place being a true signature combination of sexuality, intelligence, and attractiveness.

The black woman's image is slowly infiltrating white-dominated media, which today no longer links sexuality and intelligence exclusively to white women. Sulky, attractive women with brown skin and visually pleasing curves and long slender legs, and black women in successful roles are incorporated more and more into advertisements. Black women demand more from society and from black men. Many are choosing to remain single rather than to partner with a black man who does not fit into their own positive patterns of success, image, self-sufficiency, and economic independence.

These trends are seen increasingly in young black female adolescents. National health statistics show that more young black women are finishing high school, delaying marriage and pregnancy, and pursing college educations, while many young black males remain stuck within stereotypes. Black women are achieving goals and combating myths, while black men remain content to fulfill their prophesized destinies.

While other ethnic groups are usually able to define their own roles, those of black men are still commonly defined by how they are viewed and defined by others. The term *stuck* is not used lightly. Looking at life from behind the veil and not emerging for fear that we will not live up to our own expectations is what is meant by being "stuck." Those expectations are defined by a society that, in the past, expected blacks to fail. Perceptions of black men today still often become self-fulfilling prophecies. Although it is probably true for some segments of the black male population, being content or in something of a comfort zone does not ring true for many black men.

The term *veil* has been used in literature by authors such as W. E. B. DuBois and James Baldwin to describe how it feels to be a black man in a society where rules have been historically applied from a Caucasian perspective. If black men still believe that they will ultimately fail, then they question the wisdom of coming out from behind the veil in the first place. Black men do find, in reality, that once the veil is lifted there is no stopping us from achieving anything we put our minds to. We no longer live in the past. The future is brighter than ever when black men seize the moment and allow education, not sexuality, to dictate decisions.

Consequently, if our image is the sum total of all our fused ideas, it is our ideas that will give us the energy necessary to succeed. The energy used to form our attitudes and behavioral patterns is the same energy that drives us sexually. Our resulting success depends on our own self-image. The relationship between forming an idea as sexually driven has a direct bearing upon whether or not we are able to use this sexual idea to succeed. Thus, it would follow that our success is dependent upon just how the images of ourselves are formed and subsequently become ideas. If the sources are based solely on sex, they remain unhealthy, and our success will be limited.

Just how much do we, as black men, depend upon others to form the ideas we have of ourselves? Though many think otherwise, outside influences greatly determine self-worth, attitudes, and behaviors. But what can we do to change the way others perceive black men? Perhaps the solution is nothing more than monitoring our sexual urges and forming a nonsexual image of ourselves—as strong and successful—for others to witness. Our decision-making must be reality-based and not impulsive. We must change in a profound way how others see us. We must replace the sexual element that has driven black men for centuries with a more positive, intellectual demeanor. By doing so, this might dispel the myths and stereotypical images that others see and reflect back to us.

In addition to outside influences, black men must look deep inside in an effort to make changes on both conscious and subconscious levels. Choosing to ignore negative comments prevents us from forming and internalizing the dubious images within us. One alternative response to ignoring negative comments is turning them into an evaluation and simply verifying its authenticity. For example, when I entered medical school at the age of thirty-four, I was very apprehensive and felt inferior to all the other younger students. Throughout my life I had heard that black men were not smart enough to become doctors. Although I can't specifically remember who said that to me, I suspect it was a collective of negative people whom I encountered growing up in the ghetto. Even though I had already obtained a master's degree in education and my mentors over time had taught me differently, there was still a part of me that questioned my abilities. When I started my apprenticeship into medicine I couldn't help thinking that the white and Asian students were somehow smarter than I. This negative thinking was so ingrained that I seemed unable to change my suspicions. After the first couple of exams, however, I realized that we were all on the same level. While it is sad that it took exams to make me realize this, they were not the most important part of my epiphany. As I began to evaluate myself, all of my fears were eventually eliminated. Some of my eventual questions even contained a little humor: Were these non-black students really smarter than I? . . . Was it true that black males were incapable of becoming doctors? . . . What makes them different from me? . . . More important, what makes them the same as me? . . . Don't they all put on their pants and underwear the same way I do? The first two questions were answered by my intellectual self with no's, but my insecurity as a black male made me uncertain still. As I asked myself what made the other students different from me, I could really not come up with anything other than the fact that their skin color and hair were different and the Asian students spoke a great deal of Japanese. Although they were younger, that just did not seem to be a big deal.

Even more obvious were our similarities. They were sweating the tests just as I was. They had gotten into medical school by taking one of the hardest tests known to man, the Medical School Admissions Test (MCAT), and so had I. We were all in medical school.

Of all the black doctors and leaders in the field of medicine I had read about, there still was not enough to convince me of my true potential. It was not until I had finally passed the tests at the top of my class that I was able to confidently continue to do well. In my last year of medical school I was elected class president, an honor I came to cherish.

As in my situation, keeping in mind that even the smallest of personal tests carries great reward can push us toward success. It is not going to always be a medical school test or a school election. It can simply be pushing one's self past the traditional comfort zone and expanding one's knowledge base. An honest appraisal of what it is that can be achieved using self-evaluation questions repeatedly empowers.

A further example of a black man honestly evaluating himself comes from a patient of mine. A successful, middle-aged contractor, he had been married to the same woman for twenty years; when I asked about his secret for a good relationship he related the following: "You know, Doc, I went to my girl's [now wife's] house to meet her father and mother. I was seventeen years old and from a neighborhood where drugs and crime were terrible. I really had it in my mind that her parents would not like me because I was from the wrong side of the tracks and it was because of this, I originally thought about not even showing up. Anyway, as I walked up the steps to her house, I just told myself that just because the men from my neighborhood were 'dogs' did not mean that I was one. And since I chose not to be a 'dog' could I hold my head high in front of her parents? Doc, it worked because I felt confident that I was a good person and that I would want to meet me." He chuckled, "In fact, her parents really liked me which only reinforced how I felt and coming from the other side of the tracks didn't seem to make a bit of difference. They called me a gentleman and ever since then, I have never forgotten to ask myself those kinds of questions over the years." Self-opinion is true only if one believes it; an honest self-evaluation can determine this. How one incorporates these positive statements into one's own image and idea of self is what matters. Responses to negativity in any form are internal first, and we are free to agree or disagree with any negative issue we face. Resentment and an over-compensatory need to prove the negative wrong are common initial responses. Much energy, however, is required for each of these responses and can produce unhealthy attitudes and behaviors. Black men need to learn how to ignore the surrounding negativity and take small steps toward adjusting these negative images.

I encounter many poor and disadvantaged black women and men in my medical practice. Some have healthy self-images; others do not. Those who do have positive self-images and are unmoved by what others say about them also have a propensity to place little value on the stereotypical images of blacks. One of my patients, a well-groomed and proper elderly woman, once said to me, "Those old black tales [myths] don't mean nothing—it's the same thing that the Germans said about black men during World War II, that black men have tails. They [Germans] must have been really scared of our black men." Certainly all is not lost for us. In fact, we have the power to refuse to acknowledge these negative images of who we are as sexual men, and we must stop doubting our self-worth and contribution to the world. People tend to appreciate the demeanor of others when it is positive and consistent. When a black man's actions contribute to harmony within the social order, attitudes about that man change for the positive. Over time, it is possible that the stereotypical images many ethnic groups harbor about black men will change from animosity and fear to respect and ultimate acceptance. Black

men with healthy self-images could very well change the evolution-
ary course for black Americans and perhaps influence the way all
non-black Americans perceive us.

Resistance to the organized mass can be effected only by the
man who is as well organized in his individuality as the mass itself.

—Carl Jung, *The Undiscovered Self,* ch. 4.

Chapter 3

THE BLACK MAN IN RELATIONSHIPS

Mine ear is much enamoured of thy note;
So is mine eye enthralled to thy shape;
And thy fair virtue's force perforce doth move me
On the first view to say, to swear, I love thee.
—William Shakespeare

The proverbial phrase "Man is not supposed to be alone" assumes a long-standing notion that relationships are innate, or "meant to be." However, to the many black men incapable of maintaining loving relationships or who choose to be alone, this proverb holds little significance. A great number of black men travel life's journey befuddled and confused, unable to recognize the secret to loving someone else. The solution to this sad dilemma, from my now enlightened perspective, is to truly know oneself completely. In order for one to be able to commit to another, particularly on a long-term basis in a monogamous relationship, one must love the other with all of one's self, and must love one's own self, first.

While this might appear on the surface to be fairly uncomplicated, it usually proves difficult in reality, especially where there exists a limited frame of reference in one's life. In other words, for us to really know ourselves we must come to terms with the inner aspects of our personality, understand what makes us tick, and know what types of stimulation propel our actions. Once this is achieved, we then must be able to embrace and accept both the good and not-so-good aspects of ourselves, which is what enables us, finally, to have a greater sense of what makes us who we are.

Becoming vulnerable to our own emotions and feelings is not something that black men typically learn to do. To the contrary, we have been taught for centuries that physical strength and sexuality comprise the cornerstone of our success as "real men." The consequences of this mentality can be tragic, impairing the black man's perception of himself in a profound way. Yet a disproportionately large number of black men tragically believe that love and sex are joined, thereby creating a sense of self deeply rooted in physical sexuality.

One example of a black man basing his self-confidence and personal attributes on his sexuality occurred during a visit by a man's wife to my office. After treating her for an unrelated health issue, I observed that she was unusually uptight and pensive. When I asked her if there was something bothering her, she became, like many people, apprehensive about sharing an obviously very personal issue. After reassuring her that I was there to help, she finally said in a strident tone, "I really need some advice about my husband. He has been so cold lately and he doesn't talk to me the way he used to. We almost never have sex anymore and I feel he is drifting away from me. Could there be something medically wrong with him, Doctor?" I suggested she convince her husband to come in for a consultation, which was successful.

Upon examination the man proved to be in good health. After probing a bit more, I asked him if there were any problems at home or in his relationship with his wife. Contemplating for a moment, the man let out a long sigh and answered, "Oh, Doc, I just don't know if I measure up. I am fifty, and my wife is only thirty-seven." He further explained that his first wife had been his childhood sweetheart and both were virgins when they married. He had never felt challenged or that he had had to compete for her love.

After his first wife passed away, he went on to marry his present wife who had been with other men sexually before they met and married. He then said, "You know Doc, just the other night she suggested that we improvise and make love a different way." He went on to say in a low, sad voice, "She must be thinking about one of her old flames." He felt pressured by his imaginary competition and chose to withdraw rather than to fail any self-concocted comparison tests that could, by his account, threaten his manhood. This man's sense of self and perception of love had merged together. He defined himself and his relationship with his wife according to his sexual performance. As odd as it may seem, he could not clearly see that his present wife loved and valued him not for his skill as a sexual partner but because he was a wonderfully compassionate and caring man. Clouded by his misguided sense of self, he placed no merit on these attributes as factors of love.

This man was different from the many black men who stop coming in for treatment. I was lucky with this particular patient because he continued to return to see me on a regular basis once trust had been established. He was able to talk with me about what he was feeling and as a result he became more secure in his relationship. He definitely had a breakthrough, an experience that occurs when change in an attitude or behavior helps a person get better or feel more comfortable with themselves. Since I see many men expressing what turn out to be pseudo-breakthroughs in my clinical setting, I am often wary of their continuity.

As mentioned before, sometimes when a patient is told what the real problem is with his health, he never comes back for follow-up. Many black men are reluctant to see a doctor anyway, and either pride or fear takes over when they are confronted with an illness. Other times, like most people, the effort to change or to receive treatment may be overwhelming enough to not even bother, so they do not return.

However, this particular patient did come back to see me in the office. He and his wife entered into marital counseling at my urging and are much happier today than they have ever been. While we don't really discuss it much anymore, once in a while he'll say to me, "Doc, I may not be gettin' any younger, but I'm sure gettin' better," and together we laugh.

This patient represents an inordinately large number of black males who overemphasize sexual prowess as a precursor to love. A continuous pattern of inability to separate sex from love creates barriers for these black men that prevent long-lasting, wholly loving relationships.

Another case involving a young female patient poignantly illustrates this point.

Distraught and morose, this young woman described a caustic encounter with her boyfriend: "He moved out, that bastard left me." Perplexed, I asked her what had happened. On many previous visits they had both come into my office together, always acting affectionate and loving toward one another. In fact, I had noticed their playful teasing and jovial name-calling when they came in for visits; they always made me grin. Although some of their verbal exchanges were cantankerous at times, they never appeared to offend each other and they seemed very happy together.

She answered my inquiry: "We were joking with each other as usual and I said, 'You can't satisfy me with that little dick.'" She went on to say that after she made this statement, he had become infuriated and immediately had left the house. Visibly upset, she sighed, "I just don't understand it. I have called him dumb, an idiot, and even talked about his mother, but he has never, ever reacted like this to *anything*." It became immediately apparent to me that her statement about his sexual organ was a direct insult that reached to the core of his sense of self. Unknowingly, to his ears she had told him she didn't love him. Even though she had made the comment facetiously, he had taken it very seriously, experiencing a crushed self-worth. After hearing this explanation, she realized the error of her ignorance and set about positively addressing the issue. Following several recommended counseling sessions, this couple, I am happy to report, reconciled. While residue from that incident may resurface, they are now equipped with the tools necessary to confront any doubts head-on. Although I referred them to a counselor, I kept abreast of this couple's progress via professional correspondence with their therapist. Uniquely, they showed up at every session and followed the therapist's recommendations for communicating with one another. It seemed that even though they were in the habit of calling each other names and criticizing each other as a way of showing their love, both parties actually felt terrible when the other one reciprocated. Their history was difficult to overcome, but they managed to find and implement other avenues of expression for their love for one another. While I have not yet had the opportunity to speak personally with her boyfriend at length, this female patient has told me time and again that she has learned so many things about him. There is no wedding date set, but happily she assures me I will be invited.

Relationships are at times arduous for everyone. But for black men, who tend to define their sense of self in terms of sexual prowess, it becomes more difficult to determine the boundaries of healthy relationships. Without an honest evaluation of one's self, there is no possibility of defining relationship parameters. A sexually based relationship is destined to fail in the long run.

Reflecting on past relationships, I, myself, cannot avoid recounting a multitude of failed associations with women. Unable to resolve and save two marriages, I remain saddened by the knowledge that I was a catalyst for the dissolution of each. Sitting in my office, surrounded by an assortment of degrees and certificates that hang neatly on the walls, I contemplate that extensive schooling and intellectual achievement were not enough to sustain my relationships with others, nor did they nurture an understanding of myself. After several years alone with time for self-reflection, it is only now that I am able to approach my mate in a more honest manner and to accept her as my equal. Giving of myself, and knowing that she accepts every part of me, has enabled me to grow as a man. Because of this new success I now know that maintaining a loving relationship is absolutely possible. The macho, self-serving man that I used to be failed. My improved understanding of love and my enhanced respect for my mate's reciprocity has transformed me from a hard-to-please individual into one who is more good-natured and more accommodating in my daily actions.

Historically, black men have practiced what they have seen or been taught throughout their lives and bring this chronicled road map along to our relationships. Some are brought up in homes with fathers who practice the proverbial phrase, "Do as I say, not as I do." Some experience that "iron fist that sometimes slugged us to prove a point," and some grow up in single-parent families with either a mother or grandmother.

Growing up in a loving, two-parent home is not the norm in the black community. Many young black boys observe a father who disrespects and abuses his mother verbally and/or physically. The role of the macho man becomes permanently engraved in the minds of those children, only to surface again in his adult relationships.

On the other hand, black men who are taught to love and respect women by observing their own family bring very positive and healthy perspectives to their relationships. Although not the rule, there certainly exist the exceptional men who encountered abuse in their homes but still went on to contribute to wonderful marriages, vowing not to let it happen in their own homes.

Religion also tends to influence how black men behave toward women. When a patient of mine mentioned that he was having problems in his new relationship, he added that he was troubled by not being able to figure out why. He told me that he had met the person of his dreams, but once she had moved in, serious problems began. The young black man had been raised in a family who belonged to a special sect, in which men were taught to treat their wives and other women as second-class citizens.

He told me that his father had forced his mother to always walk behind him and he had not allowed her to work outside of the home. Raising children and being at his beck and call had been her role in their marriage. As a young child he had not questioned their relationship, but as he grew into adulthood he began to suspect that how his father treated his mother was wrong.

Upon leaving his childhood home, he chose not to follow the religion in which he had grown up. However, he confided, he had not been successful in disengaging himself from behaviors like his father's in relationships with his mother and other females in the family. When his new girlfriend construed his behavior as offensive, sexist, and chauvinistic, she left him. He was crushed, but has since sought therapy in an effort to prevent the same things from recurring. The combination of his particularly strict religious upbringing and the negative behaviors of his parents had not provided the tools he needed to exist in a healthy relationship.

In contrast, another patient was raised in a very religious home in which his father and mother were very spiritually connected. This man experienced little trouble in his own marital relationship. Sometimes I reminisce about the day he sat in my office, gushing about how much his father loved his mother and all of the romantic things that he still did for her—even after twenty-five years of marriage. He attributed the love shared between his parents as a direct result of their mutual faith in God. That young man's personal experience and religious upbringing encouraged a special respect and love for women. His values came directly from observing his parent's interaction with one another on a daily basis. It was easy to wish that my own home life had been like his.

Education can have a major effect on how black men view themselves, their sexuality, and the scope of their relationships. I sometimes meet men who have not finished high school, and many who cannot even read. More often than not, these men have experienced turmoil in their relationships because they felt ashamed, and overcompensated for their lack of knowledge. Educated women are intimidating, and these men's insecurity is displaced to other areas. Instead of using logic to deal with difficult situations, their emotions sometimes emerge as anger and aggression toward women.

This does not mean that a highly educated man is less prone to aggression, but it does indicate that those men possessing the tools to seek knowledge are better equipped to change primitive negative emotional behaviors. Education can unlock answers that aid black men in their quest for healthy relationships. In my own case, the more I learned about what a healthy relationship should be like, the more I was able to incorporate this knowledge into my own attitudes and behaviors toward my mate. While my relationship is not without its challenges due to our own differences it could prove disastrous if I still related to her as did my father-model to my mother.

For black men, relationships come in many forms and contain various meanings. Successful relationships hinge on how black men feel about themselves, the women in their lives, and the concrete definition of each relationship. Many influences have an impact on the way a black man feels about being in a relationship, perhaps the most important being how he views women as a whole. From a psychological standpoint, how a black man feels about women has been significantly influenced by his history, religion, and levels of education and understanding. How he perceives his mate and defines his partner's role in the relationship will determine the relationship's chance for success and happiness. Ideally, both partners will be genuine companions first and lovers second. A person does not enter a relationship merely because they love someone; they do it because of how the other person makes them feel about themselves. Without an honest sense of self, the relationship will be precarious from the onset, built on a foundation of dishonesty and sexual stimulation.

History has certainly played a major role in determining how black men relate with black women. During the time of slavery, body and strength defined one's worth as a black man. Although the black woman worked beside the black man in the cotton fields, she was relegated to housemaid and servant to the black men and children once back in the slave quarters. We can imagine how some black male slaves adopted the false notion that even though both were slaves, the black woman, essentially powerless, must be inferior to the black man, thus creating for him his own sense of mastery.

Clearly it is not remarkable that this type of destructive interaction developed, given the circumstances. However, because those shackles no longer physically bind, we black men must break free from the persisting "slave mentality" in relating with our mates. Our collective sense of self has suffered tremendously as a result of this narrow-minded thinking; we must successfully re-think and re-establish our approach to relationships.

In my own past, when I labored under such a slave mentality, I would find myself filling with doubt in a relationship, asking, "How could she love me, particularly when I neither love nor understand myself?" Once I started down that rocky road, I would begin to lose respect for the person who loved me. The feeling of no longer being able to trust her love would create a compulsive need to project my hidden personal resentment upon my unaware partner, causing her my pain. Similarly, as a result of his own need for power and control during an era of desperate self-doubt, the enslaved black man imagined the black woman to be subservient to him. In this way, while he was a subjugated slave in the cotton fields, he viewed himself as royalty in his slave quarters.

Whether or not black men are aware of what they are doing or are simply emulating their own parents remains a mystery. Perhaps black men are extremely aware of what is going on, but do not believe they are responsible for the chaos in their relationships. While in my past I was certainly well aware of what I was doing, realizing that it was wrong was the turning point for me in establishing successful relationships.

My sense of safety always came before the person I was with. There was always a fine line between my sense of manhood and society's perception of my blackness, and my own ability to change that perception by doing what was right. Changing my ways to incorporate another person into my life on an equal footing was not acceptable to me until I finally realized that it was the right thing to do, instead of acting on prescribed notions of manhood that had been dictated by my peers.

Do black men know they should rectify these negative situations in their own lives? Sure they do, as I did, but I was unwilling to act outside of what I thought was the norm, or how it was "supposed to be." Social learning says that a person will emulate those people that he or she feels more comfortable being around; the people that are the most accepting. If a person who acts negatively is surrounded by similar people, then it stands to reason that breaking out of that negative mind-set will not happen unless something very profound occurs, like moving to a new neighborhood or starting a different job, or even moving to a different state. More education can also promote this, although even those with a good education can be prone to negative behavior toward their mates.

In essence, even though I had a master's degree in education and subsequent medical schooling, I was still unable to disregard memories of my early childhood when my father dominated the household. That idea was so intrinsic to my being that to change it would mean to sacrifice a part of myself and learn something that I was not comfortable with—placing another person's well-being on the same plane as my own. Once I began to act differently from what I had learned as a child, my life became increasingly calmer, happier, and more predictable. The woman in my life is happy and content with who I am as a person and she sometimes says that she cannot imagine me any other way than loving and caring.

Religion also contributes to the difficulty black men experience in relationships. Traditionally, the Bible has had a great impact on the lives of black people, especially during the days of slavery. Biblical interpretations and the resulting religions have influenced black culture by defining the black man's role in the family as well as in his everyday interactions. Most important, how the black man has related to the women in his life has been influenced by religion.

Unfortunately, the roles of many women in important ancient books have not always enjoyed favorable interpretation. For example, in the Book of Genesis, Eve has been blamed for the expulsion of all humanity from the Garden of Eden; Adam's own ill-fated choices tend to be disregarded. Because of Eve's weakness for the forbidden fruit and her subsequent transgressions, the pain of childbirth and menstruation is the stated punishment bestowed upon her by God. Other biblical stories have been interpreted similarly: a woman named Delilah was blamed for Samson's loss of strength and libido because she cut off his hair; Mary Magdalene, a prostitute, and without Jesus's intervention, would have been stoned to death for her actions.

Akin to the biblical Eve, the first woman in Greek mythology is Pandora. In this particular story, the god Zeus, angered by Prometheus for stealing divine fire from the gods and giving it to man, created Pandora and sent her to live among the mortals. Out of curiosity she opened a forbidden box, freeing the evils of the world, the consequences of which wreaked havoc on all of mankind. Like the biblical Eve eating forbidden fruit, Pandora has become associated with the term *femme fatale*.

More often than not, the ancient books of influence portray women as schemers and tricksters. Black men have embedded these characterizations in their psyche, believing that most women behave in the same way as Eve and Pandora, and they become angry when women are defiant and, on occasion, blame these women for their own social distress.

Although white men taught Christianity to black male slaves, the primary tribal religions of blacks did not have its roots in these biblical teachings. As more and more slaves became assimilated to America, bible teachings about these women were incorporated into the hidden slave religions with African roots that they practiced when the white slave master was asleep. Consequently, many black men believed that all women were prone to adverse behavior and began to look at women with skepticism and distrust. Much of this was borne out of western religion. Power and control come into play in Galatians 3:28 where Paul, a disciple of Jesus, first says, "Neither man or woman, all is one in Jesus," but later declares that women should be subordinate to their husbands. He says, "They [women] should learn in silence and refrain from exercising power over men."

I can surmise that black men do not study history and religion and then actively tailor their behavior to copy the past. However, the role in which I saw women was greatly influenced by these specific biblical doctrines, as well as the education I received. If a woman is perceived as subordinate and not entitled to a black man's respect, there is less chance that there will be open communication and honest love within a relationship. If black men continue to see the black woman as a femme fatale, then they prevent themselves from developing a true loving partnership. Fear replaces feelings of love as a form of protection from being betrayed. I know this to be true because it was once a part of me. As I became afraid of betrayal, I needed to protect myself by projecting anger toward my mates, in the form of physical strength, powerful control, and conquering with my sexuality.

One of the fathers of psychiatry, Otto Fenichel, wrote about castration anxiety in his book *The Psychoanalytic Theory of Neurosis*. Castration anxiety is the fear men have for the potential loss of their penises—not necessarily in a literal sense, but figuratively, in a mental sense. Fenichel says that this fear of losing one's penis produces anxieties that later influence a man's behavior when dealing with the opposite sex. The potential loss of his penis represents the potential loss of manhood or sexuality. Thus if he were unable to have sex, he would not be a man or experience love. This leads to fear that love or the object of love (i.e., female) can be lost if the object (penis) has no purpose, much like a female who loses self-esteem because she loses a breast.

Working as a psychologist prior to medical school, I encountered a black male patient who had severe mental illness and great emotional pain when dealing in relationships with women. I was treating this emotional infirmity as well as his addiction to drugs and alcohol. He was thirty-nine years old and lived alone. He was a son of a World War II veteran and did not have a good relationship with his father. This patient's self-esteem was constantly challenged by his father. As far back as he could remember, he was repeatedly degraded and never complimented or supported by his father. In fact, his father would consistently tell him that he was not a man. Many of his father's war stories frightened and confused him; one, in particular, would plague him for much of his life: When he was a young child, his father once told him that while fighting the war in Europe he encountered prostitutes who placed razors in their vaginas to castrate American soldiers.

Although this story was peculiar and seemed unbelievable, it had an impact on the way this patient later interacted with women. As he grew older and adjusted to adolescence, he became afraid of women and developed castration anxiety. Shying away from intimacy, he feared that if he became too close to a woman and had intercourse with her, he would lose his manhood, if not his penis. So he drank and used drugs to alleviate these anxieties. As he became a young man, he chose to be with women who appeared to have morals but didn't and who did not care about their personal appearance. Castration anxiety was not present and because of his lower expectations, love would not enter the sexual relationship. Highly educated and professional women fueled his anxieties and sense of inadequacy. However, even with these shallow women—some were prostitutes—he was unable to care about them or to have intercourse with them. This case is extreme and uncommon, but I have encountered many similar cases that explore the same issues, although to a lesser degree.

Black males can suffer quietly from mild castration anxiety when they enter into an intimate relationship that they perceive as challenging to their sexuality or manhood. Understanding why this short circuit occurs can enable black men to reach a higher level of consciousness to counteract untoward behavior they use to compensate for their genuine fear.

You should increase your understanding of what defines a relationship and what part you can play in making yourself healthy and more successful in relating to your mate. A deep understanding of why you view the women in your life the way you do is necessary. What are your expectations when establishing loving relationships?

My deep understanding of relationships has allowed me to mature and to enjoy a healthy, loving, and mutually rewarding partnership. This understanding involves four major phases that black men should use to develop a long-term, loving relationship: (1) attraction, (2) sex and infatuation, (3) the barrier of control, and (4) the merging of the self (his and hers). In the phase of attraction, many black males "only look with their eyes" instead of being drawn to the positive qualities of a woman. He simply finds her visually pleasing; a black man with a poorly integrated sense of self will be stimulated and respond only to what he sees on the surface. Some men get stuck in the sex and infatuation phase of relationships. They cannot give up the rush of the initial conquest and, therefore, cannot make the transition to unselfish love. The sex and infatuation phase is totally self-serving and relationships that do not proceed beyond this phase are destined to fail as well. The barrier of control is the phase when men jockey for control in a relationship, especially if the sexual act has been accomplished. The term *barrier* means the boundary line that each person in the relationship sets. Many black males are under the misguided impression that after sex, or the "conquest," the battle is won and a relationship or commitment has been formed—there is no need to do more to please the woman. He believes that he can now rest on his laurels and there is no need to be loving or attentive. This attitude often prevents relationships from evolving into the final phase: merging of the self, both his and hers. This phase is the true union of two people working as one, both maintaining a sense of individuality and commuting to the commonality of a long-term loving relationship. This is when the fear of losing control and one's self is no longer an issue in the black man's mind and he can truly consider selfless love as no longer being a threat to his manhood.

THE PHASES OF RELATIONSHIPS

Since there are different phases to a relationship, a thorough understanding of each is necessary for black males to succeed in mutually fulfilling relationships with women. However, before discussing these phases in detail, it is important to reveal the intricacies of the black man's personality.

As we have already seen, in order for black men to be able to relate to others, we must first and foremost understand ourselves, by realizing that we are black men who are capable of love and being loved, period. When black men accept this fact, we free ourselves to understand the other people in our relationships in an open-minded and compassionate way.

Love of one's self stems from a continuous effort to improve upon that which God gave you, enhancing those qualities of your personality that are healthy and disposing of those that are unhealthy and nonproductive. A sense of harmony from within generates an outward calm, allowing people to open their minds to others. For example, a teenager loves his old car and because of his love and commitment, he shines and buffs it at every opportunity. He works on it day in and day out and the end result is a sense of accomplishment and satisfaction; his hard work and commitment have produced the very best possible results. Like this teenager, the black man should work to shine and improve all aspects of himself to create a well-integrated personality. The motivating force for this work is a love of yourself—a genuine feeling of self-worth, acceptance, and love for the person that you are. Those seemingly "soft" feelings should never be construed as "feminine" or make you feel any less of a man. In fact, if you open yourself to those feelings, they should make you feel part of something worthwhile and deserving of the love that another has to give. What is more worthwhile than loving yourself first? Perhaps black men will say that loving someone else is of primary importance, but this is a distorted answer that lacks insight into what can be felt and accomplished for another person if, in fact, you fulfill your own needs first. With this in mind, you will be free to exercise your feelings toward another person and the anger and solitude you may feel from within will be replaced by reciprocal feelings of love and acceptance.

There are many theories that seek to define a person's personality, or self. My understanding of personality could perhaps be misconstrued as antiquated by those who study contemporary psychology; however, my interpretation is simple and thus enabled me to understand myself, as well as to gain insight into the personalities of other black males like me.

Imagine that your personality is divided, like a sliced pie. The self is equally partitioned into slices that represent the important individual aspects of your personality. This imaginary pie of your personality is comprised of slices that encompass your mental, spiritual, physical, emotional, and sexual selves. Each segment, or slice, should be of equal importance. And likewise, each segment should uniquely influence the total composite of one's behavior. When this occurs, your personality is well integrated. In order for black men to achieve well-integrated personalities, they must work to develop each segment of the pie with an honest and equal effort. If there is not a balance of effort toward the mental, spiritual, physical, emotional, and sexual sides of yourself, then your personality is off-balance and poorly integrated. All too often black men look for women who add to those parts of the pie that they do not possess themselves. Your personality could remain unbalanced throughout the course of your life and leave you feeling empty and unfulfilled personally.

In my medical practice, I encounter many black men who have poorly integrated personalities and many spend much of their effort developing their physical and sexual sides. I often speak with young black men in the local schools about the importance of developing all aspects of their personalities. This can be difficult when the media proclaims sex and "machoism" as "cool." Peer pressure pushes these young men in the direction of collective behavior and away from individuality and self-growth. A group of young black men are often perceived as threatening or as searching for prey, which only perpetuates the negative stereotypes. When groups of young blacks band together, in such ways as participating in sports or helping others and the community in a positive way, they feel a need to explore other aspects of themselves. The result is a better understanding of their selves, as well as a positive acceptance of others. I tell black men that love is a natural reward and it is the gift they receive when they have worked hard to equally integrate all the pieces of the pie.

Attraction

The first phase a person encounters when relating to others is attraction. Herein, vision plays a major role, especially when one person becomes attracted to another, at least in the inception of a relationship. Visual stimulation is a precursor to attraction, unless, of course, a person is unfortunately blind. If this is the case, then the other senses (i.e., touch and smell) compensate, heighten, and play the significant role. Even the sighted individual may be alerted by a scent that initiates the attraction; however, it is the visual aspect that strengthens the allure. Several systems within the body work in concert to receive the visual stimulus and assist in determining the quality of the attraction and the length of time the initial attraction is maintained.

Before the visual image can have personal meaning, specialized nerve pathways must deliver the image to the brain and place it on receptor sites. The design and function of these sites are predetermined by genetics and enhanced by experience. Conscious and unconscious factors influence the sexual stimulation produced by the reception of visual images. When the interwoven mechanisms of this complex system are studied, the euphemism "Beauty is in the eye of the beholder" is most appreciated.

The visual system and its impact on behavior greatly influence many black males. "I first look at the butt, that's what turns me on" is one of the numerous trite phrases we heard in our focus groups, indicating the significance of initial visualization as a precursor for attraction and highlighting the relationship between vision and sexual attraction.

I attempt to stay abreast of publications that pertain to sex and black people. For many years, African Americans were absent from studies that were done by luminaries like Hite, Kinsey, and Masters and Johnson. Only recently have I begun to see articles and surveys about black male sexuality in magazines at the supermarket checkout lines and in bookstores. However, the subject matter is limited and the scope of the problem is swept under the rug in an attempt to soften the issue of black men using sex to guide their lives. I sometimes question the survey design as well. For example, I once read a survey that was administered by a black female author who found that 99 percent of black males said that they were attracted to black women and thought they were sexy when they (black women) were self-confident and self-assured. The survey indicated that beauty and a goddess-like form had little to do with their attraction to them.

Being a physician and researcher, I am somewhat incredulous when I read these studies and often wonder who these black males were and where they resided. I question why my findings were so different, since my focus groups were always compiled of a cross-section of black males with different educational levels, and who lived in different areas of the country. Most important, I think about how I would answer the very same questions and certainly feel as if the results of those surveys are skewed merely to sell the magazine. It is important that I present to you, the reader, legitimate data and information that can bring reality to African Americans, no matter how harsh or gentle it may be.

A problem can be resolved only when a person realizes that something is wrong, and only when he accepts it, can he begin to deal with it head on. Denial is so common that it distorts the real truth. I honestly believe that most of the black males taking the magazine surveys respond to questions in an arrogant, boasting way in order to seem "cultivated" and compassionate to women. My own pathology with women was no longer sugarcoated once I accepted that it was I, and not the women in my life, who had the problems. I wrote this book because I know many black men have the same type of problems that I had with love, relationships, and lives ruled by their sexuality. Many will disagree with me but only because they are idealistic and not attuned to the real nature of the black male. My findings may differ from some of the seemingly unmethodical and sensational literature we read while standing in line at those supermarket counters. I find it a shame that black women buy magazines containing the sensationalized surveys in the hopes of finding a black man like those who respond. Perhaps many buy them in the hopes of finding clues to unlock the feelings that are buried deep in the black man's soul.

I am not proclaiming that visual attraction is a factor indigenous only to African American men. It is obvious that most people possess preconceived notions as to what is sexually stimulating. The problem arises when these preset patterns of thought have an unhealthy origin. As a result, this pathology influences behavior during the establishment of a long-term relationship.

People tend to be attracted to others who possess certain predetermined qualities. They discard the people who do not "fit" with their image of "attractiveness." If this mind-set has an unhealthy origin, then the initial visual attraction becomes distorted. Some origins of an unhealthy mind-set include adverse role modeling of parents and their attraction for each other, an overabundance of media-induced images of attraction and sex, or internalization of society's superficial image of what is deemed attractive. What we "see visually" and what "actually is," are often significantly different. But many black men enter into relationships for only visually appealing reasons.

Instead of being attracted to positive qualities when they first encounter another individual, a black male with a poorly integrated personality will let in only those images he has learned to consider "attractive." His negative mind-set, caused by initial negative sexual experiences, is stimulated by those experiences alone. Just as the pedophile is only sexually stimulated by children, black males who "only look with their eyes" have adopted societal myths and unhealthy sexual attitudes that influence what attracts them to a prospective mate. A pattern of attraction that is primarily visual and possesses no mental depth is both unhealthy and unproductive; it often leads to relationships based on superficial attitudes toward beauty. These relationships are the first to fail. They begin with unhealthy behavior; they progress to lack of communication; they are based on a misunderstanding of each other's needs and often lead to divorce. These relationships can produce children who consistently repeat the pattern of behavior learned from the previous generation. It is necessary for black males to understand and admit to these behaviors so they can begin to understand what constitutes healthy attraction.

One of the most interesting series of focus groups I've observed was one with the same group of black men throughout the course of the series. The focus group ran for five meetings. Out of the fourteen men who started, ten remained through the final session. Although there was a wide range of ages (the youngest was eighteen years old and the oldest sixty-one) and a variety of socioeconomic levels (unemployed to business managers, etc.), they had all become close and quite open with each other by their final meeting. Of those ten men, five had admitted to choosing their mate based solely on "her looks" or "how good she looked." Of these five men, one had divorced and remarried—only to have that relationship last but two years.

The average length of time in relationships of the remaining four who had chosen women based on their looks was less than a year. The other five men answered that they had chosen their mate for reasons other than looks. The various answers were "self-confidence, intelligence, and traditional values." Four of those men had remained in their relationships for more than two years and three in the latter group had married those women and never divorced.

I asked the first group (who had chosen women for their looks) what caused their relationships to fail. One replied, "She was not what I thought she was." Another said, "I found someone prettier." Remarkably, a third replied, "I already had two girlfriends and the only reason I approached her was because she was beautiful and a challenge." Other reasons were "she was boring," "she was selfish," "she was a bad cook and housekeeper," "she never wanted to have sex," and—unbelievably—"she was just too smart for me, I couldn't control her." These were the most common replies and these are just a few of the statements that illustrate how superficial their choices were and how little a true, loving relationship meant to them.

The phase of attraction should be understood to allow for observation and appreciation of each other as complete individuals, with less importance placed on the visually pleasing aspect of the attraction. This includes the intellectual, spiritual, mental, and emotional parts of another's personality. How a person thinks and communicates, as well as their beliefs and value systems should be thoroughly understood before entering into any long-term commitments or relationships. For some black males, the only communication is the language of the body and the sexual response that occurs from the visual communication. It is my intention to not only point this out to black males, but to deepen their sense of self and heighten their understanding of this phenomenon so that their relationships can begin on firmer ground. It is also important to realize that the pattern of basing relationships on visual attraction alone must be broken so that the black family unit can survive and flourish in a healthy, communicative fashion that perpetuates understanding, respect, and appreciation for each other. If you truly love yourself then you will be attracted to the loving aspects of another person who possesses the same attributes; this attraction will be reciprocal. A visual glance and drool may not offer the time necessary to discover the total aspect of love and what it has to offer. Attraction to all segments of a person's personality is imperative in sustaining long-term relationships.

Sex and Infatuation

As one progresses along the continuum in relationships, the transition from one phase to another may not always be simple. The next phase is that of sex and infatuation.

Much has already been said about the influence of sex in relationships, especially when referring to black males. In an episode of the sitcom *Seinfeld*, Elaine, one of Jerry Seinfeld's close confidantes, was featured sharing events of a date she had the night before. Her rendezvous was peculiar because her date was a homosexual male friend who had to convince his boss not only that he was worthy of a promotion, but that he was straight as well. He and Elaine succeeded, but during the course of the evening, Elaine became infatuated with her homosexual escort. She shared her sparkling recollection of the evening's events with Jerry, a now-platonic friend. After hearing the details of her encounter, he smugly replied, "Dates are always good dates when there's no possibility of sex involved."

It is unfortunate that so much emphasis is placed on sex in the initial phases of relationships because it can prove detrimental and can cause serious repercussions. Sexual compatibility, coupled with visual attraction, contribute to the intensity of relationships and lead to infatuation. There are other factors involved in the preoccupation that people may have for each other, but it is sexual stimulation that fuels the fires of a new relationship. Infatuation, as defined by Webster's dictionary, is a foolish, unreasoning, or extravagant passion that is short-lived. The expense of an unhealthy, perpetual focus on another can be a loss of self.

Not so long ago, I spoke to a group of black males, all junior high school students, about teenage pregnancy and its impact on African Americans. I discussed the role and responsibility of black men and also touched on the plausibility of their achieving a healthy relationship that will last a lifetime. Many of the kids laughed out loud, snickered openly, and shook their heads with an "it won't happen to me" look when I told them how their lives could change forever. As I told them that they, as young black men, were being labeled "impregnators" by social scientists studying young black women having babies, the boys were bored to tears and yawning. They reminded me of a group of narcoleptics watching *The English Patient*. The boys didn't seem to care or to believe that this phenomenon was happening around them in great numbers and that it was just a matter of time before some of them would be looking back and wishing they had listened to me. It became evident that I was indeed competing with peer influences, collective behavior, and media hype laced with sexual innuendoes. Some asked questions, but the questions were not geared toward prevention; they were more focused on how far could they go without getting a girl pregnant. Their obvious preoccupation with sex and conquest at different levels was disconcerting to say the least. It is indeed an uphill battle.

A sexual focus drives a person's thoughts and provokes irrational behavior, which leads to quick judgments about love. This behavior can be just as obsessive as an addiction to drugs. This phase is filled with fantasies and illusions of what good sex could be, not what actually is. The illusion can be an unhealthy beginning to a relationship that could abruptly end just as it begins.

This unhealthy way of relating to others can be troublesome for those who have not achieved a wholesome integration of the various parts of their personalities. Instead of progressing on the continuum toward a healthy relationship, nonintegrated individuals become trapped in this phase that focuses on sex. Thus, unreasonable and unhealthy characteristics extend into other phases. The infatuation phase precedes the other phases. Pathological behaviors may begin to manifest as unrealistic expectations of the original goals and reasons people come together in the first place. It is both dangerous and detrimental to a possible long-term relationship because the fantasy of the infatuation is manifested in the relationship as "what could be" or "what was" and not what "actually is." This causes nothing but pain and constant conflict for each person in the relationship and the ideal of what their relationship is actually based upon. Infatuation causes both individuals to lose sight of the purpose of commitment and partnership. The relationship never ultimately evolves into the true phase of unselfish love. An unselfish love involves commitment, true love, and the same values and goals. A partnership that is built on infatuation, much like a house built on sand with no firm foundation, never ultimately evolves into the more advanced and verbally communicative forms of altruistic devotion to one another.

The Barrier of Control

The barrier of control follows the attraction and sex and infatuation phases. This phase separates the men from the boys; it separates the shallow and superficial relationship from the effort-burdened, well-integrated relationship. If this phase can be hurdled successfully, then a relationship has a very real chance of making it.

It is during this phase that males usually jockey for control, especially if the sexual act has been accomplished. Many black males are under the impression that after sex or the "conquest" the battle is won and a relationship or commitment has been formed. He thinks he has established some power base for which he can dictate the directions in which the relationship should go. He can now call the shots. At this point, a nonintegrated black male may demonstrate how macho he is, portraying himself as "the man." Cuddling and compliments begin to diminish, he no longer feels it necessary to pick up after himself or to assist with daily household chores. Instead of a need to establish equal empowerment for both, an unhealthy male feels he is entitled to control his mate. This couldn't be farther from the truth. It is imperative that black men know that women are fully aware of them as men—that's why they are with them in the first place. Women don't want to be controlled, they want to be loved for the things that they *want* to do for their mates, not the things that are *expected* of them.

To a lesser extent than males, many females may also become emotional and less tolerant in their expectations of how the relationship should progress. They may also complain more and make strong attempts to justify why they wanted or were attracted to a man in the first place. This negative focus toward the male in a relationship often stems from insecurity and is perceived as unimportant if a man empowers her in a relationship. This is not to say that women do not have misgivings, if the relationship has achieved equal empowerment, but this negative focus tends to subside.

It is imperative to work hard to understand that it is during this phase that black males must make a sincere effort to set aside insecurities and the need for control, and be willing to give up a part of themselves. In this way, they can effectively merge with their mate into a state of "one-ness." Black males must understand that having sex with his mate entitles him to nothing. In fact, out of respect for himself and his mate, he must become a giving person and attempt to identify her needs while accepting her differences as a woman. There must be an elimination of barriers and a free exchange of ideas with loving behavior. Actually, if the phase of the barrier of control is understood and embraced so that empowerment is equally accomplished, then the relationship has a chance to become a successful, long-term union. The only way that this can happen is through honest communication.

People depend on words and body language to relate to and take charge of the environment around them. It is with words that we express feelings and convey information. Conversation can affect others and influence whether a relationship is, or is not, successful. Chapter 9, which discusses communication, is a valuable tool to help move through the phases of a relationship.

The Merging of Selves

If you are successful in accomplishing the preceding phases of a healthy integrated relationship, then your arrival to the last and final phase, the merging of self and others, in a true love union can be virtually guaranteed.

Once you have debunked the old favorite myths about your "self" and the need for control, instead of a loss of self or losing your manhood, you will gain lasting fulfillment with another person. The power of love is an enriching force that inflates the self; it does not lessen a man's capacity to be whole. Black men full of anger and resentment, should seek to replace all of this unnecessary negative energy with love. Whenever there is equal empowerment and the two individuals merge together in a strong union, then the love is stronger. The journey begins with two passengers in the same coach with equal responsibility for the relationship's direction. Individuality is maintained but the direction and power of the union is a whole unit with two equal parts. As the author Kahlil Gibran states in *The Prophet:* "Just as two pillars hold up the upper foundation of a building but are not next to one another," a relationship functions when each person is secure in their individuality but both work together for the sole purpose of sustaining equality in the relationship. There should be a side-by-side effort to achieve the common goal of maintaining the strength of the relationship. During this phase there is no room for codependency or for control over your partner.

Society has placed an importance on relationships and deems it "normal" to maintain one. I have encountered many of these "normal" people who are in successful marriages or loving partnerships and often marvel at how often these people will say "My husband this . . ." or "My wife that . . ." when they begin their conversations. It hasn't always been like this for me. When I was single and between failed relationships, I resented those people who would talk lovingly about their mates, including them in conversations with me as if they were standing right next to them. Of course, this resentment was fueled by my own inability to form a union like theirs. Others' references to their mates are many times construed as an initial statement of "Yes, I am married and I am normal" to those people who are poorly integrated and unable to sustain long-term, loving relationships. This is not to say that those people who talk about their mates are boasting to the world about their normalcy, but that is how it feels to those whose sense of self is weak.

I think back to my favorite episode of *Seinfeld,* when the characters are invited to a Long Island party. Elaine, a single woman in her thirties, was bored to tears sitting on the sofa. Directly across from her was another woman who smugly asked, "Where is my fiancé, has anyone seen my fiancé?" After she repeated this question several times, Elaine, who was unable to sustain successful relationships, replied in her usual funny way, "Da dingo ate your fiancé!" Taken aback, the lady said, "I beg your pardon!" and Elaine, satisfied with herself, exclaimed again, "I said, da dingo ate your fiancé!"

In the past, I was somewhat like Elaine in that I was envious and annoyed at others who were happy to flaunt their successes in relationships. Today, I am embarrassed to admit that I actually reveled in the misery of others when I heard of a breakup or divorce. As crazy as it sounds, the dissolution of their partnerships seemed to soothe and justify my own poorly integrated sense of my self and my ensuing unhappiness.

The fact remains, loving partnerships are normal and people are not meant to be alone. This includes black men. And this is of paramount importance if the African American family is to survive and thrive.

It is by understanding that it takes individual work from within to form successful families, that the African American family can be a wonderful union of two people working together to make each other's lives the most fulfilling that it can be.

Chapter 4

THE BLACK WOMAN'S PERSPECTIVE

No black American man at any time in our history in the United States has been able to feel that he didn't need that black woman right against him, shoulder to shoulder—in that cotton field, on the auction block, in the ghetto, wherever that black woman is, is an integral, if not a most important part of a family unit.

—Maya Angelou

What does a black woman want from her man? The answer is remarkably simple and perhaps remains the same for any woman who shares a place beside her man: a relationship of joint empowerment, as opposed to struggling for control and the potential for combat. The African American woman wants her mate to listen carefully and hear more clearly what she has to say about herself. Not only does she want her thoughts and feelings to matter, she wants to enjoy an emotional connection, not just a physical one, with her mate. Black women want sensitive and caring partners and the opportunity to experience the world around them with men they trust, while growing and learning as a family unit.

Even though many black men present a macho facade, most truly want a loving and supportive woman to encourage and to challenge them in positive ways. However, current statistics show a 60 percent divorce rate for blacks, as compared to 50 percent for the rest of the U.S. population combined. The question, then, is why are black men and women distancing themselves from one another? As the numbers continue to rise, the fear remains that the concept of the healthy black family will be crushed altogether.

One of the more poignant pleas traversing the airways shortly after Rodney King was almost beaten to death by several Los Angeles police officers was, "Can't we all just get along?" The violent actions by the officers sent negative emotional waves across the country. The incident illustrated just how powerless many African Americans are when confronted by a judicial system comprised of an overwhelming majority of officials seeking to bend the law to their advantage. People from all walks of life were aghast at the acts of brutality perpetrated on Mr. King, and the statement he made not only described the notorious incident but penetrated other aspects of black life as well.

When black relationships are observed, one can't help but hear an eerie echoing of King's words "Can't we all just get along?" The following excerpt from *Brothers, Lust, and Love,* by William July II, reveals a side of the black woman that many black men are fully aware of:

In silence, I rode seven floors alone in an elevator with a black woman. Our eyes met momentarily as I entered the elevator, but, in a sharp and fast move she quickly focused her attention on her watch. On the surface, what may have seemed to be a casual time check wasn't that at all. It was a well practiced cold shun. To be honest, that move hurt my feelings. But I still managed to mumble a hello which was rebuked by her disinterested ears. That cold gesture was her greeting and good-bye; the extent of our communication. By avoiding eye contact and filling the elevator with her tense vibes, she made it clear that she didn't intend to say a word to me. But all of that was unnecessary. I wasn't interested in flirting, asking for her phone number, or diving into bed with her. I simply said hello.

This scenario clearly demonstrates that if black males and females continue in this haphazard mode of relating, using silence to cope with one another's presence, the black family will likely disappear. It is apparent that black women have been scarred, and are leery when interacting with black men, due mainly to the many hardships they or their friends have experienced in past relationships. Because of the black man's machismo, black women often question the sincerity and maturity of black men. They have a tendency to anticipate rude approaches and become defensive when accosted by sexual innuendoes, particularly when meeting for the first time.

African American relationships are often viewed by other ethnic groups in society as primarily sexual in nature, and perhaps black males have done little to dispel this myth. Of course not all black men are irresponsible, selfish, and sexually promiscuous, nor are all black women martyrs and scapegoats in relationships. Yet black men continue to allow the stereotypical view to determine how they relate to women, instead of working hard to change this way of thinking. Also, the black men who interrelate with women and focus on the family have been said to be "the minority within a minority."

If you want to hide something from a brother, the saying goes, hide it in a book. Often in relationships, black men possess a seemingly know-it-all attitude that can typically paralyze the woman. Although she may be more educated, hold a better job, and have a firmer grasp of what family means, she often turns to her mate for leadership, and ends up following his train of thought. This discrepancy may limit the woman's capability to resolve problems in the relationship and can negatively affect an otherwise harmonious home. There is much to be learned when black men become more receptive to the ideas of the women in their lives. As one begins to understand that being a life partner does not lessen one's manhood, he will be able to disengage from the role of macho super-stud and become a better husband, lover, and father. After all, that super-stud image eventually fades with age and is often replaced by wishful thinking for what once was.

Black women abhor the persistent and manipulative ploys that are intended only to get them into bed. There are a great number of African American women wary of this scheme. Ideally, black women should possess the self-awareness necessary to recognize that infidelity and the inability to be monogamous define immaturity. It is no secret to them that it is a boy who will play games, while a man works diligently to secure himself in a solid, monogamous relationship.

It is evident that there is more to a relationship than routine, emotionless sex that climactically shows the female who's the man. Though part of the sexual act is a way of showing power and control, men also have a tendency to show a woman that they love them through the act of sex itself, which does not create an emotional connection from a woman's perspective. She requires affection and non-sexual interactions in order to feel truly loved and respected.

When sex is the only type of affection in a relationship, the black woman finds the relationship to be void of love. Obviously, this can sabotage the relationship and causes the woman to withdraw, so the black man vies for even more control, using sex as a way of gaining even more power. He often feels as though she will "see" his love for her when they engage in physical sex. When she doesn't, he sometimes resorts to more violent forms of control, such as physical force and even rape, equating the violence to love.

A black patient confided to me that her husband, who had a long history of physically and emotionally abusing her and who was being treated for impotence, would suddenly achieve an erection when beating her. This puzzling pathological link of rage and sex results from a subconscious attempt at control and a warped response that is sometimes sexual. It demonstrates a negative image of manhood, and is totally devoid of the calm, verbal communication and unconditional love that more secure black males are able to offer to their mates.

It has been argued that this link between sex and rage is actually suppression of sex and racism. Calvin C. Hernton argues in his book *Sex and Racism in America* that some black men are made to feel that blackness is ugly because of the mark of oppression. White-dominated society fueled the oppression, and when black women, angered by black men, on occasion blurt out insults and racial epithets in defense of themselves, they often unknowingly reinforce it. Perhaps the black man's erection as a result of his anger signifies freedom from the feelings of castration placed on black males from the reputed virtues of white society. In any case, the results are never positive, nor is this pathological transfer of negative sexual energy ever fulfilling or consequence-free.

A black man once jokingly but sternly said to me, "They [white people] can take my car, my money, and even my women, but they can't take my hard dick," as he pointed to his genital area. Although he was laughing when he made that statement, it was not difficult to see that he absolutely believed it. He also stated that he felt that he could "do anything when my dick is hard," which he believed kept him in charge.

Interestingly, the brain centers which affect emotions like anger and lust are connected and in the same location. Because of their physical anatomic relationship it is plausible that both emotions come into play when anger or aggression provoke an erection. The feeling of being less of a man, or castration anxiety, would definitely have an impact on the libido. Castration anxiety is a fundamental fear that men demonstrate when they are fixated on their penis as a "symbol of their manhood" and a measure of their self-esteem. It serves a "purpose" and when a woman negates the value of the penis in the relationship, the male perceives himself as less than a man or has lowered self-esteem. Achieving an erection while exercising aggression and displaced anger (anger that should be directed outward at that which is doing the oppressing, rather than physically inward) probably has some liberating aspect to it.

While this is not an attempt to justify acts of aggression, it is an attempt to understand them. It certainly does not negate the fact that some men who achieve erections while exercising aggression have far more severe emotional problems than simply a feeling of freedom. An erect penis symbolizes strength, power, and liberation from perceived forces of oppression that could castrate or lessen this symbol of power. Relating freedom from castration anxiety by virtues of white society to the aggression and erection theory is not a textbook analysis, but rather an observation of many black male patients over the years. Achieving an erection while angry is more common than one might think, but not all acts of aggression produce erections. Conversely, not all erections produce acts of aggression.

Black women must realize the necessity of loving and respecting themselves before they can expect black men to respect them. All too often black women are unhappy and dwell on the negative characterization of the men in their lives, rather than focusing on making themselves happy first. Unknowingly, women tend to shift the blame for their own unhappiness. This tends to create a vicious circle of negativity that permeates relationships. If black women are not happy with themselves, how then can they be happy with anyone else? Certainly a black woman's low self-esteem is caused in part by black males' acting out in controlling, angry, or emotionally disengaged behaviors, which constantly eat away at a woman's self-image.

Picking apart the black man's faults, however, is not the way to improve one's self-image. Positive change can begin only if black women unselfishly encourage and positively challenge the men in their lives without always criticizing their faults. It is also important for women to take personal inventories of themselves before they even attempt to find fault in another person, especially their mates. They must give love and respect unconditionally in order to receive the same kind of love and emotion. Unless there is a history of uncontrolled anger or abuse, positive encouragement of another will generate self-love and encourage reciprocity from others. All people know that they have flaws, and can be acutely aware of their own faults.

Many times chronic fault-finding in someone we love sheds light on a much deeper issue. When we fall in love, it is because we are in love with the person that we *think* we know. It is the same for both black men and women. The newness is still there and since one is exploring the other in the most positive ways by nature, there is no need or desire to look at the negative aspects. As the relationship progresses, one realizes that a partner is not the perfect person he or she was originally thought to be. This does not have to be a negative thing unless those imperfections are continuously pointed out to each other.

In the beginning many faults can be overlooked, because each person is so happy to be with the other. But after a period of time, in a relationship both men and women may start to focus on the littlest of things, instead of on what brought them together in the first place.

One example is a female patient with whom I was discussing some problems occurring in her relationship. When asked what she thought might be the primary problem, her not-so-surprising response was, "He doesn't do anything right. When he washes the dishes, he doesn't do it in the right order and when he washes the clothes, he doesn't separate them before putting them in the washer. I always end up doing it over again."

While this might seem as very trivial, it actually reveals something much more important. Instead of focusing on the fact that her mate was actually participating in the household chores by doing the dishes and the laundry, she was looking at the negative ways in which he was going about it. She was not satisfied with the way her mate was doing things, thinking that they had to be done her way or no way at all. While some people think that their way is the only way there simply is no right or wrong way to achieve something.

Loving relationships between black men and women do not have to contain a power struggle. A relationship is really about accomplishing the same goals and working together to reach them. Each person must realize that a contribution made by the other person is equally valuable, regardless of whether it is an issue of who brings the most money into the household, who takes care of the children, who does whatever household chore, or who pays the bills. As long as everything gets completed, what difference does it really make?

Trivial fault-finding is unfortunately a common occurrence in relationships. Taking a self-inventory can quiet this tendency, by asking such questions as: Am I doing everything I can to focus on the positive things about my mate? Am I looking at what I could do differently in order to place the most important person in my life in a positive position in my thoughts?

Remembering that everyone has their own unique style of doing things is one of most productive ways that we can relieve ourselves of the negativity in our own lives. By removing negative attention from our mate, we are able to redirect the energy inward and do our own rearranging. We place a great deal of pressure on ourselves when we attempt to control the world around us. If something does not go as we think it should, then it is our own responsibility to change it. This is a double whammy to the relationship because the person who is attempting the task also feels responsible.

Simply put, to try to control how someone else accomplishes something is a form of devaluing the other person's choices and actions. It is done in such a subliminal way, some people do not even realize they do it. Years of this type of communication can certainly break down a relationship, so the "my way is the best way" philosophy must be tossed out the window.

Another example of this problem is the man who tells a woman to do something for him rather than kindly asking her if she will do it. One of the biggest problems black men face is understanding that we have been socialized to be aggressive leaders of the family. Yet women especially appreciate being asked, rather than told, to take care of something. Being asked implies that a value is being placed on the action that is requested; being told is perceived as an order, and no one really welcomes being ordered what to do. Black women deserve to be respected for what they do for black men and vice versa. A simple change in how a need is expressed makes all the difference in the world to the loved person.

More often than not, people tend to focus on another's faults because it seems easier than confronting their own. How often has the phrase "It's easier to tell someone how to do something than it is to do it ourselves" been uttered? Instructions on how to accomplish a goal or how to carry out a task often fall on deaf ears, and everyone eventually becomes frustrated. If a person must do something a certain way for good reason, the proper avenue is suggestion instead of instruction, unless of course that person is actually requesting assistance.

Unsolicited advice is often perceived as a demonstration of little faith. Over time this begins to wear on a person's self-esteem, which can be shattered by this type of constant barrage. Although one might mean well, logic argues that if the person requested to do something requires assistance, he or she will simply ask for it directly. Being respectful and challenging one's mate in positive ways applies here. If one partner asks for something and the other decides to act on the request, he or she will readily ask for assistance if needed. This reciprocal respect and valuation of the other's talents is a way of validating the uniqueness between partners.

Remember when you first met and there were certain things you did to impress the person you wanted to get to know better? Everyone reaches a comfort zone in a relationship, and understandably so. Demands of jobs, school, children, household tasks, and family responsibilities interfere with having sufficient attention for those things that once attracted you to one another. Having unrealistic expectations can ruin communication between two people. Even in their infancy relationships can be fraught with similar issues.

A case at hand involved a conversation with a female friend. She shared that she and her boyfriend had been having significant problems since they formally committed themselves to being a couple. She expressed that she did not think he was being open enough with his feelings, and that maybe their relationship was not going to work out after all.

After gathering a little more information and listening to her side of the situation, I realized that her boyfriend had really not changed at all. What had changed, however, was her idea of what he was supposed to do and how he should behave in the relationship. There was something about the designation of "couple" that made her believe he should begin pouring out his heart to her, report his whereabouts, and make plenty of time to be with her.

After talking with her further, she too began to realize that the problem was not his behavior after all. Gently I identified how she seemed to have her own expectations of what was supposed to occur between two people when they become united as a "couple." She said that the two things that drew them together were the same things that she had begun to find negative. His calm, slow approach to things had become laziness in her eyes, and his laid-back demeanor had been erroneously interpreted as his not caring about her. As she came to the realization that it was her ideas that were new and not her boyfriend's behavior, she had to laugh at the ironic twist in perception.

Regardless of whether it relates to exclusive dating, a committed relationship, or marriage, the truth regarding perception remains consistent. Perhaps this is just one of the reasons that some black men shy away from committed, long-term relationships. Preconceived expectations can result in a convoluted thought process, often with the belief that the other person will conform to meet those ideals. This way of thinking is destructive to a relationship and will erode its foundation faster than anything else.

Ideally, in the beginning of a relationship, there seems to be magic in the air. Both the man and woman love to make sure they are seen in their best light. Both are there for one another, and no matter what is shared, both make an attempt to listen and always find something positive to say. In the beginning, both people find themselves feeling accepted and cared for. What more could a person want in a relationship?

Oh, yes, there is also the fun. Laughing playfully together, sharing private jokes, and feeling comfortable and safe in the time spent together tie up the package beautifully. Feeling this type of joy and excitement, most couples are inclined to begin a building process to see if this could be the person to share a future with. It is at this point that both decide to seek a more formal relationship. It is often at this point that the music stops and preconceived expectations take over. Just like the flash of lightning in the sky, the rain begins to fall. Both people begin to express such sentiments as "Well, now that we are boyfriend/girlfriend, you should . . ." or, "Who was that you were talking to on the phone?. . ." "Why didn't you . . ." "If you were a good man, you would . . ." or, "Since we are together now, we should start . . ."

The final problem with these expectations is that they seem to increase each day. There is always something else the other person is supposed to be doing, or saying, or buying, or thinking. Once this negativity sets in, it is destructive. It is not, however, irreversible. Taking a self-inventory can turn harmful thinking into the anticipation, rather than the expectation, of an enduring relationship.

The idea of the black woman's self-inventory receives specific mention following an encounter with a black female patient, who was beautiful but obese. The incident occurred during my residency in family medicine when she came into my office complaining about a back injury. After taking her history, I focused my attention on her weight in relation to the nature of her back problem. This was obviously a sensitive area for her as she immediately became irritated with me. Although I knew after several tests that her excess weight was the cause of her symptoms, she would hear no part of my suggestion that she lose some of the excess weight; instead she wanted me to give her something just to kill the pain. She became so irritated, in fact, that she filed a complaint with my program director, who called me into his office to determine my motives. After I explained my diagnosis in detail he said to me, "Look Dr. Smith, don't you understand that fat people know they're fat and that it can be a painful flaw in their psyche?"

Much like my bringing this patient's painful feelings of inadequacy to the surface, a mate sometimes brings imperfections to the surface, which only reinforces already low self-esteem. This works both ways and it is important to note that when men and women assist one another in overcoming their own adversities, a positive relationship trend begins. Most black women would welcome the sensitive side of their mates. They want an opportunity to experience the world around them *alongside* their mates rather than simply following their lead. Relationships between men and women prove to be a positive and loving journey if the life-partner ideal is recognized and followed.

It is necessary for black men to give black women what they want most: better communication seasoned with a softer, more supportive and loving side. On the counter side, black women must give men respect, encouragement, and positive feedback. Let's break the cycle and dispel the image of the black male as macho, a super-stud, and allow for the opportunity for love and growth in our relationships. Black men need to listen. It is by revealing a softer side that good lovers can become great lovers, and good fathers can become great fathers. It is through unconditional, supportive love that true life-partner relationships thrive.

As revealed in other chapters, I have conducted many focus group discussions and administered surveys in an attempt to gain better insight into the inner dynamics of black people in relationships. The data accumulated are both revealing and, sometimes, shocking. Specifically for this chapter, I conducted a survey of three hundred black women to find out how they felt about their relationships and the black men in their lives. A self-reporting questionnaire, the survey subjectively required the respondent simply to fill in the blanks. Confidentiality and objectivity of the respondents were well maintained: the women were instructed to seal their own responses in envelopes. The questions related to common issues that had come up during previous focus groups, and the answers were returned to the surveyor to be given to me for data analysis.

Eighty-eight percent of the black women surveyed filled out every question. Those that were not completely filled out were invalidated. Most of the respondents ranged from twenty-five to forty-four years old (68 percent). Thirty percent were high school graduates and 24 percent had attended some college. Twenty percent also possessed a bachelor's degree. Sixty-two percent of the respondents had never been married but many of these women did indicate that they were involved in a relationship. Twenty percent were married and 14 percent were separated or divorced. Seventy-two percent of those who were married were involved in their relationship for one year and longer. Note that the percentage of respondents who had never been married mirrors the national statistics for single-parent families, and that, quite unremarkably, of those who reported being unmarried, most had at least one child.

Most black women reported making less than $21,000 a year. Fourteen percent reported making over $30,000 but less than $40,000 a year.

The survey requested the following information:

1. *Name three things that you like about your mate.*

Most of the respondents (22 percent) said that looks were the number-one priority, followed by the ability to provide well (14 percent), and a good personality (14 percent). Two percent of the women offered varied responses, such as humor, supportiveness, religion, and cooking skills. Only 1 percent stated that they liked their mate's parenting skills, understanding nature, responsibility, good communication skills, and affectionate manner. (Incidentally, 3 percent of the women chose their mates for a relationship because of the sex.)

2. *Name three things you dislike about your mate.*

As remarkable as it seems, many of the same individuals who said that their mates were good-looking, great providers, and had likeable personalities also said that they exhibited too much control (12 percent), were jealous (10 percent), insecure (10 percent), unfaithful (10 percent), and lied to them (6 percent).

Although I doubt that this is normative for all black women, I am saddened to see that those surveyed chose their mates for the same superficial quality that black men do: looks. It's no wonder that these relationships fail. If black women changed their primary priority to what is really important to sustaining healthy relationships, communication and nonsexual affection would rank higher. If black females seriously demanded that potential mates possess certain relationship values, unfaithful and dishonest black men would simply be kicked to the curb. Those ethno-phrases "Hey brother, talk to the hand," and "Look man, I can do bad by myself," would be more appropriate instead of settling for any old "brother" just to feel loved. (Incidentally, three percent of the women chose their mates for a relationship because of the sex.)

The third directive required the respondents to:

3. *Name three things that attracted you to your mate. If you are not in a current relationship, name three things that attract you to a potential mate.*

Of all of the respondents, only 1 percent was not involved in a current relationship and those answers were not analyzed due to the small sample size. However, of those in relationships, 50 percent answered that looks were the number-one factor of attraction. Eighteen percent reported that the way their mates communicated was their primary attraction and 12 percent reported that their mate's personality first attracted them.

4. *Name three things you would like your mate to improve upon. If not in a relationship, name three things that turn you off about a potential mate.*

Again, since only 1 percent were not currently in a relationship, the sample size was not statistically significant. However, of those in relationships, 35 percent felt that their mates needed to spend more quality time with both them and their children. Twenty-five percent indicated that their mates needed to stop lying to them and 15 percent said that laziness was a problem. Other answers included mates who needed to take better care of their appearance, who needed to communicate more, and who were no longer fun to be with.

Even though women were asked about ways their mates could improve themselves, it became apparent that money was not necessarily an issue. In fact, motivation and becoming more family-oriented were of primary concern. When mates lied and stopped talking about their feelings, a downward spiral of resentment began in a relationship. Once this occurs, the fault-finding begins.

5. Do you think your mate tries to control you?

Surprisingly, this question was split down the middle with 40 percent answering "no" and 40 percent responding with "yes." Twenty percent responded that they were not certain if their mate was controlling.

What was most perplexing about this question was not that the women actually tolerated the control in the relationships by staying in them, but that a great deal of women did not know the difference between control and leadership. Many of the 20 percent that responded this way made additional statements such as "he is only controlling when he is angry," "he controls where I go and who I talk to but other than that he's not controlling," and, "I let him think he's in control but he's really not."

These statements are examples of the game-playing that occurs in relationships that are neither mature nor particularly satisfying. I can only surmise that women who stay in controlling relationships do not have a sense of who they are as women and do not recognize that they deserve more than having someone make all of their life decisions for them.

6. Who makes most of the important decisions?

Forty percent of the women who were in relationships indicated that both partners made the important decisions, 35 percent said that they were the ones who made the important decisions, and 20 percent stated that the men made the important decisions. Five percent did not respond to this question.

The responses to questions 5 and 6 inspire both surprise and ambivalence. First, I am surprised that nearly half of the women did not feel that their mate tried to control them. It is my observation that most black males use their physical power to control their relationships. The 20 percent that answered "not sure" revealed a commonality that could be related to those who did not feel as though their mates controlled them.

Second, I feel hopeful about the number of women who did not feel controlled and who were able to make decisions together with their mates or alone. Perhaps a significant number of men did not think it was important to be involved in decision-making within their relationship, or perhaps they could feel comfortable with the decisions that were made by their mates. Or maybe some men felt the women to be of superior intelligence and therefore better able to make decisions. If this were the case, I would suspect that the man tries to control other aspects of the relationship.

7. *Name three things that would improve your relationship.*

Of the 78 percent that responded, 40 percent of the women answered "better communication," 20 percent said "more romance before sex," and 18 percent indicated that more quality time spent together would improve the relationship.

These answers match what they would want their mate to improve upon, except for the 20 percent who answered "more romance before sex." Romance has long been an issue in relationships between men and women, but the fact that this answer appeared so often shows that women are not necessarily happy with the approach black men take prior to sexual contact. Going back to the way black men show their love through physical contact, I might offer some insight to this dilemma.

Given the fact that women want more from their mates in the way of emotion and sharing through verbal exchange solidifies the fact that black women need to hear more of our true feelings. How do black men accomplish this? I believe that it takes a great deal of practice, but the more it is done, the easier it becomes. Simply telling a woman how you really feel about her without actually touching her is one of the greatest gifts you can give her. She will cherish this as much, if not more than, any of the physical sex you share with her. In fact, not only will she remember those words, she will grow to respect your need to be a man in other areas of your life and will encourage the maleness in you. This verbal sharing does not mean that you are less of a "real man." In fact, it makes you more of a man in the black woman's eyes. She will readily accept your faults with dignity and respect, rather than reminding you of them.

8. *Has your mate shared his history of past relationships with you?*

A surprising 56 percent answered "yes" to this question. Thirty-four percent answered "no" and 10 percent did not answer.

Those not answering this question might have considered it too personal or too much of a reminder that their mates were once with other women. I did smile at two of the respondents' sharing that their mate was a virgin and that they were waiting to be married before they had sexual relations. This indicated that there are still some black males not viewing sex as more important than other aspects of their lives.

For the next question, what can be said? Those black men, who might be perceived as secretive and conniving, shared their sexual histories with their mates.

The next question created even more antagonism:

9. *If yes, was he promiscuous? And how so?*

Seventy-seven percent of the women said that he was not promiscuous. The 20 percent who said their mates were promiscuous also stated that their mates were only involved with one or two other women prior to them. The black men told them they were not promiscuous, were committed to their previous relationships, and that they had had only one or two other sexual partners. As you will see, these statements were diametrically opposed to what black men said when they were privately surveyed. What they told the women in their lives and what actually occurred were two totally different things.

10. *Would you say your sex life with your mate is:*

(1) Very good (2) Good (3) Bad (4) Very bad (5) Doesn't apply

Forty-six percent of the women described their sex life as "good" and 24 percent reported that it was "very good." Only 2 percent indicated that sex was "very bad" and, other than the two people who said their mates were virgins, the rest answered "bad." Those who represented the "bad" and "very bad" responses indicated in detail that more romance and longer foreplay could make their sex life better. Since many of these relationships were formed on the basis of physical attraction, it is no wonder that the sex was considered to be "good." This does not, however, indicate total satisfaction. Given the fact that 62 percent of the respondents were unmarried, one can contemplate whether or not these relationships will last beyond the physical attraction when the sexual contact wanes. Those who are married or who have been married in committed relationships for a long time know that physical sex may or may not continue to be a significant factor in the relationships. Rather, the majority of the married women said that their sex lives were "bad." This reveals the true pattern of complacency in committed relationships. These relationships tend to shift the focus from physical intimacy to emotional intimacy and this is when black men tend to become dishonest. Commitment and emotional intimacy are not things that black men historically embody or practice openly with their mates. If relationships between black men and women can survive the transition from physical intimacy to emotional intimacy, the likelihood of a long-term relationship that is honest and committed will increase. Lack of commitment occurs when the black man is challenged to become vulnerable to the black woman. Many times this results in the breakup of the relationship.

11. When you and your mate argue, what are the major topics that you argue about?

Even though most women, 26 percent, argued about money with their mates, this was the only time that money came into play in the survey. Certainly one or two women said that they would like their mates to make more money in response to a previous question, but this issue was not profound. When two people have few money management skills and do not agree on how, where, and why money should be spent, arguments are likely. Considering the personal diversity of those in relationships, this figure is not surprising. Fourteen percent argued about the lack of quality time spent together; this was a common theme among respondents throughout the survey. Six percent argued about their "mate's whereabouts" and "where they were when not with them." This coincided with the dishonesty that many encountered in their relationships. Other popular responses were alcohol and drug use (4 percent), control issues (4 percent), insecurities of the male (4 percent), and 2 percent of the women said they argued about consistent infidelity.

Most couples will have problems about various aspects of spending and saving money, but money problems are often related to issues of control. Some black men have confided that they often get even with their mates by spending too much money or by sabotaging the budget to keep their mates dependent. Many black men do not realize that this not only interferes with the cohesiveness of the relationship, but it also hinders the stability of the family.

The fact that the black women surveyed even had to argue about their mates' whereabouts leads back to the question of why the black men are lying in the first place. Why are they deceiving black women? Why do they feel a need to stray? And most important, why do black women put up with this type of behavior from black men? Is it that there are too few black men to go around? Or do black women feel that it is their only chance to feel loved? During the course of this book, many of these questions are answered in detail; some cannot be answered at all.

Looking closely at the issue of black male sexuality and its effect on relationships from many different angles not only evokes thought, it brings to the surface many issues that have been buried for centuries. It is time to get these issues out in the open so that black women can feel love with black men, love that is honest, secure, and focused, instead of some sort of game. As Maya Angelou so eloquently said, "No black American man at any time in our history in the United States has been able to feel that he didn't need that black woman right against him . . ." And this doesn't mean physically. Black men need to know that it's okay to become life partners with black women, that by doing so we become stronger in our abilities, guided by a source of strength unique to black women.

Chapter 5

THE BLACK MAN AND HIS FAMILY

> The only perfect love to be found on earth is not sexual love, which is riddled with hostility and insecurity, but the wordless commitment of families, which takes as its model mother-love. This is not to say that fathers have no place, for father-love, with its driving for self-improvement and discipline, is also essential to survival, but that uncorrected father-love . . . is a way to annihilation.
>
> —Germaine Greer

One early spring day I heard the sounds of laughter filling my waiting room and I went out to see what was happening. A young African American father had brought in his three young children for their yearly checkups. He was cuddling the baby and the toddlers were playing happily at his feet. Their joy had spread to my smiling office staff, who were instinctively drawn into this circle of family intimacy. I, too, became almost giddy. The image of a loving, involved black father was so powerful we all wanted to warm ourselves in the glow of his open and genuine affection for his family.

Later, the opportunity arose to talk with this father privately about his thoughts on our reactions to him and his children. It was quite apparent that both the staff and I were captivated by the warmth and love they had displayed in the waiting room. I asked him how he felt about the family in general and how he regarded the importance of the family for the black man as well as for himself. I let him know that I do not often witness a black man behaving so warmly and attentively toward his family.

Since he had been to my office before and his children were used to the staff's entertaining them, we were allowed sufficient time to discuss these questions. The children were very well behaved and as the father proudly stood nearby, he talked about his familial beliefs and opinions.

He began by saying that without his family he would be nothing: "I'm here today because I wanted to help my wife. She had to go to school and the children needed to come in for checkups. That's my job, to do my share." After being married for twenty years, his wife had decided to go back to college to get the degree she had put on hold when she began raising the children. He smiled when he said, "Doctor, I am very proud of her; she's going to be the first in our family to have a college degree."

He went on to relate that his childhood family had been negatively affected by the absence of affection and attention from his father. He had vowed to himself that when he had his own family, he would show them he loved them and would devote all of the time he could to insure their safety and happiness.

"You see, Doctor, my family defines me as a responsible black man and without them I would not be this person. I never played or acted silly as a kid and now I do because of the children. They make me this way." From his perspective, it was his own family who taught him how to be kind and how to love, especially his children. They had given him something that he never had, which included an intact family unit that would pave the way for generations to come long after he was gone. He really believed in his heart that he could change the future of his children and their children by adding so much love and affection to the equation of the family that they would never feel the same kind of alienation he once felt as a child.

He loved his wife and children unconditionally, and believed that because his wife had gone back to school, in essence, the entire family was in school as well. It was viewed as a group effort, not as something that just his wife wanted for herself, but as something to benefit the whole family. He concluded before he left, "Doctor, I see it as my duty to see that everything goes smoothly while she works and is in school at the same time. It's just as much my duty to contribute equally in our family and not hold my wife back because of some sort of ideal that a black man shouldn't do certain things in a household. That's such an ancient way of thinking. By the way, Doc, it makes me happy to see my family happy." And with that, he and his children left and I was left with the definite knowledge that this was truly the ideal role model of a responsible black family man who had overcome emotional hardship.

This man's focus on family provides a meaningful illustration for African American males. The black man's understanding of his own sexuality affects his family; his attitude toward women influences his children, especially his sons. As a youngster, I dreamed of growing up to be a man of valor, to be heroic and brave. Because my own father, perhaps influenced by slavery's historical upheaval of the family, was not a role model for this image, my ideals developed through reading Marvel comic books and watching television. My father, who abused alcohol and drugs and, eventually, my mother, cast fear and rejection into my heart. His unpredictable nature and argumentative style led me to resent who he was as a black adult male. As a result, I actively searched out other black men from the community I could respect and rely on to balance my perspective and teach me how to behave in healthy ways.

The black family of today continues to struggle with the legacy of slavery and its fracturing impact on the family unit. Historically, white slaveholders caring more about commerce than human rights constantly separated black families, which in turn limited solid familial bonding. Despite this abomination, many African Americans did not abandon hope for family unity; even during early oppression the black family ideal endured and thrived.

The unending hope of our ancestors has threaded its way through countless generations, enabling the black family to survive. It is actually in today's fast-paced, non-value–oriented society that the threat of extinction of the black family unit exists. It is not clear when the black family began its shift to single-parent households with absent fathers. It is unknown why the black man began to displace his responsibilities as husband and parent. What is clear today, however, is that the black man's primary focus tends not to be on maintaining an intact family unit.

Some social scientists believe that the early industrial period in the United States occurred during the initial voluntary splintering of black families. During that era it became necessary for both parents to work outside the home to make ends meet. Jobs were scarce and those that were available paid discriminatory wages. As new immigrants with white skin blended into the dominant white society, they took away jobs that had been held by black men. Black families were typically unable to sustain the financial pressures of an evolving world economy and the subsequent psychological stress, which led to the disintegration of communication between husbands and wives. Black men began to allow themselves to become sidetracked from the traditional family ideal of sticking together through thick and thin. In attempts to cope with their resulting anger and loss of self-esteem in not being able to provide for their families, some black men turned to alcohol, gambling, and other risky activities. Many men simply gave up on themselves and left their homes, never to return and likely believing their families were better off without them.

Unquestionably, more opportunities exist in today's society than ever before for African Americans to prosper and succeed. Unfortunately, many black men possess limited skills and lack the education necessary to advance in an ever-increasing technological society. Black men repeatedly find themselves in unstable employment positions that over time deprive them of their manhood and injure their feelings of self-worth.

In addition, a great number of black men with limited formal education father children early in life. What happens when young, undereducated men have children of their own? For the most part they demonstrate instability and erratic behavior, as opposed to accountability and responsibility for their offspring's future. Often leaving their mates and children behind, these men pursue physically stimulating alternatives, trading responsibilities for more sex. It is no secret that, for black men, sexual conquest has long created an illusion of being more powerful. As a result, they make more and more babies in a hopeless attempt to prove their manhood, only to abandon more women and children.

My direct response to these tragic men: "Brotherman, what are you thinking? Don't you see what you are doing? Or do you even care? How do you define yourselves as men? Impregnators? Aren't you concerned about having a family who has values and a future? Are you as black men thinking about whether or not African Americans will survive into the twenty-first century and beyond?" Most likely, they are not. Too many black men are destroying the ideal of the black family, pushing it to the brink of extinction. According to the United States Census Bureau, approximately 70 percent of black children are being raised with no father present. That is an enormous figure, considering that African Americans make up only 12 percent of the total population of the United States. If African Americans do not instill hope, accountability, and perseverance in future generations, the annihilation of the black family seems inevitable.

An encouraging look back in history to the tribal families of Africa illustrates the possibility of successful intact families complete with predefined familial roles. Order, dignity, and values allowed each member, including the head of the family (usually the man), to contribute in beneficial ways to their society. When members did not pull their weight, they were banished along with their entire family or, worse, sent off alone and their families executed.

African tribal men knew the importance of contributing to their societies in positive ways; why should it be any different today? The responsibility of the black man to insure the unconditional survival of his people goes beyond a commitment to his family. It must extend into black society in general. The residual pain black men leave behind when they abandon their families in pursuit of meaningless sexual gratification also creates chaos in their extended families. Grandmothers, aunts, and even sisters or brothers are left with the responsibility for picking up the pieces.

After interacting with black men, women, and children on a daily basis, listening to their sad stories and watching them from birth to death, I have come to realize how important it is for black men to do the right thing. I am more frightened than ever for the black family. While solutions may not be simple, one is self-evident: black men *must* stop impregnating young women, making babies they won't take care of, simply to feed their sexual egos. We have the power to divorce ourselves from our sexually oriented image. We know that impulsive sexual behavior is usually imitated by offspring who are raised with the knowledge of why their fathers are not present. We must be men who love our mates completely and unconditionally, who have pride in our blackness and value our children's futures. Surely we are not such a small minority that no one would hear us or bother to listen. Raising our black children to maturity while developing a healthy sense of self must be our number-one priority.

It is frightening to consider what the future might hold for black families with no fathers in the home. The survival of black culture depends on black men. The role of "Daddy" is a huge one to fulfill, but future generations of black families cannot exist without him. Women left to raise children alone become overwhelmed with the responsibility of playing the roles of both mother and father. Children are forced to search for father figures elsewhere, sometimes in teachers and coaches, sometimes in street pushers, gang leaders, and those very same men who left other women and children. Suffice to say that it is strongly desirable for young black men to have role models who make a positive difference in their lives. In my own life, had responsible black men not intervened on my behalf, I might have wound up in the same prison where my father died.

The oldest of six children with an absentee father, I was looked up to by my two brothers and three sisters for guidance and a concrete definition of the world. The problem with this role was that I had no frame of reference for myself, so I simply "winged it" with my siblings at first. Although my father was in our lives occasionally, he was both inconsistent and irresponsible. Venturing out into the world around me made me realize that my biological male parent was not much of a father at all. In fact, I'm not certain how I knew, but I did know that there was more to a family than a mother who struggled alone with a house full of kids. I can only surmise that it was through observing my friends' parents and my school mentors that I began my journey toward understanding.

A childhood epiphany, which I still remember vividly, occurred right after I turned six years old. Television was new and was inevitably becoming my best source of information. Some programs like *Father Knows Best* depicted a father who was friendly, loving, attentive, and responsible. Since my own father did not demonstrate those characteristics, I immediately knew that something was different about my family. Once I began attending school, I listened to my friends talking about what they did with their fathers on weekends: going to baseball and basketball games, the theater, or out to have fun spending time with Dad. My father, in contrast, was nowhere to be found. The joy I felt when encountering those families helped me develop my positive outlook for black families in the future. All of those families, whether black or white, shared a humanity that transcended skin color and made them unique. It wasn't about race; it was about the concept of family togetherness, love for one another, and mutual support that made them special to me.

Some people may think that shows from the 1950s and '60s like *Father Knows Best* or *The Adventures of Ozzie and Harriet* may be outdated and corny by the hip standards of today. However, looking past the old-fashioned dialogue to the heart of the messages, the focus is on the family and how each member works together in support of one another. The message of love these old shows conveys could not carry more endurance and importance. The concept of love for the family is not constrained by time; it is everlasting, something we all would be wise to strive for so that we might preserve it for generations to come.

The other children always seemed happy and more engaged socially, which left me feeling alienated and fueled my growing anger and resentment. Constantly I worried myself with why they had a father and I did not. I wanted what they had, and made up my mind at a very young age that I was going to be a part of that environment somehow. Forging my mother's name to permission documents, I signed myself up for Little League baseball and the Boys' Club. I simply did not care that my mother and siblings thought me a defiant oddball; I would leave when my father would periodically, briefly, enter the household. He would respond by accusing me of disrespecting him and wanting to be like a white person.

The simple fact was that I wanted to have one of, and to be like, those fathers, some white and some not, who were more 'normal.' I already knew the difference, and recognized that it was not color-coded. My father did not know the difference, and did not want to be bothered with me other than to see me blindly obeying his orders and commands. His abuse of my mother was more than I could stand and I found my refuge at the local Boys' Club. I refused to acknowledge him as my father because he had nothing positive to offer and, at any rate, was absent for the greater part of my childhood.

My father's abandonment of me and the guidance I yearned for served as powerful motivators. I began to etch places for myself in happy environments and to escape the dysfunctional family I had been born into. Defining myself was my number-one priority as a boy who knew he did not wish to be like his father when he became a man. My gift of foresight, observing those early television images, and having a great number of friends with healthy families allowed me to recognize early that there was a different way of living and that it was within my grasp.

Participation in organized sports and the Boys' Club required me to be away from my house for long intervals; I spent any extra time with my friends and their families. Excelling in sports brought no family members to my games or practices but it did bring notice from my friends' parents. They were honorable men who truly cared and they began to welcome me with open arms into their homes of loving, emotionally available and healthy families. These fathers, both black and white, showed me an entirely new world—the same one that existed on the televisions shows about wonderful fathers, but this one really existed and I could touch and feel it. They allowed me to see things from a whole new perspective.

I'll never forget the first time I sat down at the dinner table at a friend's house and was offered a beautifully laid out meal. All of the family members began to ask each other about their day's activities, and they included me. In fact, it was with glowing appreciation that I responded to the father's interest in me. This gathering was a new experience, and their warmth filled my heart with hope. I listened to the way the father's voice resounded with proud admiration for his sons and witnessed the way the mother smiled when her husband talked.

Other fathers similarly included me in discussions about the future, including my college plans. I had never seriously considered college; it seemed so far from what I was exposed to from my father. I watched in amazement as the same look they gave their own children appeared on these men's faces when I began to talk tentatively about college and my future goals. When I appeared unsure of myself, they generously gave me their time and attention, listening to my trepidation. By offering me guidance and the emotional support I was lacking from a male role model at home, they pointed me toward the pathway that would lead where I wanted to go. I found that I wanted to be like them. Reflecting on these early interactions with my friends' fathers reinforces my observations of the demise of the black family unit. The energy that my friends' fathers enthusiastically expended on me, not my father's commanding ways, made me passionate to achieve. I wanted to make them proud of me, and they were. Addressing my insecurities, they assured me that I was capable of succeeding in college, and in life. In turn, I shared this invaluable encouragement with my siblings, who thankfully listened and are equally successful in life. Even though I carried some of my father's traits into my marriages, it was those early experiences with my friends' families that gave me hope and pride in myself as a person.

Distressingly, not all black males have similar access to mentors and father figures; instead they fall prey to the street's negative role models. I consider myself one of the lucky black men who escaped the oppression in childhood that my own father, and perhaps even society as a whole, tried to enforce. As black men, we must step into the role of mentor for the young. Ask most African Americans about their family life and chances are they will answer, "My mother [or grandmother] raised me," and/or "I never knew my real father."

Strong black women have done their part honorably to bring us where we are today. They have proudly taken on the role of caregiver but they need our help. We owe it to them to take responsibility for our children. Real men simply do not leave their families behind. It is not "cool" to be a "player" and it is ludicrous for black men to make babies and then abandon their families.

Fatherless families appear to be more common in Northern than in Southern cities. Perhaps this is because the South has preserved more of the cultural roles that grew out of the days of slavery, or because Southern culture tends to accept large families, however extended, as the acceptable norm. Some studies show that in large metropolitan cities in the North, West and Midwest, the number of single-parent black families is on the increase. Furthermore, there exists a large number of single-parent households in the South as well. The difference is that Southern black families seem more cohesive within the extended family, with grandparents playing a large role in the raising of fatherless children. Even in the Bible Belt, two-parent families are breaking into scattered families with children forced to parent themselves. Some studies indicate that a great number of these children rebel, use drugs, and often fail to finish school, which supports the argument that two parents have a greater probability of guiding and nurturing their children into successful adults.

To illustrate the invasive, long-term effects of the disjointed family, analyze the following story of the irresponsibility of one black man and the effects of his behavior upon generations.

As a physician I constantly see my own upbringing reflected back to me from patient histories, so I will use my own family as a prototype. Although I did not know my great-grandfather, my grandfather was a wayward alcoholic. By the way my father physically abused his own children, I feel confident in making an educated guess that he experienced extensive physical abuse from his own father. My grandfather was a poor role model; my father mirrored his behavior. Both of them drank, used drugs, and were ill-equipped to be role models.

As we all learn from and imitate the behavior of our parents, it is perhaps fortunate that I produced no sons. I distinctly remember when I found myself behaving like the man I had vowed I would never emulate. A longtime mate had told me time and again that I treated her badly but I took not one word she said to heart. Arrogantly, I had decided that she was just weak and could not handle the commands that a man "normally" gives his mate. I also had assumed that she would never leave me, and that she needed my control because she couldn't take care of herself. I was very wrong. She did leave and went on to become very successful on her own, without my continued "assistance." Sometimes I battle hating myself for such past hurtful behavior, but doing so won't change the past—which is why it is important to change the future. Other black males, hopefully profiting from such stories as mine, will abort the cycle of repetitious mistakes like those of my grandfather, my father, and myself.

Who gets the "short end of the stick" is predestined if an irresponsible black man paves his family's path to destruction. For generations, black women have been burdened with keeping families together, and accordingly have suffered unjustly. For many women, mind and body have reaped the consequences of many years of sweat and tears; their death rate from many diseases, such as diabetes and stroke, is on the increase. Although there is limited scientific correlation between absentee fathers and black female disease rates, it could be argued that the stress of single-handedly raising a family is a significant contributor.

Probably the most worrisome dilemma for many black mothers is how to help their young black children grow into responsible black men without a father figure in the house. Some women must work two or three jobs to make ends meet, affording little opportunity for quality time with their children. Further, social scientists have hypothesized that black mothers spend more time with daughters, preparing them for their own eventual absentee-husband dilemma.

What attention is given to male children leans toward the external, such as assigning household chores, rather than an internal focus on the self and the importance of responsibility. These black boys are not often taught the significance of black family unity, or how to love themselves. There remains a critical need for both male and female black children to experience responsible black fathers who can help them discover who they are. These fathers must help their children grow up without succumbing to unhealthy outside influences and negative stereotypes. In order for our children to understand what it means to *have* a family, we have to show them how it is to *be* one.

My own father ultimately deserted his family after intermittent stopovers. He was eventually arrested for and convicted of armed robbery, and died in Trenton State Prison when I was fifteen years old. While this tragedy has served to sadden and embarrass me, it has also, ironically, served as a blessing. As an adult physician, I treat and counsel many black men who share a similar paternal history with me, and many of them feel encouragement and, at last, hope through our discussions.

In *Sexuality and Racism,* the authors share an image that touches close to home for many black children:

> After my father was gone a very long time, my mother invited a tall black preacher to a dinner of her special fried chicken. After the preacher arrived and not really understanding right away the reason for this, I began to resent him much like my own father. I learned quickly that he demanded things to be his way by how he spoke to my mother in a commanding tone. Even though I was very young, my stomach was turned by his macho, controlling attitude towards my mother.

My first reaction to this story was "How could this be happening to our mothers? Isn't one time too many?" Because black men often display such controlling natures toward their families, the cycle of resentment and emotional instability seems inevitable in the black male child.

At this point it is important to emphasize that even a horrific, unstable, or inconsistent family life does not dictate failure for the black male. The sociologist Emmy Werner studied the offspring of chronically poor, alcoholic, abusive, and even psychotic parents in an effort to understand how failure was passed from one generation to another. Her study contributed to the creation of what is referred to as the Resilience Theory, as its results remarkably showed that one-third of the children studied grew up to be emotionally healthy and competent adults.

Like Werner, I focus on the black man's return to the family because of the survivors; we learn from those who have succeeded. Teachers, extended family members, and community leaders alike are capable of helping to pave pathways to resiliency and success, as opposed to leaving the outcome to fate and determinism. Hope lies in the fact that there are people who have faced childhood adversity and have overcome the odds. Much of their resilience can be credited to the intervention of others who may or may not have been family members. Consider the potential success all black children might enjoy if their own fathers stayed home or returned to their families as that "intervening variable." That could change their perception of the family unit as one that stays together.

Conclusively, then, not all black children without families are destined to fail and become social casualties. Whereas I used to harbor resentment for being a product of my disadvantaged and dysfunctional family, the help of a psychologist redirected me toward the path of gratitude. Because I had been able to successfully compete with others who had the advantage of a low-stress childhood, I began to rethink my position. Overcoming the adversity of my background became one of my personal goals; I began to consider that perhaps I might have even reached the position of first black president had my father been present, emotionally healthy, and supportive. Since becoming a physician and interacting with others functioning at a disadvantage, my gratitude has grown and I realize that I am indeed resilient. The thought of the number of black children with similar potential is staggering; all they await are encouragement and guidance toward a successful future.

It is true that the black family of today is still coping with the legacy of slavery and the value conflicts that deeply saturated its spirit. Just as the events of the Holocaust affect the lives of present-day Jews, so has slavery enflamed the emotions of blacks for generations. Emotional scars from that period have left ugly images in the minds of many present day blacks, and most likely have influenced in part the destructive patterns of behavior seen today in the black male in his relationship with his family.

Many black men have the same feelings of anger, distrust, and fear that their ancestors had for an oppressive system controlled by whites. In order for black men to break slavery's cycle of destruction upon their minds and in their lives, a series of mental adjustments must occur to compensate for the emotional pain that many of us feel.

First of all, anger must be replaced with love. Anger is a very unhealthy emotion that can lead only to the destruction of the person who incessantly feels it. Long-standing anger, left unresolved, builds into resentment, which is also unhealthy. In the black man's case, although slavery ended and the civil rights movement of the 1960s helped blacks to move forward, the pain of slavery lingers.

Black men must learn to let go of this cancerous emotion and move forward, not continue to look backward. Placing blame on white society is a way to justify the anger, but it still festers, eventually harming the person doing the blaming. Changing the way they view themselves by creating their own destinies is the only way for black men to overcome the feelings of victimization borne of oppression. Taking the stance that there are no victims in adulthood (other than those who have crimes committed against them) focuses attention on the individual and blocks the fear of being without choices.

When one loves oneself, the roots of resentment do not exist. This love of self is then naturally transferred to the family and with this love, the emotions of trust, realism, and confidence replace fear. When the black man gives his family genuine love and affection, he enjoys confidence in himself, and feels capable of succeeding honorably in a system that has wronged his people for generations. Imagine the virtues gained by the family who shares his life. Embracing our black women and children should be our primary concern because a cohesive family has the power to resolve conflict. In doing so we are good role models for our children, who will learn to overcome obstacles through the learning process. The black man must perceive his mate as his strongest ally, not his enemy, if the family is to survive.

Role models within the family also contribute to the substantial awareness of sexuality among black adolescents. Increasing social tolerance permits our black youth to have more knowledge and curiosity than ever before. Black males are generally described as permissive in sexual behavior and most often teach this pattern to their children. Moreover, as children tend to mirror their parents, the black male child, who typically wants to be like his father figure, will grow to disrespect women when he sees his father, grandfather, or a significant member of his family do so. Black males can demonstrate their sexuality to their children not only by being physically indiscreet, but by their actions and words as well.

When a father is present in a black family, his children learn about relationships from observing interactions between him and their mother. Eventually they recognize the difference between cohesiveness of the family unit and one that is unstable. The importance of structure, commitment, and intimacy is paramount to a healthy marriage between a black man and woman, and to the future of their children. Both environment and childhood perceptions of adult role models are significant factors in determining future behavior and success in relationships. Unconditional love and deliberate nonsexual affection are critical for our black children to witness.

It is unfortunate that open nonsexual displays of affection are uncommon in many black households. How then can black parents expect children to learn affection as a normal behavior between husband and wife? Holding, cuddling, caressing, and kissing in front of the children are not typical—usually they occur out of their sight. Children can be left emotionally unfulfilled and forced to form their own conclusions on intimacy. They often reach conclusions through such informational media as television and movies, which often portray more fantasy than reality.

Love and intimacy tend not to be openly discussed in front of black children, thereby leaving the male child, specifically, with a distorted idea of how to relate to women as an adult. As opposed to nonsexual affection, confrontation seems to be the norm in many black households. Dissension is often accusatory, distrustful, belligerent, and expressed by black men toward their mates in front of the children. Black boys see their fathers as physically macho men showing emotionally charged anger or indifference; they are often controlling and even sometimes physically abusive toward their mates. When this behavior becomes repetitious, black children eventually perceive their mother as merely the bearer of children or as the provider of physical satisfaction for father or father figure. Children raised in families that have discord rather than show love openly can become destructive, cycling into a pattern that spans generations.

Scholars have argued that oppression of an entire racial group, particularly with respect to black males, results in compensatory attitudes and behavior. These attitudes can be positive or negative depending on the history and experience of the black men involved. Women alone often have trouble providing a stable financial and even loving household due to socioeconomic stress. Often a boy in a female-dominated household becomes confused about his role as a boy. Early feelings of powerlessness and dependency may develop into disrespect for his mother as he experiences the difficulties black mothers face when trying to meet the needs of their male children. Later, this disrespect extends to black women in adult relationships.

A more positive prediction suggests that if black adults share the same goals and values and are committed to one another, they will build the fundamental foundation for a secure family unit. The offspring of couples who possess these characteristics will likely become healthy, stable, and committed individuals who will manifest these qualities in their own lives and develop fulfilling relationships with others. Children will also build their own strong family units that are naturally equipped to deal with the stressors of life, including the perils of racism. People who belong to cohesive families do not usually feel as though the world owes them something, nor do they feel resentment for others when things do not always go as planned. As masters of their own fate, they tend to be confident and to approach negative situations in a positive manner, seeking to accomplish what they can to improve things. Children raised in a loving family and who are taught the value of honesty and hard work are more likely to overcome the barriers of racism.

The role of father, therefore, and the loving manner in which parents relate to each other is important for the psychological growth of the black male. Ideally, early perceptions of their world will be positive and wonderful. Acceptance is received from fathers who have love, not anger, in their hearts and who realistically interpret events and interactions with people as they actually occur. These fathers are unblemished by insecurities or preoccupation with their sexual selves and possess well-integrated personalities.

As an example, I can recall a rare occasion when my father took me shopping for sneakers. Shopping with my father was always a nerve-racking event because I always felt as if I were walking on eggshells in fear that I would anger him somehow. When the mood struck him, we were expected to be ready to leave immediately. His sternness and unloving ways frightened me. What could have been a blessed outing turned into one packed with anxiety. While we toured the stores, my father referred to our surroundings in a cynical, rather resentful way. The experience revealed how he viewed himself.

If a store security guard casually glanced his way, my father would say, "Look at that, the man thinks we'll steal something." He would tell me how much he hated everything and, in fact, rarely expressed his genuine likes. However, as contrasting as night and day, my father's demeanor would alter noticeably when an attractive woman crossed his path, his scowl miraculously transforming into a deceitful seductive grin which showed all his teeth. He would say slyly, "Hey baby, what's your name? You're lookin' good," in a voice much different from the one he used with my mother and me. I watched his eyes while he inspected these strange women and wondered what he saw in them that he didn't see in my mother, his wife. This different tone of voice seemed to make him act strangely as well; he turned into a seductive, loving, and generous person. When we left the store, he always returned to his usual moody, grumbling self. These trips had a great impact on my emotions and subsequently influenced me later in life in my own relationships. I came to realize how he wasted so much of his affection on things that did not matter to anyone but himself.

Those early shopping excursions greatly influenced my early perceptions of how men behaved. I have often wondered why many young men operate from negative mind-sets before they are old enough to defend themselves with common sense and a positive attitude, especially when dealing with the women in their lives. I believe that black men must accept responsibility for softening the future perceptions of our sons. Any of our own emotional baggage of the stereotypical black man must not blemish their reality.

The Social Learning Theory proposed by prominent sociologists suggests that children learn by gender modeling. It is postulated that boys learn their roles as adults through interactions with adult men, modeling the behavior of the black men closest to them. The good news is that if the father is present and emotionally healthy, black sons reap the benefits of their fathers' insight and life experiences. The responsibility clearly lies with the attendant black man, biological father or not.

Black men with healthy personalities tend to have a positive attitude about life. In my experience, if my father had been more respectful to strange women I would have learned the same respectful behavior through observation. Unfortunately, there are many black men like my father with very little to offer in the way of being a positive role model. Men who are available and eager to share their positive attitudes with young blacks are helping their own sons and their friends or are involved in programs sponsoring support for black children and families. But there are too few of these sorely needed mentors to meet the needs of all black male children. Men who understand the significance of raising young black men to be responsible and to value the family instill neither doubt nor fear in children, nor do they encourage a macho sexual posture. Healthy role models do not define themselves in sexual or physical terms. Rather, they emphasize the spiritual, intellectual, and emotional selves and strive for growth in every area of their lives. How blessed are those children who have a black man offering them a positively wonderful outlook on life!

In the African American community today, there is a great need for mentors to help meet the needs of the increasing number of black male children without fathers. The importance of mentors in the black community cannot be overstated. Today it takes a community to raise a young black child, especially when the father is absent from the home. Mentors are important because they provide a guide for the young black man to follow; they act as a surrogate father who knows the safe road to success, devoid of many of the dangerous pitfalls that keep a young child from reaching his potential.

Most effective is the black man who lives his own life in the way that he guides a young person, with consistency and concrete boundaries for what he believes. Hillary Rodham Clinton identified it perfectly when she coined the phrase, "It takes a village." If black men form a bond of commitment with just one Boys' Club or other neighborhood organization, committing just a couple of hours a week to a young black male child, that child's life could be forever changed. It is easy to shrug and say, "It's not my problem," but it most certainly is. It becomes everyone's problem, or the future of black men will be filled not with positive, but with destructive, outcomes.

Another ongoing social atrocity is that too many young black males continue to be exposed to the wrong people: unenlightened peers, street hoodlums, black men who are devoid of healthy attitudes and an honest conception of their true role in America. Many of these unfortunate men are struggling with survival needs or are emotionally impaired, and are thus disinterested and unqualified to steer a black child in the proper direction. Those black men who are integrated and do not embrace myths regarding black males are devoting their attention to their own families, so they are often unavailable to provide a role model for others.

Perhaps not much can be done for black men who have already chosen to follow in the footsteps of those who harmed them early in life. If true, how distressing. We, as black men, must take off the blinders that prevent us from seeing what's really happening to African Americans; black families are slowly dying and are destined to become extinct if something significant is not achieved.

Black males have been misrepresented and misunderstood for so long that society believes unhealthy behavior is our norm. We absolutely must take the bull by the horns, stop talking, and start making things happen.

Strategists and urban leaders continue to map out numerous avenues of unity for helping young black males, such as the Million Man March that took place in Washington, D.C., in October 1995.

The event was well publicized and attended by black men, both young and old, and of all religious denominations and belief systems. It sparked a fire of brotherhood in the minds of these men as a collective commitment to atone for negative attitudes and behavior.

Weeks after this historical event, black male patients as well as some of my own friends were still glowing. They talked about how "being with all those positive brothers" had changed the way they perceived themselves and their families and given them a renewed sense of commitment. The collective fervor, however, was unfortunately short-lived, fading as time passed. It was really strange when patients who were initially motivated appeared complacent when I brought it up in conversation months later. Speculation considers that this occurred because nothing structured was in place for the aftermath of the collective unity. Men returned to their homes and sons, to schools and jobs, only to find that their lives had not really changed that much at all.

Even though the march on Washington was a great event, there was no guidance for follow-through at the local level. Except for the black men who used the Million Man March to further their commitment to their families, the motivation for the celebration remained in the past. We must accept responsibility for not continuing the momentum of the Million Man March's historical message. What happened? And how can we discover new ways of raising awareness so the theme stays alive? While the answers to those questions are beyond the scope of this book, the questions raise issues for every black man to think about. Without a plan, the only way for success to continue is with luck, and luck cannot be depended upon for long-standing success.

It is vital for the future that we shift our focus from how we were raised or how the system is against us to producing a new generation of loving, honest and responsible black men who will be respected by the world as "real men." Being a family man is one of the most important, courageous jobs a black man can have. The rewards and benefits of taking responsibility for our black family unit generates greater, longer-lasting rewards than does the impulse of sex. The next time we witness a young black male child languishing in life, we will do a world of good to reach out our hand and change his direction, "one child at a time."

Chapter 6

SEXUALITY, RAGE, AND THE BLACK MAN

Rage cannot be hidden, it can only be dissembled. This dissembling deludes the thoughtless, and strengthens rage and adds, to rage, contempt.

—James Baldwin

One of my patients, a middle-aged black woman, confided to me that her mate was being treated for impotence. She further revealed that this man had a long history of physically and emotionally abusing her and, in spite of his condition, would suddenly achieve an erection while beating her. This confusing link between rage and sex is not uncommon, exemplifying a manifestation of power and control that is overcompensating for a negative image of manhood.

This chapter offers a glimpse into the often overlooked, unfortunate, and disturbing violence occurring in more and more African American relationships. There is a significant number of black men whose personalities are adversely affected by a covert or hidden rage deeply rooted in their psyches. A lack of awareness coupled with an absence of tools to control the anger yields a powerful disturbance in a black man's interpersonal relationships. A feeling of hatred aroused by anger rapaciously eats away at the self-control of the man who possesses it.

Anger dilutes a positive human spirit, causing a black man to behave in ways he will no doubt eventually regret. In black men's lives, hostility often leads to chaos. Uncontrolled anger and rage result in domestic disputes and repeated calls to authorities, thus cyclically reaffirming negative stereotypes of the black man. Dispelling this public belief is no easy task due to the severity and complexity of the sources of the black man's anger.

My inner-city medical practice affords a window onto the violence and anger that dominate the lives of many black men. Meticulous attempts to delve deeply into the root of a patient's emotional problems yield the conclusion that an angry black male with nothing to lose feels pressured to fulfill public expectations. If one repeatedly tells another that he is worthless, over time he will begin to believe it. This is precisely what happens to the black man who feels powerless to change his feelings of poor self-worth.

It is a twofold tragedy in that much of the black male's aggression is displaced onto his mate. Abuse—verbal or physical—is a symptom of the powerlessness and desperate desire for control that many black men feel. Women all too often bear the brunt of their angry mates' physical and emotional assaults. Several black female patients of mine have developed both emotional distress and psychological disease (i.e., mental illness and psychosis). They suffer physically as well; morbid obesity is often a result of the anger and violence suffered at the hands of their mates.

Disruptive and abusive relationships sometimes cause those on the receiving end to have fear, which often results in neurosis. Symptoms of neurosis progress to psychosis if no intervention occurs. For example, one of my patients, a severely depressed woman suffered deeply at the hands of her abusive boyfriend, both physically and emotionally. She even ended up in the hospital for her injuries and emotional stress. After she told me that she was hearing voices and suffering hallucinations that told her to kill her boyfriend, I admitted her to the psychiatric unit. Milder case studies have shown that women also can develop compulsions, such as eating to obtain a sense of pleasure and contentment, to compensate for the pain of a terrible relationship.

Regretfully, this cycle of anger, violence, and abuse is very familiar to me; I know the pattern all too well. Growing up with an abusive father left me riddled with anger and malice. Thankfully, God intervened in my life, as did many good friends and colleagues, and I was able to redirect my anger toward more positive endeavors. Realistically, not everyone recognizes his destructive pattern, and it distressingly survives through future generations of his family.

The black man's rage extends beyond boundaries imagined by conventional society. Those who experience and survive abuse carry the deepest understanding of how it invades the human spirit. Others are often exceedingly confused by the senseless acts of violence and rage reported by newspapers and televised news shows. Most other ethnic groups, including whites, plainly do not share the black man's historical beginnings. Without justifying the black man's acts of violence or abuse, it is my conjecture that it takes one angry black man to know another. Many of us share the same sad stories.

One night, I awakened to odd sounds of *thumps*, as if someone were batting a stick against a rug in an attempt to beat out the dust. Along with the *thumps* came muffled screams. My brothers and sisters and I jumped out of bed and ran to the living room, where we came to an abrupt halt in horror. There on the living room floor sat my mother, my father hovering over her like a monster, a rolled-up newspaper in his right hand. Upon closer inspection, that newspaper materialized into a wooden table leg he had broken off an end table.

After turning on the lights, my sister ran to the aid of our mother. Blood was everywhere. Fear permeated every cell in my body; in fact, I could not move from being frozen in fear. My trepidation was so great that I felt total helplessness. I have wrestled with this memory for many years, questioning my inability to go to the aid of my own mother. I was merely seven years old when this incident occurred, my sister barely five.

Still, to this day, that moment haunts me for many reasons. What is peculiar—and even more embarrassing to think about—were the feelings of anger I had projected onto my mother, the victim, for allowing something like that to happen to her. I asked myself, "Why couldn't she have fought back or made some sort of effort not to have this ruthless person in our lives?" I was angry with my mother for not doing more for us, instead of looking at why that incident was happening. As I grew older and became more emotionally healthy, I realized that my mother (or any of us) was not responsible for my father's rage.

In turn, I began searching for an answer as to why my father would display such intensely angry behavior toward someone he was supposed to have loved. Like many young black males in similar positions, I became the next victim of the anger and violence in my home. Through the many angry confrontations between my mother and father, I remember vividly my own feelings of apprehension when my father would return home, usually intoxicated and full of rage. Upon entering the house, he immediately let everyone know that he was the "man of the house and therefore in charge," even if he had not been there for many days. Repeatedly, while my siblings and I watched, immobilized by fear, he proved his manhood and sexuality by beating his wife. Sometimes he pushed her, sometimes he yelled and demeaned her verbally, but most of the time he simply used his fists or anything that resembled a bat. It was by aggression and attack that he achieved his place as head of our household, not through honest affection.

Because of these experiences, I am not shocked when I read news articles about young black men doing what my father did. I no longer condone this behavior; I abhor it. Being a survivor who has gone through the process of recovery, I now understand how these violent acts could have occurred. To this day I do not think my father realized that our obedience and deference to him were simply the result of our paralyzing fear. He died alone, in Trenton State Prison, perhaps wondering where things had gone wrong.

My father's anger toward my mother profoundly, deeply scarred my soul, emotions, and spirit. Sadly, such rage and violence dictates the eventual fragmentation of the black family and perpetuates the sexual anger of the male abuser. He then compensates for his "failure to keep a woman in line," or subservient, by increasing his outward violence and thereby proving to himself and others that he is a "real man." Often this anger is displayed sexually and, in addition to the verbal and physical abuse that the woman suffers, she is often secretly exposed to sexual abuse within her own marriage.

Once violence begins in the home, the cyclic infection spreads to the children. They are passive victims, affected by the aberrant, nonloving behavior typically exhibited by the black male parent. Often the mothers in these relationships are not affectionate with their children due to difficulty in overcoming their own emotional torment. The children are emotionally affected by the violence and are at increased risk for repeating the cycle in their adult lives. If one has not experienced love, it is usually very difficult to express. In homes where affection and love are absent, the children often feel unsafe and unloved, suffering long-term consequences. If the cycle is to be broken, every African American must work in concert to develop alternatives for young blacks who find themselves in similar situations. Black men must learn that love and respect are the norm and that rage and acts of violence within their families are no longer acceptable.

Plausible explanations for the phenomenon of rage, resentment, and the levels of anger that black men are exposed to are abundant. The dynamics of these explanations could very well fill a library with a lifetime of sensational reading. The few social scientists who place most of the blame for the angry, violent behavior of black males on socioeconomic factors seem to receive the most media attention. This is partly because most of the black men they study tend to be low on the socioeconomic scale. Although these scholarly theories may contain partial truth, they do little to adequately explain further why some black men who grow up within impoverished communities and single family households do succeed in life and do gain control of their anger.

The reality is that black men need not submit to the belief that they are stuck in environments affording limited opportunities for success. Factors such as positive peer influences, organized activities supervised by caring adults, and significant participation by mentors can save a child from the negative influences of disadvantaged beginnings. Furthermore, through the intervention of caring individuals, black men can be shown alternatives to their anger and positive and productive ways of managing stress.

In our black neighborhoods, no matter how hard we attempt to dilute the fact that there is violence around us, there always exists a safety issue. Many black male teens are either murdered or incarcerated before reaching adulthood. According to the United States Census Bureau in 1995, 56.3 percent of black males who died were victims of homicide. In addition, over half of the prison population in the United States is black. Typically, the males who grow up in dangerous environments rarely feel secure and fight to defend what little territory and sense of self they do have. Limited opportunities within many urban black neighborhoods offer few or no avenues for black men to exercise their talents, without violence, in productive and effective ways.

Aggression is not foreign to black culture. In African history, men would engage in combat to prove their manhood. The more muscular opponents who were able to wrestle their challengers to the ground received the most respect and gained status. Similarly, today's society finds large numbers of black males pressured by a need to prove to others that they are "manly." Much like our ancestors, this validation is carried out aggressively. The need to certify one's manhood in this manner unfortunately explodes into a force of destruction. The ensuing consequences of aggressiveness negatively affect the black man's life and family, and society as a whole.

The black man's anger and violent behavior have done little to help the plight of African Americans. In studying couples, I have found the black man's anger repeatedly to be a major feature of relationship difficulties. Although I have met many intelligent black men more loving and less angry than I, there is a persistent element of latent, unresolved anger eventually revealed by the man in counsel. Actualized professionally and intellectually, these men still detrimentally display anger within a relationship. However, unlike their less formally educated counterparts, more educated black men express their anger in increasingly covert ways. They become passive-aggressive with their mates, practice infidelity, intimidate and control their women by any means available, much as I did in my earlier years of anger.

Rage came easily to me because I had grown into an angry black man under the influence of a caustic father. Indirectly expressed anger took the forms of cynicism and pessimism. Yet today I battle residual anger, for the time lost when I was neither loving nor being loved; I offer my story in earnest so that other black men might benefit and never know such a loss. At times, as if having never learned anything from past transgressions, I still find myself confronting others harshly when my expectations and demands go unmet. A great and satisfying difference, however, is that when I am aware of doing this I immediately attempt to modify the untoward behavior before someone is hurt.

Although professional, well-educated black men tend to avoid physical confrontation and do not usually carry weapons, aggression and anger find other ways to demonstrate manhood. As a black man with my own share of macho aggression problems, I stubbornly retain hope for myself and other black men to conquer this destructiveness. Still, noticing details while observing black men display negative behaviors is part of my daily office routine. Unable to set aside these incidents as "just a part of life," I feel the heavy weight of how black men contribute to their negative societal perception.

For example, one day I awoke in such a great mood that I decided I could successfully implement an approach different from my usual fault-finding regarding myself and other black males. I decided that for this day I would view everything from a positive, encouraging perspective. After putting on a cheerful yellow bow tie, I drove toward work at my usual moderate speed, obeying limits in order to avoid accidents in the congested inner-city traffic. My pleasant frame of mind was suddenly challenged when loud honking demanded my attention. In my rear view mirror I could see two young black men apparently annoyed by my "slow" driving, tailgating until they could pass me—unfortunately, not an uncommon experience. I could not relate to their caps turned sideways or the loud music blaring from their open windows. But what made me feel uneasy were the obscene looks they gave me; they were clearly pissed off.

Peacefulness now interrupted, I struggled with my mood as I approached my office. Several policemen surrounded a black male, and though I could not hear the conversation, the officers appeared close to anger. Turning into my office driveway, I glanced back to witness the police officers grab the young black male and throw him against the car where they handcuffed him.

Still struggling to maintain my original decision to remain positive, I greeted my first patient, Ms. J, a thirty-six-year-old black woman. Ms .J, a friendly person who had been coming to this office for some time, did not look happy that day. Attentive to her change in disposition, I listened as she complained of a bad cough, adding, "By the way, I just left the courthouse and got a restraining order against my boyfriend. He cut up the furniture and threatened to kill me." When asked why, she responded, "I told him that I wanted to go back to school and that if he did not stop drinking I would have to ask him to leave." She was obviously saddened by her decision yet, strangely to her, she felt motivated to start a new life without the abuse. "I can do better by myself," she explained.

Following these events occurring on the same day, I found myself resenting all black men. I imagined how white people must feel when they witness such acts or are the victims of violence by black men. I began to deeply fear that stereotypes and myths would never be erased from the public mind; "WE" brothers would remain stuck in the mud of a macho slave mentality. I considered how black women appeared to be moving toward success while men languished, defining ourselves by physical means.

Hostility has limited the social progression for black men, providing distorted negative images of them. Other ethnic groups appear to view African American men with fear and disdain, preventing a healthy support system and potential alliances. As a counselor for a boys' program once observed, the character traits most likely to draw him to and mentor a child were friendliness, courteous manners, and a smile. He maintained that an angry, disrespectful child is least likely to acquire assistance.

Public perceptions, including fear of the black man, have virtually alienated him from many ethnic groups. This alienation must be dissolved for him to progress and to ensure the proliferation of the African American family unit. Through the creation of a support system, not only from within black society but from all of American society, black people can achieve what is rightfully deserved, thereby strengthening society as a whole.

It is not difficult to understand the factors that can lead to the destruction of families and relationships. The following equation leads the way: add up the negative factors and obstacles faced by black males; then add the lure of quick money from the sale and subsequent use of drugs; economic barriers from uneducated and disadvantaged single-parent family structures; insecurities from feelings of despair. The whole (destructive fire of rage) equals the sum of parts (fuel). Compound the parts with an outpouring of critical public opinions that classify black males as lazy, sexually charged, and violent and the stage is set for the end result . . . an angry black male with nothing to lose. He yields to the pressure of fulfilling public expectations.

As stated before, women are the ones who are left to bear the brunt of physical and emotional assault, to make ends meet, and to promote harmony within the family unit. Becoming frightened and angry, they either succumb to the man's power and control or they fight back. Like my patient who decided not to be part of an abusive relationship, many fight back by leaving and ending the relationship. The women may, in fact, become angry and aggressive toward mates and children, preventing any reconcilable hope for the relationship.

The breakup of the family unit adds to another evolution of the anger cycle, particularly when children are involved. The mother may begin to blame herself for the problems in the relationship and start to abuse or neglect her physical and emotional selves. Since she rarely seeks help, the self-demise of the black woman continues until the single mother becomes a liability instead of an asset to the family unit. Black women who are more fortunate, who have family and financial support, might suffer less but their battle is not without casualties. In their plight to be self-sufficient, they must play two roles in raising their children without the normalcy and comfort of a loving relationship.

Solutions to our problems as black men, and women, can be identified and implemented only if collectively, as a people, we can muster up enough courage to say "We have had enough!" If each black man would take responsibility for the future of just two black male children, situations would begin to improve. As mentors and possibly fathers to these young boys, we could begin to guide and reform young black males into happier and more serving individuals who would be able to succeed in life. We could teach them what's necessary to become real—happy and healthy—men: work hard to achieve what you set your mind to.

If black men learn the satisfaction of achievement, their self-esteem will soar; and if they feel better about themselves, they will be less angry. Black adult mentors will become a part of the journey these young males make as they move toward their destination. By addressing the pitfalls and potential life experiences that could make reaching the children's goals difficult, mentors experience the journey, too. Important values—a willingness to work, using the mind to persevere, working not only for money but for self-improvement— come to life through a mentor who truly cares.

All too often the young men I meet in my practice see little or no value in hard work. Many seek a shortcut to success and subsequently get into trouble. Generally, these kids are unmotivated and work only on conditional terms, if pressured or if the reward for their effort will meet some selfish need. There is very little pride in setting a goal which will push and stretch their personal limits, so they miss out on the result of achieving such goals: an unconditional love for self, one that cannot produce an angry adult.

There is an unfortunate number of unmotivated young black males who inform me that their parents never work, thereby failing to teach them its value. In contrast, the resilient boys, even those living in the ghetto, who do demonstrate good work ethics have a parent (usually a mother) or parents who have worked hard all their lives to put food on the table. The children who grow up with hardworking parents understand the value of work and therefore have a greater chance of success. For example, the successful professional athlete who gives thanks to his mother, a hard-working religious woman who taught him the value of hard work at a very young age. I believe any child can make it with hard work, along the avenue Thomas Edison described: "Genius is one percent inspiration and ninety-nine percent perspiration."

Another solution to the black male problem is the encouragement of a religious commitment. Black men, especially young ones, have seemingly turned their backs on God, or a "higher power." Most of the young black males I meet have little or no religious commitment. The successful ones go to church or belong to an organization that does charitable work and instills the importance of a power greater than the child. These young blacks grow up experiencing love and the importance of giving of themselves to another human being. They are less physically and sexually oriented; therefore, the macho stereotypes do not apply to them.

These young, happy, and healthy black males usually excel in their classwork and are liked by their teachers and adults, who feel privileged to witness their accomplishments. These males are not enticed by gangs and other groups that foster peer pressure and allow no individual thoughts or expression. It follows, then, that another solution, encouraging the individual, is geared toward achieving success and personal growth.

One day on my way to a fourth-grade school presentation, I realized how unsure I was about what to teach a population in such great need of adult guidance. The topic I had chosen was individuality versus peer influences, but the problem was how to present such a subject to a group of youngsters who would most likely be rude and disinterested. I decided to tell a story:

In an ancient time, nestled within a small coastal village of the Far East, a certain community of people were modest and humble, blessed with a cornucopia of special talents that enabled them to prosper. Of all their gifts, one provided the villagers prestige and considerable export revenue. Known as "the beautiful little place by the sea where the shoes are made," this small hamlet made shoes for most of the Old World cities and towns. It was also during this period in history that shoes were made for vanity's sake and not simply usefulness. Beginning as an item of necessity, shoes became fashion accessories with style and provocation. Since shoes were a major commodity, it was only natural that footwear creativity would emerge.

Salah was a hardworking man, devoted to his family. He had a son who had not yet reached adolescence; he was a curious child, especially quick to learn new things. He particularly loved the way the older boys of the village made their shoes and spent most of his time watching those boys work. The young son dreamed that he would one day be able to make shoes, bringing honor to his father. He often wondered if he would prove himself worthy when the time came.

Unfortunately for this young dreamer, a family tragedy occurred and his father had to move to a faraway land, taking his family with him. Although their new village in the faraway land was very different, the little son was saddened. The main reasons for his sadness were the remoteness of the region and the impassive, noncreative nature of the people. No one even wore shoes.

As time passed, memories of his former home became more and more vague. He could barely recall how those beautiful shoes were made. Nevertheless, he began using his imagination, and, unknown to his father, isolation from the other villagers caused him to pour himself into making special shoes. These shoes were a personal project he would work on until his fingers grew numb. What he could not recall, he improvised, creating shoes unlike any others and, certainly in his eyes, not for public inspection.

As weeks and months turned into years, he maintained this tenacity in his work. When the son was not helping the family and his father with chores, he slid away into the little warehouse behind the garden to make his special shoes. With only his own thoughts for company, he wondered if he would ever return to the home he once knew.

Finally, one day, through a twist of fate, his father decided that he wanted to return to his former home as he was growing old and tired. The son, now a young man, became very excited, although the excitement was tinged with a sense of apprehension. Knowing he would have to work so that his father would not be required to, he wondered if his special shoes would be welcomed into the little town where he grew up. He questioned whether he would fit in or simply be ridiculed and laughed at. He contemplated whether or not his isolation, self-reflection, and hard work would pay off. One thing was sure: he had grown as a person and had developed a great spirituality that enabled him to feel happiness, security, and peace. As always, he could rely on these feelings, even if his shoe-making skills were not appreciated.

When he and family finally arrived back home, they were met with cheers and love and when the villagers saw the old man's son with his shoes, they marveled at the excellent craftsmanship and ingenuity of his designs. His shoes were unlike any they had seen before. The styles of the shoes were unsurpassed, and his work reflected his skill. The son's shoes were both durable and serviceable: greater distances could be traveled and more places explored. The sale of the special shoes would also provide an income. In his many years of isolation and quiet tenacity he had become an innovator of shoes and displayed a genius that the world would applaud.

I was happy to see that more than half the group comprehended the theme. Their questions were profoundly appropriate and many identified with the boy in the story. One girl said that she was able to know herself better and that she got more work done when her friends were not around. I was convinced after this discussion that young blacks are aware of individual pursuit and that negative peer influences can be detrimental to one's individuality.

The central theme of the story revolves around the premise that one must concentrate on oneself first. Perhaps if black males were more centered on their own talents and did not attempt to seek outside stimulation to fill idle time, their own personal skills could be honed and practiced, allowing a productive and healthy integration into society. Rage would diminish, too. Peer influences are not positive if the personalities within the group are not moving forward toward improving themselves intellectually, emotionally, and spiritually.

In fact, much of the untoward behavior displayed by our youth is the result of negative peer influences and collective behavior. If these could be replaced with organized, adult-supervised activities rooted in humanitarianism, young blacks would greatly benefit.

Adults must light their paths. When young black males find themselves at the crossroads of very important decisions, a wrong turn makes the difference between reaching self-growth and individual thought, and failure. By screening peer influences, we can increase the probability of healthy interactions. We then insure the survival of our youth.

Yet another solution to the problem black males experience encompasses limited structure and routine. Many young males have no positive organized activities in which to participate. As a boy, I attended the Boys' Club and the Boy Scouts to learn about life and how to relate to others in a positive manner. Today, boys sometimes feel that these activities are for "sissies." In fact, those who do participate in organized activities usually do so only on basketball courts and in other athletic fields that sometimes erupt into violence.

A patient of mine who is a guidance counselor stresses that the students who do well and who achieve honors for academic excellence almost always benefit from routine and structure in their lives. These students adhere to a schedule and manage their time efficiently. No one has to tell them that it's time to study. They take pride in developing their inner locus of control. Their focus is unencumbered by the negative influences of their peers. It is common to see these black males neatly attired, and their rooms tidy and clean. Adults like them, and when they walk into a room and smile with a Denzel Washington dazzle, those in the room are captivated and seem to forget all the negative stereotypes about black men.

The final solution to be implemented by mentors of black males is to create teachers. Why not have these boys teach younger children, and by doing so, let them become smarter and more responsible? An example of the success of this approach lies with a previous patient of mine who was a rambunctious, disobedient boy at fifteen. His mother could do little to control his outbursts of temper and behavior. He was most certainly headed for the penal system unless something major was done to avert him. Although quite intelligent and quick to learn, sadly he felt school was not worth his effort.

Around the same time I was working with a family with a seven-year-old boy not blessed with the same intelligence as our juvenile delinquent. This younger boy's mother was troubled by her son's inability to read. Since I knew both families well, I decided to pair these two boys in performing a rather enticing experiment. On two afternoons a week, the older boy would teach the younger one to read. (Of course, I had to pay him for teaching with Knicks basketball tickets!) During the next several weeks something magical occurred: the fifteen-year-old became a teacher and taught the seven-year-old to read. Not only did the older child come at the appointed time and prepared, he began to prepare his lesson plans with diligence and improvised to keep the interest of his pupil high. My theory that kids do well when they feel important and acquire responsibility had worked. The teen teacher began to do well in school himself, stating wisely, "Now I understand where my teacher is coming from." He even said to me one day "Doc, you don't really have to get me tickets . . . Psych!" The success of this experiment was not all my doing. The boys' mothers both helped considerably. Not only did they agree to what I wanted to try, the idea became their own and they acknowledged the value of how it could help their sons. Without their support, it is possible that the boys would not have done so well.

One of the boys' mothers told me that every night just before bedtime she would go in his room and ask what he had learned that day and, after listening to him, also assured him that he could accomplish whatever challenge that came his way. She kept supporting him and telling him how proud she was of him. Using me to demonstrate that I had a great deal of faith in them, the young man was able to see that he was just as capable as the next guy. The other mother followed a similar approach.

If more adults were to use this same paradigm to help young black males gain self-esteem and act responsibly, a considerable change would occur. First, the boys would become less angry, and second, they would be less physically oriented. And by the way, that fifteen-year-old is now a freshman at a prestigious university and is getting honors. His major? Secondary education.

These are merely a few solutions to a big problem; other black adults have their own. The point is, African Americans have to make an effort to work together to change the behavior of young black males. In doing so, we not only save a generation, we save an ethnic group from potential extinction.

Both mothers and fathers are responsible for the future of their children. Parents face many barriers that can prevent a black child from being a part of the societal prescription for success. Not all, but a large number of black parents find themselves unable to pay for tennis lessons, organized sports, club activities such as Boy Scouts, and other culturally enriching activities that can provide safe alternatives for a child. It is a community of black families that will provide the proper guidance for children to walk the road to success. If parents don't do everything possible to ensure their children's success, then it becomes possible that the children may never truly achieve what they are capable of. What could most certainly work is a system that runs parallel to the one that has been in place in white society for years, tailored in a culturally sensitive way and geared for the specific needs of the young black male.

An example of this parallel system of values is the parents of the superstar tennis pros Serena and Venus Williams. Both their father and mother made a conscious decision to be different. . . to be different by first thinking positively before they interacted with each other and their children and managing anger in a constructive way. By making an effort to communicate their honest feelings with one another in front of their children and with them directly, they produced a valve system that was open and flourished. Their parents prepared the young sisters for success from the very beginning of their lives. Requiring more from their children, while showing them consistent love and commitment, created two very driven and talented black women. They chose to have their children follow their own system of success, a system that was uniquely tailored for them.

Another example is Tiger Woods, the professional golfer whose winning ways and committed father have made headlines many times. Tiger Woods openly shows affection for his parents and states that without his father and mother's pushing him to be the very best he could be, he would never have reached his high level of golf success. His father's dream for his success influenced his work ethic and value system, convincing him that he could do anything very well if he simply chose to. Tiger Woods' father and mother paved the way for his success by carving out a path for their son that was uniquely his own.

While becoming a parent like the Williamses or the Woods can be difficult, it does not have to be done at the same level. Parents who exercise tenacity, love, and consistency often produce children with similar characteristics. Making a commitment to oversee all children's activities up to and throughout their teen years helps keep them from becoming a statistic of the system. This social hierarchy historically set up by white society, does not always serve the young black man's needs, and sometimes totally excludes him.

Chapter 7

SEXUAL DYSFUNCTION, IMPOTENCE, AND THE BLACK MAN

An identity is questioned only when it is menaced, as when the mighty begin to fall, or when the wretched begin to rise, or when the stranger enters the gates, never, thereafter, to be a stranger. . . . Identity would seem to be the garment with which one covers the nakedness of the self: in which case, it is best that the garment be loose, a little like the robes of the desert, through which one's nakedness can always be felt, and, sometimes, discerned. This trust in one's nakedness is all that gives one the power to change one's robes.

—James Baldwin

Early one morning before my first scheduled patient, I sat in my office thumbing through a stack of medical journals, basically minding my own business and savoring the quiet time. I was in the middle of catching up on important recent medical updates, hoping to ease feelings of guilt stemming from my article-reading procrastination. Behind the closed office door I had unexpectedly begun to enjoy an impression of the room's whispering to me, "Alone at last," when I was startled by a loud knock at the door. My medical assistant uncomfortably announced the unscheduled arrival of two black men, who had seen my car parked outside and hoped to get in to see me before office hours began.

Annoyed at first, I managed to put my feelings aside and agreed to see them both. What happened next afforded me yet another unique look at a facet of black men. Neither of the men disclosed to my assistant the importance of being treated right away, sans emergency. Seated in two different exam rooms, one waited patiently while I saw the other. When asked why he had come to see me, each man remarkably answered with the same word: *Viagra*.

These two hard-working, generally healthy men were seeking the new blue "wonder drug" marketed by Pfizer only a week before the impromptu office visits. Both men maintained that they needed something to boost their sex life. It seemed extraordinary that both men had come to see me for the exact same thing at the very same time. Through years of treating these patients, I had not been aware of any medical problems or marital discord that would have affected their respective sex lives. Yet there they were, staring boldly at me in hopes of obtaining the wonder drug perceived as necessary to ensure their proper sexual performances in bed.

After that experience I began to wonder just how many more men would emerge from their private closets to ferret out that "magic blue bullet" named Viagra. It had not taken long to find out; soon thereafter I was being asked several times a day for Viagra. Surprisingly, men who had not admitted their impotence before the release of this drug were now discussing their sexual problems. The nature and scope of the impotence problem became very apparent to me in the ensuing weeks. Impotent black men sought my assistance in droves and I began to realize that it was a much larger problem than I had realized.

Black men usually fit into two distinct groups when it comes to impotence: those who have diseases like diabetes, high blood pressure, and heart disease and are impotent as a result; and those without diseases who feel a need to increase their sexual state and desire. Those in the first group, who experience legitimate impotence as a result of disease, are often reticent when it comes to revealing sexual dysfunction. Those who do not show clinical evidence of erectile dysfunction are requesting Viagra "to make things work better." Whatever the situation, impotence must be clearly understood by black men as a treatable condition marked by the presence of preexisting factors that cause it.

The emergence of Viagra has provided me, as a practicing physician, the considerable opportunity to acquire more complete sexual histories from black men, and to clearly define impotence for them. Impotence by definition is a loss of sexual drive, lack of erection, or the inability to achieve orgasm, and it affects black men to a greater degree than men of other ethnic groups. This last variable is largely credited to the prevalence of cardiovascular disease and diabetes among black men, conditions capable of causing impotence or sexual dysfunction.

For a black man, the psychological impact of being unable to achieve an erection can be devastating, especially if he is uninformed about the nature of his condition. Obstacles faced by the African American man in today's society are already overwhelming. Consequently, when a black man is unable to perform sexually, he is confronted with a "failure" that can emotionally parallel death. Impotence can deeply wound a man's psyche. Emotional and physical dysfunction often result from this inability, even affecting men in apparently stable relationships. Significant torment erodes a black man's sense of self when he realizes that he cannot perform the one basic function that has driven, motivated, and served as the center of his life: sex.

Yet diminished sexual performance truly need not lessen the integrity of a black man's definition of his manhood. A patient I treated for impotence told me that he considered himself a failure—nothing more than a eunuch. He found himself compensating for his loss of sexual prowess by becoming more aggressive with his wife and children. Like many black men, he was directing frustration and fear toward his mate in the forms of anger, resentment, and indifference toward her. My message to him applies to all black men: Impotence is not all in your head. It is a treatable physical condition that can be effectively managed by a qualified, knowledgeable physician.

Proper information about impotence and sexual dysfunction allows black men to identify any possible underlying physical cause and encourages them to seek competent medical assistance. Four types of impotence exist: loss of sex drive; the inability to achieve an erection; the inability to achieve orgasm; failure to ejaculate. These conditions are not occasional problems. They occur repeatedly and consistently over a period of time.

Impotence is certainly not just a black problem; thirty million men are affected in the United States alone, with causes including drugs, alcohol, smoking, and stress. When asked if it isn't an "old man's problem" I consistently respond that no, it does not have to happen when a black man gets old and yes, it can be successfully treated.

Many of my patients attempt to conceal the pain of sexual problems, not only from me but also from their mates, by adopting a greater-than-average macho persona. Because men will avoid romantic encounters that may reveal their perceived sexual inadequacy, the women in their lives are left baffled by the decreasing intimate contact and distancing in their relationship. This result emphasizes the importance of black males' understanding that they are not alone and, in fact, can take control of their situation by treating impotence as a physical problem.

Discussing impotence and sexual dysfunction requires a sensitivity I always combine with three major facts: First, impotence affects black men more often than white men or men of other ethnic minorities. This can be attributed to the higher rates of diabetes and cardiovascular disease in the black community. Second, black men place great emphasis on their sexuality in relationships and therefore may have problems at home. Finally, it is merely a myth that the black man possesses infallible, super-sexual prowess.

In taking thorough medical histories I make it a point to bring up the topic of sex with black male patients as a means of discerning any simmering problems. If I did not ask questions, many of these men would never inform me of their problems in the bedroom. Ideally, every physician would ask similar identifying questions.

One of the most intriguing aspects of consulting with black males about their sexual problems is the dramatic change in atmosphere once the examination-room door closes. There is a literal transformation from macho, overconfident, and aggressive demeanors to heightened anxiety and submissiveness. This "disrobing" of the inner self, the shedding of persona, strips away many stereotypical defenses and leaves these men feeling vulnerable and exposed. Once the catharsis begins, the black patients are in a unique position of addressing society's stereotypical myth and confronting their sexual selves with candor.

While this type of intimate situation creates discomfort in men of any ethnic group, for the black man it falls just short of emotional paralysis. This reason alone generates reluctance to go to doctors or to place himself in any potentially similar situation. Although there are many men, like me, who do not define themselves solely in sexual terms, an alarming number of black men continue to do so. Perhaps the reason black men have difficulty discussing sexual problems is because problems with sex equate to feeling vulnerable. Early in life, black men are socialized to be strong in most situations, particularly around other black men.

In illustration, I recall from childhood how black boys behaved in a predictable pattern. A big, strong, athletic kid, I was generally chosen to be captain and thus had to decide who played on which team when we played basketball. Inspecting the other boys lined up for the picking, I remember gloating and feeling self-important while they stood with their chests inflated, standing as tall and erect as possible in hopes of being chosen. Sometimes I still find myself assessing men this way, no doubt due to the way black men are socialized, many others probably do the same. Black men inspecting and measuring one another, sizing each other up and in effect choosing sides again, is certainly no new custom. In African history, black men challenged each other regularly in order to establish gender tasks.

Doctors and professionals who are not black do not usually link this behavior with a criterion to determine health issues. Thus, it is to our advantage to investigate various personality traits of black men in order to explore the impact that impotence has on their lives. In my experience, black men fall into four roles, or categories. The first group consists of the "pure jocks," men who are big, strong, and athletically inclined. Black men who fall into this group tend to grow up relying on aggression, unknowingly buying into the black male myth involving aggression, dominance, and conquest. While some are smart and develop psychologically healthy habits early on, many develop into a "jock," and often pick pretty women they can control. Once these black men believe they have conquered a woman, the adrenaline rush of the pursuit ends and they often go searching for another woman. Pure jocks, as in times of slavery, define themselves in terms of physical prowess. Consequently, the loss of their physical sexual selves through impotence can cause significant psychological problems.

The second group encompasses scholars with good study habits. They are not athletically inclined, and get good grades. Organized sports and aggressive activities are not, for the most part, of interest to them. They don't get their kicks abusing women and are considered by the pure jocks to be effeminate. These black men have grown up instilled with a sense of focus and purpose. They use their minds introspectively and are not angry black men. Impotence among this group of black men is usually addressed promptly and with the desire to understand why they are experiencing their symptoms. Their loss of sexual function, the motivating factor for these men seeking help from a physician, is still secondary in importance to the state of their health.

A third group of black men might be considered the "cool crowd." Everyone usually likes the very social black men in this group. Their gregarious nature usually takes priority over such things as schoolwork, organized sports, and other organized activities. Proms, parties, and lavish social events are the most likely places to find these men. They would much rather be jet setting than pursuing academics. Black men who fall into this category most closely fit the stereotypical descriptions of black men. They work and/or use their savvy to acquire money to feed their image as womanizers and studs. Probably the most psychologically impaired by impotence, this group instantly loses identity and manhood when their penises fail them.

Finally, black men in the fourth group grow up in families with limited income; they endure horrible hardship, and are considered to be disadvantaged. Sadly, many black men fall into this group. Too often they must grow up quickly, thereby becoming serious-minded. Parents of these boys may even carry emotional pathologies which affect their lives considerably. They don't necessarily buy into preconceived stereotypes of black males, but are nevertheless angered and disenchanted with themselves and their lives. They sometimes grow up to take their anger out on the women who love them, and blame society as a whole for their misgivings or misfortune. Many of these men subsequently become lawbreakers and end up in jail. Impotence experienced by the men in this group can often be connected to their anger and stress levels or other psychosocial issues. Although not always the case, their anger, coupled with a loss of sexual function, can push these men over the edge and they commit crimes, sometimes with violence.

These categories of black men are not scientifically proven, but they provide me with a consistent approach in a clinical setting to obtaining information about their sexual behaviors. Taking their personal histories into consideration enables me to gather a great deal of information regarding their sex lives and any other problems that they may be having. Sensitively doing so establishes a foundation upon which to build an alliance and an understanding of where they are coming from. Realistically, it is also important to note that the prototypical features of the black men in these groups is not static: scholars can be jocks and the disadvantaged can grow up to be scholars and achieve great success.

The following case studies exemplify black male representatives from these groups. Note how a change in demeanor and approach to the patient encourages him toward a better understanding of his sexual attitudes and behaviors. It is also interesting to try to identify the group from which the black male patient seems to have emerged. Perhaps the most interesting question to ask is "From which group did I (or my spouse) originate?"

Case One: It may sound odd but I always become suspicious when black men come in to see me for "only a checkup." Remarkably, unless their family or spouse have coerced them into seeing a doctor, it is rare that they do so until symptoms become serious. So when Mr. G, a thirty-five-year-old black man, came into my office for a checkup and began to complain about his energy level, I noted with interest that he did not appear tired at all. In fact, Mr. G had just been playing rather rambunctiously with some of the children in the waiting room. I asked this six-foot-five ex–football player with a very muscular frame, "How much can you bench press?" He looked at me, perplexed, and indicated, "Me?" Smiling, I said "Yes, you. You look like you can lift at least 300 pounds. I started body building two years ago and I still have problems lifting 225 pounds. You are not messing around with steroids are you?"

Instead of answering, Mr. G shifted the conversation toward his professional football career, fame, "the babes," and his past, during which he had possessed what he wanted and done as he pleased. He had married a professional cheerleader and had remained with her throughout several of his personal indiscretions. He also slid in that he could lift 550 pounds. During the history he informed me that problems had surfaced in his relationship and that his wife's demand for intimacy was beginning to take its toll on their marriage. His statement that "she wants to have sex all the time" seemed to explain his earlier "energy" quip. He sadly stated, "Doctor, not only have I failed as an athlete but now I have failed as a man." Fighting tears, he confessed, "Doc, I can't get it up anymore." The man admitted that he was, in fact, depressed. He worked part-time as a security guard and bouncer at a club and had started drinking a great deal after hours. Night after night he would drink until he was drunk, intentionally arriving home late to avoid any discussion that would lead to an argument or entice intimate contact with his wife.

During the examination he interrupted me several times to discuss sports. He asked what I did to stay in shape, and begged me to tell him what he should do. I assured him that I would be able to determine the best course of action after all of his test results were in. Finding nothing pertinent during the examination, lab tests subsequently found Mr. G positive for cocaine. He returned the following week, appearing in better spirits and reporting that he had begun to exercise again as a result of our meeting. I began by gently informing him that he did not have a disease that would cause impotence, that his liver was not healthy, and that he had tested positive for drugs.

This big, powerful man looked at the floor and began to cry. Having defined himself for years by his ability to perform sexually, Mr. G was now addicted to cocaine and depressed. Carefully, I explained that it was likely he was having sexual trouble due to his drug and alcohol abuse and not from any organic illness, and that I was referring him to a rehabilitation center. He was fully cooperative, and after a month's treatment at an inpatient center and excellent aftercare program, he remains sober. No longer impotent, Mr. G has regained his sense of self-worth and he and his wife are happily content.

Case Two: Mr. T was a sixty-four-year-old black man whose wife of many years had pressured him into seeing me. His wife, a schoolteacher, had noticed changes in her husband's behavior. He had become moody and was spending most of his time isolated in his study, reading and preparing lesson plans for his work as a professor of mathematics at a local community college. Hugs and kisses between the couple had become less frequent over the years and his lessening of affection had made his wife suspect that he was having an affair. Their children were all grown and no longer living at home. The pair had found themselves alone in a big house that loomed even bigger with the man's odd behavior. She privately related to me that on several occasions she had awakened in the middle of the night only to find him shuffling around the house for no apparent reason. She became both worried and intolerant.

Mr. T was a handsome black man who had received his Ph.D. at a Southern black university; was quiet, well-built, and in no apparent distress. As I walked into the exam room he immediately asked, "Are you board certified?" I pleasantly answered, "Yes sir, from the University of Florida." "That's a good school," he retorted. Knowing his background from the medical history he had provided, I said, "Hey, I see you're a math professor. How are your students getting along with Euclid's algorithm?" As he looked at me and smiled, the ice was broken and he began to talk.

"I have not seen a doctor in ten years. I love my wife and don't want to lose her. But the truth is, there has been a change in my body that I cannot explain." He went on to tell me that all he ever wanted in his life was to have a family, a profession, and to be a loving man to his wife. His problem began the previous year when he began to notice daily fatigue and increasing thirst. He was making frequent trips to the bathroom and urinating more than usual. Finally, he had lost his ability to achieve an erection.

Fearful that his wife would see him as less of a man, he made excuses not to be intimate with her. Frequent urination was such a problem that he had to get up several times during the night to relieve himself. Mr. T admitted that although it had been ten years since he had been to a doctor, he had read health magazines and thought that his symptoms might be related to diabetes. However, the fear of knowing the truth and having his wife see him with some type of impairment was too much for him to endure. Not only did he believe that he should not burden his wife, he thought that by staying away from her she would be unaffected by whatever might be wrong with him. Of course, quite the opposite was true.

Lab tests confirmed his suspicions and he was diagnosed with diabetes. During a follow-up conference, I informed the patient that his impotence appeared to be directly related to the diabetes. Speaking very candidly with him, I emphasized that this problem did not mean he was less of a man. He felt better knowing what was wrong, and once he knew the cause for his sexual dysfunction, an intimate relationship with his wife resumed. They both attended diabetes classes in the clinic and have since reaped great benefits from their mutual support through this trying time.

Case Three: Mr. A frightened my office staff the first day he came into the clinic. Politely and quickly he told my receptionist that he wanted to be seen immediately and would not take no for an answer. He did not smile, and though he was small, his posture was straight and he had an intensely intimidating stare. My tiny and stubborn receptionist was quick to usher the patient into an exam room. Knowing I dislike pushy patients, she gave me a perplexed look as if to say "This is a live one." When I heard that he had refused to provide any reason for coming to see me, I began to suspect a concern about his sexuality.

Prominent scars on Mr. A's face led me to believe that either he had been in a car accident or had experienced some rough times in his life. As I entered the exam room, he quickly and nervously said, "What's up Doc? What's happening?" I noticed ear phones around his neck and asked what he was listening to. "John Coltrane," he replied. Laughing out loud I said to him, "You're too young to know anything about the master." He replied, "What you talkin' 'bout? In the joint I was into Trane [Coltrane], [Charlie] Bird, and [Miles] Davis . . . all the jazz boys."

At thirty-five, Mr. A appeared much older, having been released from the state penitentiary a year before. He would not discuss his crime but said that he was now straight and attempting to get his life back on track. After listening to and conversing with him for a while I learned that he had taken drugs most of his life, never really caring if he lived or died. During his long prison term, he had redefined his priorities and found religion. He had also been told that he had severe high blood pressure and was currently taking three kinds of medicine for hypertension. After a bit of coercion, Mr. A finally told me that he had met a woman he cared deeply for. However, he was now in my office because he had not been able to achieve an erection for the last six months. "If she finds out that I can't get it up, she will drop me," he said. She knew he had been in prison, and he connected his inability to achieve an erection with his fear that his new girlfriend would think that he was interested in men and not in her. This fear was very real to him and even though his new flame would most likely never connect the two events, he believed she would and he was worried about their relationship. We discussed how his erectile dysfunction would most likely have a plausible solution and was in no way connected to his stint in prison. I encouraged him to be honest, open, and sensitive enough to trust the person he adored to understand about his past, and he slowly nodded his head in agreement.

Urological tests and a physical exam all revealed normal results. After a thorough review of his medicines I realized he was taking two pills that were known to cause impotence and I made the appropriate changes. Mr. T signed up for spiritual counseling at his church and one year later he is happily married and his wife is expecting their first baby.

Case Four: Mr. V is a twenty-eight-year-old man who had been employed as a computer analyst for several years. After graduating from college with honors, he accepted employment with his current company, and consistently does very well. An obese male, he weighs 320 pounds and stands slightly under five feet, eight inches.

The first time we met I was intrigued by his reading the *Wall Street Journal* and *Barron's* financial newspaper while waiting for his appointment. He seemed extremely shy, not really looking at me when I spoke. Subsequent conversations confirmed that he was an introvert who had lived alone most of his life. Later, I discovered that his solitary life had recently changed after meeting a woman for whom he had seriously fallen, and that, in fact, she had moved in with him a few weeks before his initial visit to my office.

Despite initial poor eye contact and abbreviated responses to my questions, Mr. V was very mannerly and somewhat humorous, a person who seemingly liked to laugh. As his social skills were underdeveloped and he appeared anxious, telling jokes helped him to become more comfortable.

We began exchanging stories. I said, "You know Mr. V, I thought I was clever when I heard that a company going public on the stock exchange was going to open at ten dollars a share. I called my broker and told her to buy a thousand shares when the market opened. She did, but to my disbelief and chagrin, the price of the stock at market open was actually thirty dollars because of aftermarket trading." With a really silly look on my face I blurted, "I almost peed in my pants!"

Surprised, Mr. V burst out laughing, not stopping until tears gathered in his eyes. He grinned at me, "I'll bet it was one of those pesky Internet stocks!" Answering in the affirmative, I assured him that I had learned a very expensive lesson that day. He took a deep breath and blurted out, "Anyway, Doctor, I think I have a disease or something and need you to check me out."

His history revealed a black man who had grown up in a family with both parents present and no siblings. Mr. V had spent most of his time as a child alone, reading high-tech books and taking his computers apart and putting them back together. Other children had made fun of him because of his size, and he had begun to shy away from people, often finding most of them shallow and obtuse. Not until he had met his current girlfriend did his feelings change. She had had the foresight to insist that he see a doctor about a problem which was baffling to both of them.

He initially had difficulty being specific, suggesting that his hormone level be checked out. When I asked what hormone he was thinking about, he said, "Testosterone, that hormone that deals with the man's sex organ." Suspecting that he was hinting at some form of sexual dysfunction, I nevertheless did not want to scare him off verbally and proceeded to testing.

Nothing terribly unusual, aside from his grossly overweight condition, surfaced upon physical examination. His blood pressure was within normal limits and results from a finger-stick for diabetes were also within the normal range. I did note that his breasts were large and that he had a very small penis, and he was very uncomfortable about allowing me to see and examine it. Blood was drawn for lab work and he scheduled an appointment to see me two weeks later. He cancelled and rescheduled twice, not actually returning to see me until a month later. Upon meeting in the examining room, he looked embarrassed and said, "Doctor, I am sorry for showing up a month later but you gotta understand that if it weren't for my girlfriend, I probably wouldn't even have come back. I just know that something bad is wrong with me and I just hate the thought of knowing it if there is."

After he made this statement, I let him know that while I understood, follow-ups were nevertheless very important. Upon hearing that his test results had all come back normal, including testosterone levels, he did not seem especially relieved. "Why don't you tell me what's really going on?" I asked. "That's what I'm here for." Before I could finish he blurted out, "I can't make love to my girlfriend because I can't get an erection when I'm with her."

Calmly, I began to reassure him that the two of us could get to the root of the problem and hopefully help him understand what was happening, and perhaps even a find a cure. As Mr. V commenced discussing his life, his eye contact became more direct and he even joked about the strictness of his parents.

He eventually confided that when he was alone he had no problems achieving an erection and, at times, would even masturbate while talking on the phone with his girlfriend. They had phone sex and both seemed to enjoy this alternative stimulation when they were not together. Yet when she was with him, it was another story. Because he was able to masturbate to climax and hold an erection while doing so, the problem did not appear related to blood flow to his penis.

After several visits spent exploring Mr. V's feelings about himself and his girlfriend, it was mutually agreed there was no organic reason for his impotence. Mr. V was suffering from performance anxiety, primarily due to his poor self-esteem and the need to perform well—a form of psychogenic impotence. Although impotence caused by psychological reasons is rare, and most cases arise from diseases like diabetes and high blood pressure, Mr. V fit the profile.

This patient had a poor body image, no confidence, and had avoided people as a result of his own emotional difficulties. Placing him on a weight loss program, I directed him to meet twice a week with a diabetic educator for diet suggestions and additional support. Even though he was not a diabetic like many overweight patients, he enjoyed the benefits of learning how to eat more wisely.

Happily, he and his girlfriend also entered couples' counseling. While meeting with her one day, I discovered that she loved him a great deal and truly hoped he would become more comfortable with himself. Never mentioning his erectile problem, she added wistfully, "I wish he would hold me more in his arms."

Following a few months of meeting with a counselor and exercising regularly, Mr. V was able to lose weight and to achieve and maintain an erection while making love to his girlfriend. They are now married and expecting their first baby. When I saw his wife one day on the street she informed me of their extreme happiness, and confided that the biggest change in her husband now is how much he likes going out to jazz clubs and spending time outdoors. She never mentioned sex, just how very much she cared about him.

Impotence affects approximately 30 percent of all men between the ages of forty and seventy and occurs most often in men past sixty-five. Too often, erectile dysfunction implies sexual failure or unmanliness, and it can be associated with anxiety, depression, marital discord, anger, and even outright violence among African American men. Just what is the pathophysiology and treatment of impotence?

In essence, the penis becomes erect with an increase of blood flow. For full erection, the blood must remain in the penis, not leaking out until after climax has occurred. Diabetes directly affects erection by limiting blood flow to the penis. Too much sugar in the bloodstream thickens the blood, which in turn damages blood vessels. With this decreased blood flow, the penis is unable to achieve erection.

In theory this sounds very simple, but it becomes complicated in practice when considering the consequences to the black man who is unable to achieve an erection and whose manhood thus feels threatened. He rarely considers the possibility of a physical explanation to determine the cause of his impotence. Quite often, going to the doctor to determine the cause is the very last thing that men do, unfortunately, when it should be the first. A urologist can perform specific tests to confirm impotence and then tailor a treatment plan. Treatment can include medication, penile injection, penile implant, or any of a variety of devices fitting around the penis in order to sustain an erection.

It is critical for physicians to take time to discuss with impotent patients the damage resulting from defining one's sense of worth in terms of an erect penis. Black men really need to become more open and honest with their mates, who oftentimes are pillars of strength. In the cases shared here, the women involved were fully supportive, understanding, and helpful, as exemplified by Mrs. G. Within a month of treatment Mr. G's blood sugar was well under control and his energy had returned tenfold. I had prescribed the "little blue pill" and with coaching and counseling he became more affectionate toward his wife than ever before. Subsequently, I received a very welcome thank-you note from Mrs. G, letting me know just how much "fun" they were having. Now when I see Mr. G, he has a radiant smile on his face and his wife on his arm, both looking like kids. They just returned from a trip to Paris and brought me a clever gift I will treasure forever, a book about *How to Love Quadratic Equations in Physics*.

For men, impotence is a sensitive subject that still need not diminish the integrity of their manhood. Black men who experience this problem tend to be affected most severely and, because they define themselves in sexual terms, tend to overcompensate in negative ways. They suffer depression, isolate themselves, display anger, and blame or ignore their mates. These behaviors jeopardize relationships and thwart communication. Societal attitudes toward sexuality have become more liberal and black males need to understand that when they buy into the black male sexual myths, they purchase nothing allowing real self-growth. Impotence affects all men as they grow older, a fact that black men need to accept and understand.

One of the biggest issues in addressing impotence involves the reluctance of many black men to seek help in dealing with illness of any kind. Not seeking help until symptoms are especially disturbing, these men find that by then treatment is no longer simple. Sexual dysfunction is at the forefront of this reticence because black men do not want to accept, let alone discuss, the fact that there might be something physically wrong with their penises.

Other illnesses fall into the same category of repression. When black men are accustomed to being viewed as strong leaders and they encounter a physical problem, they assume their strength will conquer the symptoms naturally. Overlooking or ignoring symptoms is a direct reflection of a social construction in which black men have been taught not to talk about what is bothering them. Because they have strong minds and wills, they believe they can "think" their illnesses away. Denial is such a large part of not seeking treatment that it is only through accepting that medical assistance is not a form of weakness that black men can acquire timely help with such illnesses as sexual dysfunction.

Having previously reviewed the many forces that drive a black man and his behavioral patterns within relationships, it seems clear that there is nothing more significant than his sexuality, or "sexual self." The downward spiral of a relationship between a black male and his mate can be wildly accelerated by an insecure inability to discuss serious problems. A problem that potentially involves a black man's sexuality and threatens to expose his vulnerabilities has a tendency to remain within the confines of his mind. Keeping their vulnerabilities to themselves, they outwardly express their frustration and fear as anger, resentment, or indifference toward their mates.

The four case studies share a common theme: sexual dysfunction being equated with each patient's sense of being a man. All four men were reluctant to share their feelings with the person who loved them most. Unknowingly, they had bought into the stereotype of black men as primarily sexual beings. Once the mythical veil was lifted by a better understanding of facts, each man was able to relinquish his defenses and emotionally grow in a loving relationship.

Chapter 8

SEXUALLY TRANSMITTED DISEASES AND THE BLACK MAN

Living at risk is jumping off the cliff and building your wings on the way down.

—Ray Bradbury

Sexually transmitted disease (STD) as a health issue affects millions of Americans per year. STDs and their consequences can affect not only the physical health of African Americans, but their emotional health as well. Our children today are particularly susceptible to contracting an STD in their lifetimes due to lack of knowledge, having unprotected sexual contact (not using a condom), and the prevalence of disease in society. One very important and often unrealized fact is that a sexually transmitted disease can still be passed on even when using protection if the condom breaks.

As a minority physician, I have become gravely concerned about and saddened by the careless sexual practices of many blacks. Making bad choices attributable to misleading information that proliferates in the black community, can grievously affect one's sense of well-being. When a person disregards personal safety, a potential death sentence awaits. Perhaps the peer pressures and societal influences faced by our youth today are so compelling that doing the right thing and making self-preserving decisions may seem utterly impossible.

Undoubtedly, there are many factors that encourage black males, in particular, to engage in unsafe sex and with multiple partners. Among the most obvious are music videos with obscenity-laced lyrics that encourage promiscuity, as well a feeling of invincibility; consequence is not an issue. Also likely operating in the black male's psyche is the naïve belief that a macho man dominates women. Finishing the deadly equation is a general lack of education about STDs and how they are transmitted.

Peer pressure is certainly a driving force. The black male virgin is often ridiculed, shunned, and heralded as a "faggot" because he has not had sex. Engaging in sex, therefore, becomes a common occurrence and a "passage of manhood," according to peer standards. The status of being a player sometimes carries more weight in African American social circles than even completing high school.

Throughout history, African Americans have been thought to be gifted with a talent for music and rhythm. Music has been a source of strength, hope, and emotional escape for blacks since the days of slavery. But as time passed, adverse lyrics replaced those early songs of hope, becoming instead reflections of violence, despair, and frustration. The significantly poignant lyrics in many African American songs portray the deterioration of moral values, and sadly depict the scarred souls of our black youth.

Today's music is geared toward young blacks who have turned away from the healthier rhythmic influences that were present in the late 1960s and early '70s. They are angry and careless vehicles that exploit, promote and, glorify sexuality simply to turn a profit for their producers. Many times "making love" is no longer deemed sacred and sincere within the content of the music. Tragically, the bulk of rap videos and song verses encourage sex with multiple partners and violence, and give explicit details of the sexual act itself, thereby portraying sex as no longer sacrosanct or respected.

Much of what our youth are exposed to today, whether it is music, television, or printed material, would have been inexplicably labeled "pornography" only a decade ago. Young black men sometimes idolize "gangsta rappers" and even take on their persona to make themselves appear important. Their facade and this type of rap music devalues women by calling them "ho" and "bitch," thus creating a parallel effect of negative behavior toward the women in the black male's life.

The fact that black men even assume facades is a tragedy in itself. Today's music, geared for youth, all too often sacrifices love, spirituality, and emotional bonding between two people, replacing it with domination, conquest, and the black male's player attitude. Often he feels he must sexually conquer as many women as possible in order to live up to the persona of the "gangsta rapper." The skimpily clothed females seen gyrating in the videos can wreak havoc in the minds of our already hormonal youth. These visual images are not reality-based and the fantasy they create negatively fires the spirit, deceiving our youth into thinking that promiscuity is normal and acceptable.

The music industry capitalizes on the vulnerability of our youth, and must bear some of the responsibility for preventing the potential loss of an entire generation to STDs and acquired immunodeficiency syndrome (AIDS). If the music industry replaced the theme of "Sex sells" to "Unsafe sex kills," it would certainly reach and educate our youth so that they might live long and healthy lives. Unfortunately, greed and not the well-being of youth in America remains their primary focus of business.

Another factor contributing to the young black male's propensity toward death, despair, venereal infection, and even death by AIDS, is what I term the "indestructible syndrome." Many young people, regardless of race, experience this syndrome, the feeling that nothing bad can possibly happen, because "It happens to other people, not to me." This thought process originates from being unable to see the future consequences of their actions, or a lack of boundaries for themselves. The process continues due to a deficit of knowledge about STDs and how they are transmitted.

Many federal, state, and local institutions have been accused of not extending a hand to educate our youths. These systems in particular have fallen short in their obligation to address such potentially deadly issues. The flaw lies at the decision-making level, and the tiptoeing around what is and is not appropriate to teach our youth in school is assisting premature deaths. Teaching the facts and consequences of STDs in a straightforward manner has been muffled due to budget concerns and political protocol, so much so that our children must rely on media such as television and radio for information.

Not a new phenomenon, AIDs was identified in the early 1980s.

Yet propaganda supporting the notion that the transmission of AIDS occurred only in gay communities—not the case, of course—kept the matter under wraps. If the problem had been addressed when originally determined a public health threat, it is quite likely the infection would never have spread like wildfire. Blame for the proliferation of human immunodeficiency virus (HIV and AIDS) does not belong with the gay community, it belongs to the politicians who thought it was simply a "gay disease," and doctors who wanted notoriety for being the first to discover it. Many lives were lost because of the politics of the disease.

In the midst of the battle of whose responsibility it is to teach this information to adolescents, our youth continue to die from STDs and AIDS. It is the responsibility of everyone, most importantly the educational system working in conjunction with families, to educate our youth about prevention, as well as about the consequences of contracting STDs or AIDS.

Many black youth seen in my practice are not even offered a health course in their schools or have no physical fitness classes at all. Through talking with many young black men, I have found that along with their feelings of indestructibility comes a sense of denial. When they are told they have a disease, they tend to lay the blame on another rather than claim responsibility for their own careless actions.

I have heard phrases like "She must be a dirty whore" from those who will not accept that both parties are responsible for practicing safe sex and no one is to blame. A black man, once informed of his condition, will often tell his friends that he contracted a venereal disease from so-and-so, spreading rumors and neglecting to inform his sexual partner in a proper and private manner so that she might seek the medical care she deserves. Respect is lost when the male attempts to transfer blame to the other person. This characterizes a common theme with many of the youth of today, both black and white.

The young black man's inner locus of control, which should be proactive, becomes reactive. Choosing to say no, or going against the norm of society, has been lost. Our young black men often assume that they are never to blame and sadly lack knowledge of the time it takes to initially contract diseases. They do not know that the disease can lie dormant and take weeks to become symptomatic. Ultimately, the person who is blamed may not be the person from whom he actually contracted the disease in the first place. He may, in fact, have spread the disease to the very person he calls a "whore."

Males are often symptomatic. Females, on the other hand, may not realize they have an STD unless an odor or change in vaginal discharge is present. Just like many black male adults, many young people don't seek medical help even when they sense something is wrong. Often people are afraid to go to a free clinic because of a perceived stigma should a friend or acquaintance see them there. The young black person, for the most part, is afraid that someone may spread their personal business and destroy their player reputation, or perhaps fears that the clinic may inform their parents of their sexual activity.

The infected black man will sometimes not tell his partner because he is afraid that she will stop having sex with him if she finds out they are both infected. Alarmingly, his worry that his peers will exclude him compromises the safety of his partners.

Many believe the problem will just go away. This could partly explain the increase in heterosexual transmission of HIV/AIDS in the African American population. Within a short period, I once treated six girls for STDs, all infected by the same male. Unremarkably, one of the infected girls was also pregnant. This heartbreakingly distorted thought process, in part, is simply a form of denial and has caused many precarious situations of STD to reach epidemic proportions.

All indications point to the fact that blacks (apparently oblivious to signs and symptoms of STDs) blatantly do not care. I am constantly reminded of this by certain secondary school lectures in which I have shown slides of herpetic blisters, syphilitic chancres and venereal warts to young adolescents who later told me that they had seen these lesions on people, but had not associated them with STDs.

This drives home the fact that black youths must be taught the signs of these diseases so they can identify the symptoms, seek treatment, and perhaps make more informed decisions about their sexual involvement with others. The truth is that teens are having sex. Without condoning their actions, the importance of using condoms cannot be overstated.

The argument for the necessity of such devoted attention to young black men is supported by a California study administered in the early 1980s. In an attempt to lessen the prevalence of teen pregnancy in a barrio community, forums, peer meetings, and straightforward lectures to teenagers were conducted, but only with black and Hispanic males; females were virtually excluded from the study. After an eighteen-month period, the study determined that by educating young black males, teen pregnancy rates dropped significantly. This became only one example in support of the notion that education and intervention targeted at the black male population could change how black youth perceive their own sexual responsibility and self-worth.

This California study emphasizes the fact that the male plays a major role in the dynamics of his relationships with female counterparts. His dominance and manipulative sexual behavior must be acknowledged when addressing today's problems of STDs. Educating the black male and emphasizing that he plays an active role in resolving societal issues is necessary to facilitate a healthy existence for both him and his sexual partners.

A high percentage of young black men believe, as many of their fathers have in the past, that sexual prowess is strength. In fact, just the opposite is true. Being responsible and respecting the wants, desires, and needs of their sexual partners are true strengths of a black man, opening him up to limitless possibilities of healthy, happy relationships. Because many black men take women for granted early in adolescence, the black man's insensitivity influences young women to behave the same way. They become subject to STDs and demonstrate the same irresponsible behavior that spreads disease.

Much like the black male, sexually active women, often labeled "freaks," will lie, cheat, and take on several partners, in order to receive attention from their male companions. This ultimately results in a negative outcome for the black female, unlike the respect and recognition that the black male receives from his peers. STDs are characterized by the impact that they have on their victims. The stigma surrounding someone unfortunate enough to contract an STD pierces the black family unit so profoundly that the victims often become isolated within their own family.

This only fuels the hopelessness many young blacks, the twelve- to twenty-eight-year-olds of America who are known today as Generation X, experience. For example, I am often dismayed when a parent brings a young person into my office who is subsequently diagnosed with an STD. The anger, shame, and apparent powerlessness recurrently demonstrated by the parent can be truly exhausting at times.

All evidence seemingly points in the same direction for a solution: black youths must be encouraged to depart from a road to self-destruction and be redirected toward a more positive and healthy existence that demands respect for themselves. They must understand the shame and hurt they cause their families and how it directly affects their well-being. Sadly enough, the decline of moral values demonstrated by many adults, resulting in an increase in the number of single-parent family homes, has done little to assist black youths in reaching this realization.

Efforts are under way in many suburban communities to save young people from the social perils of drugs, crime, and even death. Oddly enough, the communities that are mandating and implementing education and prevention curricula within the school systems are the very same systems that also involve the family unit in their education and prevention measures. These programs encourage dinner-table discussions and open communication between parents and children. The question to ask is, Why are the inner-city black communities not doing more to address these problems?

My professional observations of black youth, their behavior, and the interactions they have with their families lends credence to the belief that many black families are not demanding enough of their schools. Schools must teach health issues and sex education as an adjunct to home and family discussions regarding sexual safety. The tenacity of the adults involved could prove to be effective in changing the perspective of many school systems.

School boards have a tendency to argue that morals and values should be taught only in the home. This does not indicate, however, that they should not provide scientific health facts. The problem with their philosophy is that many black youths live in single-parent homes and their parent is simply not equipped with enough information to address the issues of health and sex education, thereby leaving the youth to gather information mostly from their peers. Health and sex education should be addressed within the educational system, and programs designed to deliver proper and straightforward facts about STDs and their impact on black youth. Families and society as a whole must be held accountable for the future of our children. More structured school health education programs must be strongly solicited and supported by both educators and parents alike, in addition to positive input and intervention by black health care providers.

The drug-friendly, antiwar culture of the 1960s has been replaced with what is now known as Generation X. These are the twelve- to twenty-eight-year-olds of all races, born to the baby-boomer generation of the 1960s, '70s, and '80s. For the purpose of this chapter on STDs, African American youths of today are discussed. Two distinct components of this group have emerged. On one hand are those who are goal-oriented, self-motivated, and respectful of themselves and others. These moralistic youth grasp and maintain a genuine understanding of the importance of an education and the significance of what it means to focus and achieve so that they may somehow have a positive impact on society. On the other are the unmotivated and non–goal-oriented. They are pleasure-seekers who live in the present, rather than focusing on their future and their contribution to society. It appears that this half of Generation X neither understands nor desires to participate in or keep pace with the changing world around them; they are content to perceive themselves as victims, or rebels. It is evident that they do not seem to care how they look and are reactive.

Those in the unmotivated group tend to place blame on the "system," often blaming other races, namely whites, for their position in life, and ultimately depend on public assistance. The many cases of STDs, seen in my practice and in statistical studies, show that most African Americans who acquire STDs are low-income youths in single-parent homes, often on public assistance. Many of my young patients diagnosed with STDs lack a true sense of self. STDs often encroach upon those who maintain a dysfunctional self-concept and have little or no support for their place within the family. This leads them to look for acceptance in the arms of someone else, who can be inappropriate or even dangerous.

Legitimate responsibility for this tragedy lies within the family unit, but it is again obvious that in order for the family or parent to responsibly provide information, they must be educated. How do we instill responsible sexual behavior and goal-oriented direction in black youths who think that it's "cool" to have many sexual partners and lack respect for those who can help them the most? The answer is not an easy one, but the information is out there and if parents take steps to ensure that their children have the answers at their fingertips when they need them, the likelihood of contracting an STD will be lessened greatly.

Chapter 9

COMMUNICATION AND SEXUALITY

The highest compact we can make . . . is—"Let there be
truth between us two forevermore."
                                        —Ralph Waldo Emerson

Common sense tells us that if we did not communicate, the ebb
and flow of our relationships would cease to exist. The emotional and cultural environment in which we live determines our
ability to communicate with one another; many African Americans
still find it difficult to relate to each other through honest communication.

An elderly black female patient once said to me, "Black women
come from the earth and black men come from the moon." Smiling,
I replied, "Maybe that's why a lot of black men feel like aliens around
women." Her wise input? "I don't know why young black people
have so many problems gettin' along with each other. They just need
to settle down and talk to each other without any of those games." I
couldn't have agreed more.

Communication is not simply expressing views. It is the manner in
which feelings, needs, and desires are conveyed to others, and how
they are reciprocated. The primary reason for the high divorce rate
among African Americans is the lack of true communication between black men and women. The truth is often distorted and emo-

tions are heightened during verbal exchanges, which only results in animosity and anger. There is so much talking going on that no one is listening.

Even in my medical practice I have noticed a difference in the way black men and women communicate. Many black women, no matter what their level of education, continue to articulate needs and complaints until I completely understand where they are coming from. On the other hand, many black men use metaphors to describe their needs, circumventing their specific reason for coming in to see me. To add to my confusion, some dance around the subject so much that I often feel like a dentist pulling teeth to discern the exact need. Poor levels of education can make communicating more difficult for anyone, but the crux of the matter lies with saying exactly what you mean without telling long, drawn-out stories around the subject at hand.

African American men are in the unique position to take back their families and bond together, by opening up the lines of communication necessary to survive. Black men and women have more resources than ever before to strengthen their basic family structure and raise healthy, strong-minded, and value-oriented children. But unfortunately this is not happening, basically because "black women are from earth and black men are from the moon."

During the focus groups that I conducted, the topic of communication was posed to both a group of black females and a separate group of black males. I asked the same questions to each group of young adults, whose ages ranged from nineteen to thirty. There were eight people in each group and as you read on, you can judge for yourself how wide the rift is between black men and women that makes it so difficult for them to communicate with one another. Here are some excerpts from those sessions (see tables).

I really believe that if black people are to survive, then we must begin to bridge the gap in the way we communicate with one another. Black men should shed their negative attitudes and replace them with the more loving, softer side of themselves. Macho posturing and sexual conquest is archaic and does nothing to nurture a positive, long-lasting relationship with a woman.

About Communication (Dislikes)	
Women	**Men**
He does not talk enough to me and thinks I can read his mind.	She talks too much.
When I really need to talk about something that is bothering me, he just ignores me and doesn't say a word.	She talks to me at the wrong times, usually after work, or when I'm stressed out or want privacy.
He talks loud and scary when he wants something.	She's always forgetting to do something or acts like she does not hear me.
He blames me for everything.	When I talk we argue, especially when I tell her what she's done wrong.
He talks about my weight too much.	She is not into talking about sports, that is why she is fat.
He does not talk about things that I am interested in.	She is not motivated to talk about what I am interested in.
He does not ask me how I feel about things.	She is always wanting to give me her opinion when I don't ask for it.
He walks away when I start to talk to him or does not let me finish what I'm trying to say.	I get so irritated when she just keeps talking and talking.
He does not listen to all parts of my explanation for things and is very one-sided in his views. I really think he is unable to see the big picture.	It is my way or no way. Her explanations are so long that I don't see why she spends so much time talking.

About Sex	
Women	**Men**
I like it soft and gentle.	I like to "hit it" hard, that's what she likes me to do.
I want him to talk to me more during sex. To tell me he loves me.	She always wants to talk a lot during sex. What's there to talk about?
I would like more talk after sex.	When I climax I am ready to go to sleep or watch the game.
I need more warming up and foreplay.	I would give her oral sex if she did it to me first.
He always wants me to give him oral sex but makes excuses not to do it for me.	I don't have time for all the oils and tools, that's for them "freaks."
He just wants to "stick it in." That just doesn't do anything for me.	She should want me inside of her. Now that's love and adoration for me.
Since we have been married, he kisses me less.	She kisses too much.
I can't remember the last time he gave me flowers.	She wants flowers. Flowers die and it's a waste of money.
Sometimes he stinks, I wish he would clean up more. I try to be romantic and take a bubble bath with perfume. He comes home from work or playing basketball and expects me to have sex right then and there.	She is not into being spontaneous. She always wants to set a mood, like a set stage. Hell, I ain't no actor.
There is no romance. I need romance.	She wants romance. . . . sex is romance.

About Relationships	
Women	**Men**
The desire for me went out the window after the first year of our marriage.	After a year with her, she is boring. It was so exciting in the beginning.
He tries to control me and my feelings. He won't let me make any decisions.	She is too dependent on me. I have to make sure she does everything right.
He is condescending and patronizing.	She thinks she is smarter than me.
He sees other women, I'm sure of it.	I was already involved with other women when I got married. Why should I have to stop seeing them?
All he cares about is sex.	She never wants sex anymore.
He never lets me get close to him.	She is nosy and always asking questions.
I have never seen him express his inner feelings, except anger.	She is always making me mad about something.
He only wants sex and not a true partnership.	She does not understand, I was not ready for marriage. . . . I did it for her.
He does not like my children.	She uses her kids as a tool to get things from me.
He is not honest and I can't trust him.	She is selfish.
He is selfish and macho.	She asks me too many questions like: "Where have I been?" and "What have I been doing?"
He doesn't accept me for who I am, and is always trying to change me.	She always wants me to change and be someone I am not.
He gets drunk and high and sometimes doesn't come home.	She is always going behind my back to find out who I have been partying with.

When I run the focus groups, I cannot escape feelings of guilt because not so long ago, women were saying the same kinds of things about me. I wonder how I could have been so blind about all of this for so many years and I can only surmise that I was doing a lot of the talking and not listening at all.

I do not recall my mother and father ever talking calmly, joking, or discussing issues in a civilized manner when I was a child. They often argued loudly, gesturing and pointing accusingly, making my heart race with fear. During those verbal storms, I would pray for calm, and then welcome the return of their usual silence and indifference. I remember that it was during these times that my mother would show great affection toward me, while she ignored my father with fierce determination. She would shower me with false attention, which I did not normally receive when my father was away from home. It was not until my preteens, when athletics took me away from my parents, that I had the opportunity to see how the families of my white and upper-class African American friends loved and communicated. It became painfully obvious that my family did not communicate normally. My friends' parents talked and laughed with each other and discussed different topics without ever raising their voices. In retrospect, I have come to understand just how defensive and argumentative I was when compared to the openness and cheerfulness my friends displayed. Perhaps this is when I realized that I was angry with my family.

I guess I felt responsible for the lack of communication between my parents. However, at a very young age, I was also helpless to stop the indifference. The guilt and shame would overwhelm me, especially when my friends or their parents would request to meet my mother and father. I would always provide an excuse by saying my mother was suffering from some unnamed illness. I must have said it so often that when I was fourteen years old, the mother of one of my friends asked me what kind of cancer my mother had, and did she have much more time to live.

The negative patterns which my parents exhibited while I was a child scarred me significantly. When I began to date, my manner of relating to women would, at times, mirror my father's behavior. I would be confrontational and argumentative. Even today, I must maintain conscious control of my emotions, especially when my mate disagrees with me or when I perceive that my needs or my expectations of her are not being met.

Now, as a health professional, I am seeing more and more African Americans who are enduring what I went through as a child. It is as if time has reversed itself. Couples not communicating seems to be the norm, not the exception. In order to stop the destruction of the family unit, it is necessary for us to identify our needs (not to be confused with wants); we must communicate in a nonthreatening and noncombative way. Many adults and couples blame others for their unfulfilled needs, expect others to care for them, and eventually become angry when they don't. It is important for black men to realize that there are no victims in the healthy adult world. We are in charge of our lives and enter into relationships by choice, knowing ahead of time the obligations and consequences of this choice.

Black men need to love. In order for this to occur, we must openly communicate with another person, making ourselves available to our companions for any and every word, feeling, or touch. We must express our feelings verbally and allow our mates do the same. Both people must actively listen and attempt to understand these thoughts and feelings, no matter how horrible, sentimental, weak, or bizarre they may seem. Black men must respect and acknowledge our mates; we must recognize them as a truly separate people, and like them for who they are. We must allow them to experience their own feelings—in their own way, and without judgment. It is only after achieving this acceptance of each other that two people can explore all of the hidden intricacies of the other's inner self. Freedom of expression is the key to communicating with one another, even in touchy situations. Displaying kindness toward your mate is not always exploited and revealing your true self with the ones you love, whether good or bad, often produces new knowledge, excitement, and a deeper understanding of each other. It is normal for partners to have different needs in at least a few areas. This includes spending time with other people versus spending time with each other; it includes wanting quality time together versus needing time to be alone. Having different needs doesn't mean that your relationship is coming apart.

The opposite of love is actually indifference, not hate, contrary to what many believe. When two people within a committed relationship stop talking, feeling, and touching, love diminishes. When they ignore the fact that there may be issues to deal with, the love that originally cemented the relationship begins to erode, causing lines of communication to close. Then, there is little chance of ever resolving unspoken issues and it may ultimately fracture the family. This indifference crushes the basic component—love—that can be so fragile. The result is anger, distrust, insecurity, and animosity between two people who, perhaps years earlier, professed their undying love for each other. The black family has fallen prey to this breakdown in communication, and our families end up as mere statistics. This permits the perpetuation of myths by other ethnic groups and creates baseless and uninvestigated reasons for so many broken homes.

Upon their return from a year in Germany, an interesting family came in multiple times for general exams and to update the children's immunizations. The couple's story was unique, as they were part of the "military family syndrome," in which communications deteriorate during periods of long separation as one partner completes his or her service obligation.

As planned prior to finishing high school, they had married upon graduation. The husband had subsequently enlisted in the army, spending most of his tour of duty in other countries. His wife accompanied him on most tours and after two years, they had twins. Upon meeting their seven-year-old boy and girl, I observed that they appeared to be happy, intelligent, and well-adjusted children. Yet the parents consistently seemed very distant from each other, speaking directly only to me or to their children, not to each other.

While the couple's pattern of relating to each other was not necessarily atypical of what I might expect to encounter, this couple was nevertheless behaving differently. Couples have had arguments right before coming to my office for care, no doubt stressed from preparing their day around seeing a doctor, particularly if children are involved. Yet it did not seem to be stress that was separating this couple.

Their hostility revealed an apparently deep-seated anger; they did not speak directly to each other and they seemed to dare the other to enter their own personal space. Neither could they could agree on what the children needed. Like two politicians debating a moot subject, the father said, "My son needs his eyes checked," to which the mother hotly retorted, "No, he needs his ears checked. He already had his eyes examined at the eyeglass store a month ago in Germany and if you were paying attention you would know this!"

Attempting to reduce the tension, I quickly tried to change the subject, saying "I usually examine both the ears and the eyes anyway. It's procedure, and besides, I need to make sure the Germans did a good job." I chuckled slightly after my quip but neither parent seemed amused and they simply stared at me stoically. Intrigued by their coolness, I focused my attention on the children. After finishing their routine exams and lab work, an appointment was set for their two-week follow-up.

Not surprisingly, the wife returned alone for her own lab results. When couples do not get along during office appointments, they often stop coming in together. The manner in which this couple had demonstrated their communication skills (or lack thereof) had been disconcerting. Therefore, I appreciated the opportunity of speaking with this woman to gain insight into the dynamics of the entire family.

The wife came from a large family in which she was the youngest of five children. Both parents had been present in the home throughout her life. She had been an average student, often ridiculed by her siblings and friends for not being as quick as the rest. Many of her girlfriends had been jealous of her wholesome beauty, which always attracted men.

By the time she attended high school she had learned to use her sex appeal to get what she wanted: one of the jocks on the football team. He had great looks, but neither money nor the grades to get a scholarship for college. They eventually became a couple, so enamored with each other that their whole world revolved around them, often to the dismissal of others. Her parents had been against the relationship, but couldn't prevent her from running away with him the day after their high school graduation. She was sure that their love would keep them together and that theirs would be the picture-perfect, textbook marriage.

Her husband joined the army and was stationed in Europe so he took her with him. During the first three years she began to notice changes in their relationship. They stopped talking and sharing time together, isolating her considerably because they were in a foreign country and did not speak the language.

She had almost no interaction with the other wives on the army base, primarily because they were so involved in raising their own families and she still had no children. While in high school she and her husband had spent every waking hour together; during his days in the service he began coming home after work, showering, and going to bed. She asked him why he often ignored her, offering her little more than a curt hello when he came home. He told her he loved her but that he was not the same man he used to be, that the army had hardened him.

Their lack of communication continued when they returned to the United States, and after she gave birth to the twins, her feelings of isolation resulted in resentment of her husband. On several occasions she had considered leaving him, but felt that the children needed their father. That belief, coupled with her limited skills, created a strong emotional and financial dependence on her husband. Her feelings of helplessness also contributed to overeating and a considerable gain in weight, which added to her already low self-esteem.

She told me that when she would confront her husband about his avoidance of talking with her or being close to her, he would simply dismiss it with "It's your imagination," or "It's all in your mind." Ignoring her requests and attempts at communication, he nonetheless had denied her accusations of having an affair.

"When he makes love to me it's in a mechanical way," she confided. "He rejects the idea of counseling because he doesn't think anything is wrong." Adding that all she wanted was for things to go back to the way they were when she was first dating him, she sighed, "This all has affected the children too. The kids play loudly in their rooms but when I call them to the table for dinner, they clam up out of fear of angering their father or being the cause of an argument. Also, we all just sit there eating in silence. I even heard my little boy say to his sister that if she didn't stop what she was doing, he would stop talking to her just like mommy and daddy do."

When she blinked the tears from her eyes and said, "Doctor, please help me. I truly don't know what to do," my heart went out to her. I told her that I would have a chance to talk with her husband when he came in for the results of his tests, and she thanked me and left.

A week later, the husband came in with a totally different version of their situation. He told me that he really loved her, but that things were not the way they were supposed to be.

"I can't seem to talk to her without starting an argument," he related. "We met in high school and I thought she was the most beautiful girl I had ever seen. Her parents were high-class and stuck-up but that didn't stop me from marrying her. We loved each other and spent all of our time together when I wasn't playing ball.

"I wanted to go to college but they offered me only a small scholarship and I couldn't afford to pay for college, so I joined the service." As I listened, I could tell how distraught he was by looking at his face.

"Even in the service, we had a lot of fun. We saw the world and she got pregnant. But when I was assigned to a high-priority, top-secret group, she began to change. The activities that I was involved in had to be kept a total secret, even to our wives. We would go on special missions and when I would come home she would be in the bedroom eating ice cream and watching television. Man, she must have put on a hundred pounds in just one year."

Then, with much resentment in his voice, he said, "Here I was on these trips, sometimes a thousand miles from home risking my life, and she was just eating." He confided that he thought he had lost respect for her. He had started taking some college courses in the mornings, but did not want to get into any arguments with her about his needing to spend time with her so he kept it a secret. He told me that he felt that she was not able to understand what he did and who he was becoming.

The bottom line, as far as he was concerned, was that he thought she was still acting as if they were still in high school. He did admit, however, that he did not know how to break their cycle of silence and that if he could not figure something out, he was going to leave her. The children were changing as a result of their relationship and more times that he cared to admit, he knew that the arguments between him and his wife were having negative effects on the children. Unremarkably, his son had started acting just like his father toward

his mother and sister, and had even been given a failing grade in conduct because he argued with his teacher.

When asked if he had thought about going to marriage counseling,
he abruptly said, "I don't have the problem, she does." (I had asked
her the same question and she said much the same thing: "He's the
one who doesn't talk to me.")

Although the husband told me many things about what his wife
was doing to contribute to their mutual silence, he never really focused on the fact that he might be part of the problem; he admitted
only that there was a problem. Placing the blame for uncomfortable
feelings on the other person is a common occurrence in relationships. Displaced anger or stress is one of the most common causes of
disagreements; projecting these feelings onto a mate creates great
stress and forces that person to carry the blame of a relationship with
problems.

While listening to the wife, it was apparent that she also displaced
her insecurities and stress onto her husband, and never really focused
on her own contributions to their problems. Since, in any relationship, it takes two people to communicate, each person in that relationship is responsible for his or her own feelings.

Not talking to one another was actually the least of this couple's
problems. They had never really learned to take responsibility for
themselves because they had always had each other to fall back on.
Consequently, a negative co-dependency formed . . . co-dependency
formed a feeling of being overly responsible for the behavior of another (i.e., their bad behavior causes you to feel bad or a need to "fix"
the other person). In turn, they began to believe—to embrace—the
idea that the other person was causing the problems, and did not
hold themselves personally responsible for how each was feeling.
This type of communication can proliferate over a long period of
time and eventually break down the very core of the relationship if
not addressed quickly.

They agreed to come in together to my office. When they arrived
at the scheduled appointment, I made it clear that I was not there to
counsel them but to share some insights about relationships in general. They were attentive and cooperative.

Telling them that maintaining joy and passion in a relationship depends on a feeling of connection, which is created when both people

feel they are heard and understood. I added, "It's important to remember that you both are members of a team and that the main intention is love and compassion for each other. In times of conflict and confusion, remembering this is part of knowing and appreciating your partner's perspective. This is the ultimate goal."

Our discussion centered on why people don't communicate. "One of the hardest parts of communicating with someone is really being able to recognize your own feelings and put a label on them," I explained. "In addition, being able to realize that your partner has feelings too that he or she may not be able to pinpoint is also important for good communication. Naming or labeling your feelings helps your partner understand you and therefore feel connected."

As I talked with them, I answered questions and pointed out that if knowing how a person feels is a new concept, then noticing the first clue that a person is having feelings is very important. As they were not aware of their true feelings, it was making it difficult for them to express them in a healthy way, thereby repressing the relationship. We discussed how usually the first clue is physical: a feeling of tension, a knot in the gut, tight lips, swallowing hard, stiff back, tight shoulders, clenched fists, teeth or jaw locked or tight, or being unable to sit still. Or, maybe knowing there are feelings but not knowing what they are.

This couple did not know exactly what they were feeling, which was making it difficult for them to even begin communicating with each other after such a long period of silence. During their appointment I explained that sometimes people will say one thing but really feel something else in an effort to protect the other person from any hurt or pain, and that usually this difference is communicated nonverbally. Sometimes, I added encouragingly, people only think they can read other people's emotions by looking at their faces and that many times this leads to the wrong conclusions and misunderstandings. Finally, I told them that sometimes in expressing a feeling nonverbally, we still fully expect others to understand it.

It was evident that this couple had never been taught this, and they did not understand that just because two people spend a great deal of time together does not mean that each person knows what the other is thinking and feeling. To the contrary, the only way to find out is for one person to honestly tell the other. As the couple listened, they began making eye contact with one another for the first time, as if beginning to individually realize each had indeed been assuming to know what the other was thinking.

It was not a bad guess that they had originally thought they were coming to see me to hash out their differences with a referee. When we began to discuss setting boundaries in a relationship, they at last began to visibly relax. I defined boundaries not as some imaginary lines drawn daringly in the sand with a stick, but as a set of principles. These principles define how people safely navigate their everyday life experiences, while honoring their own physical, emotional, and spiritual needs. By learning to trust themselves to honor their own needs, the couple can risk being vulnerable with each other, whether the ensuing communications leads to conflict or celebration.

Boundaries can be as simple as letting people know they need to call before coming to one's home or as difficult as telling someone that no feelings of safety exist, and what needs to change to create the safety. In this couple's case, defining the boundaries they want to establish as a couple and as individuals is of paramount importance. These boundaries then need to be respected by both partners.

After exploring all of these ideas, the couple really began to talk. The husband started by looking at his wife, for the first time in many months, and telling her that he wanted their relationship to improve and that he wanted to learn how to communicate better. He openly admitted that he had not thought she would understand his military operations and thus had never shared them with her. Since the military was a major part of their lives, he agreed he could see that his decision had caused a great deal of conflict. He also told her that he was guilty of not trusting that she would understand.

Likewise, the wife turned to her husband with tears in her eyes, telling him she loved him very much and wanted everything to be okay. She admitted that she had suppressed how she was really feeling about being overseas and feeling very alone, even though she had outwardly acted as though it was no big deal.

Both asked me for the name of a marriage counselor who could help them with their communication issues, and they followed through. It took them a long time and a great deal of working together, attempting to understand each other's needs. And it took a lot of give and take. One day they stopped by the office and showed me a "feelings list" the family therapist had given them to help to identify their feelings. They told me they were also using another list to work on practicing communication. The counselor told them to keep a running tally of positive and negative feelings on the list. The husband informed me that at the onset of counseling, most of their feelings had been negative. However, the couple was happy that they had improved in their communication and now were expressing mostly positive feelings, as outlined on the list. These individuals are models of the way intervention achieves positive results.

Their list follows for the reader's own reference. Also included is a bill of rights, author unknown. These are very comprehensive and uniquely personal studies. While the approach taken with this couple is not always successful, it opens the door for many people feeling alienated from each other. As befits a true happy ending, after taking their children to some final counseling sessions, the couple has "taken back" their family.

I also feel that it is important to address the issue of children born into any relationship since this is where young people are first exposed to the pattern of noncommunication and indifference. If the children are conceived in love, then they result from a beautifully intimate form of communication—lovemaking. However, the pressures of day-to-day life, financial concerns, and opposing viewpoints must still be overcome throughout the relationship. This tends to overshadow the initial feelings, and children are helpless to assist their parents, who are supposed to provide safety for them. Lack of expressed love in the relationship can cause a small child to painfully assume responsibility for his parents' conflict. The social difficulties of surviving are particularly difficult for children in black families at a low socioeconomic level. They may emulate their parents and, as adults, tend to experience the same painful series of events that occurred in their childhood. The cycle never seems to stop.

Black men often experience few intimate moments and poor communication due to the pressures of everyday life. Although this scenario occurs in families of all ethnic backgrounds, the black family appears to be the most affected by this cycle of noncommunicative family interaction and, more important, indifference. Fortunately, though, what is learned can be unlearned.

The Feelings Inventory/Definition List

Positive Feelings		Negative/Avoidance Feelings	
Love— feelings of attraction toward another		**Hate—feelings of revulsion against another**	
Affection for	Admiration	Animosity	Dislike
Appreciation of	Friendly toward	Wish to shun	Repelled by
Concerned for	Passion for	Stubborn	Indifferent
Compassion for	Warmth	Cold toward	Shun
Friendliness	Loving	Despise	Withdrawn
Desire—feeling movement toward that which is love		**Aversion—feeling movement away from that which is hated**	
Excited	Need	Avoidance	Escape
Eager to impress	Want	Evasive	Withdrawn
Sincere	Longing for	Bored	Shy
Curious		Uneasy	Frustrated
		Alienated	Distant from
Hope—confident expectation that you will have what you love and desire		**Despair—an expectation that something will not be attained or the inability to feel as though you are able to control something**	
Anticipate	Trust	Hopeless	Helpless
Confident	Aspire	Trapped	Defeated
Preoccupation	Faith	Discouraged	Dominated
Reliance	Competence	Disappointed	Desperate
		Insecure	Inadequate
Joy—a feeling of delight		**Sorrow—that which comes with the loss of what is loved, or the presence of hate**	
Calm	Supported	Ashamed	Sympathetic
Pleased	Delighted	Sad	Humiliated
Contented	Complete	Embarrassed	Lonely
Proud	Satisfied	Depressed	Cheated
Comfortable	Fulfilled	Rejected	Sorry
Elated	Serene	Put-down	Grief
Surprised	Happy		

The Feelings Inventory/Definition List (cont.)	
Positive Feelings	**Negative/Avoidance Feelings**

Courage—a feeling of strength that you can overcome difficulties		Fear—a feeling of dread or that there is danger present	
Assurance	Risky	Afraid	Anxious
Brave	Bold	Anxious	Impatient
Patient	Confident	Fearful	Distrustful
Enduring		Cowardly	Nervous
Spunky	Gutsy	Nervous	Cautious
Daring		Uptight	Scared
		Unsafe feeling	

Anger— A feeling of strong antagonism and displeasure toward something that blocks attainment of what is loved and desired		
Resentment	Indignation	Frustration
Irritation	Hostility	
Aggravation	Annoyance	

John Edgar Wideman, in his book *Fatheralong*, writes about the negativism that many children observe. He describes the interaction between his mother and father with disdain:

> Seeing my parents in the same room, no matter how large or small, I was forced to consider this [noncommunicative] history. How pain had supplied them with ample justification, as well as the means, to ignore each other totally. I could almost hear the hum of energy, the constant exercise of will and discipline it required for each of them to pretend the other was not in sight. Too many bitter memories formed a wall between them and from where I sat on stage, I could hear more bricks being stacked.

The childhood pain that Wideman must have felt as his parents shut themselves off from each other offers a glimpse into one man's foundation for his own family. Arguably, we must consider if pain is valid justification for ignoring the needs of our mates. As noted in the above passage, Wideman, as a child, recognized the will, discipline, and energy it took for his parents to keep from opening their lines of communication.

One of the primary reasons that the divorce rate is so high among black families (60 percent, compared to 50 percent in whites) is because there is a lack of true communication between black males and their mates. This can be partly attributed to a black man's self-image. Many black men grow up in an environment of constant conflict or indifference, and self-protection becomes more important than self-love and emotional growth.

Perhaps the first step for us, as black men, is to learn to communicate effectively with our mate. It would require us to first identify what makes us unique. Recognizing that we have something very important to offer our mates, besides our sexuality, will have a profound impact on how we relate to our mates and others. We must be fully committed to ourselves and take personal responsibility for who we are before we are able to fully commit to another person, let alone produce children. Striving for emotional, physical, and spiritual health clarifies what is necessary to achieve loving, committed, and lasting relationships.

If black men utilized the same amount of energy that it takes to ignore their mates to communicate with them instead, then the black family would not be in jeopardy. It is imperative that we incorporate self-awareness, discipline, and honesty into our lives so that we can be fully accommodating and emotionally available for our partner and family. We can create healthy relationships that will be the most rewarding interactions of our lives. Children learn from these primary examples, and we must not just talk about them, we must live them in order for our children to grow into healthy adults and ultimately have wonderful families of their own. The following are some exercises that I used in my own life that were helpful:

Ask yourself these questions:

1. Are you conscious of the consequences of all of your actions?
2. Do you strive to develop a "talking" relationship before a sexual one?
3. Are you aware of what troubles you emotionally, spiritually, and physically?
4. Are you doing anything to remedy problems with respect to these?

5. Are your reactions based on anger? And do you think before you act?
6. Do you try to control others?
7. Do you blame your parents for your present situation?
8. Are you open to criticism? Or do you get angry and defensive when things don't go the way you want?
9. Are you able to identify your fears? Do you confront them or avoid them?
10. Do you understand what unconditional love is?

As a black male, you are 50 percent of any relationship you may have. Relationships should begin with both parties being a healthy "half." Many black men count on their relationships to "cure" a poor self-image or self-esteem, whch is akin to a house being built on sand. In order for the house that you and your mate establish to be solid, it must begin with a healthy foundation. Children hold the world and the people around them responsible for meeting their needs. A child's thoughts, feelings, and behavior are based on how he reacts to the world. If a child's parents do not take responsibility for their own actions, the child begins to shoulder their burdens and learns a distorted view of what makes a family healthy.

Fulfilling relationships are hard work, but mostly individual work. Intimacy for both men and women can be frightening. Black men are taught to be strong and for many, showing weakness is not an option. Perhaps it is this strong will that won't allow us to show our tender and vulnerable emotions. Quite possibly, this is the same fear of suffocation, rejection, and abandonment that many of us felt during childhood when we observed our parents' noncommunication. Our protective armor kept us impenetrable from others. Intimacy in a relationship helps us reach the upper limits of happiness, while fear of failure or even success can cause us to unconsciously sabotage ourselves. Sometimes people even unconsciously fear being successful. If a person feels undeserving subconsciously, they will create an environment in which they feel awards and achievements are not deserved. They may even create circumstances to block their achievements (i.e., a self-fulfilling prophecy). It is important for us to be completely aware of our mate and to communicate on a regular basis in order to keep this sabotage from entering into our relationships, but it is important to communicate clearly.

We all need to be heard and understood by the people we care about. We don't always need to agree; differences do not create distance. It is important to know that you are heard, understood, and respected for who you are. No one is a mind reader; communication in the form of a smile, hug, attitude of acceptance, or having our opinions reflected back to us reinforces that we are understood. It is imperative to actively listen to your mate so they will specifically tell you their feelings, wants, and needs; this brings you closer and avoids unnecessary conflict.

From our focus groups, we gained valuable insight into the minds of African Americans, both male and female. I would like to meet the person who thinks that they can read their mate's mind. The woman in our focus group who shared this sentiment was unsure as to why her mate would not say exactly what he wanted or needed. When we asked him why he did not simply come out and say what his needs were, his answer made us all chuckle. He said, "I don't always know what I want or need but my wife always has the answer for that." After an open and honest discussion with each other, this couple realized that after ten years of marriage, they really needed to be more direct in sharing their needs with one another and each promised the other that they would work on it.

Although during our focus groups there were many episodes of laughter, there were serious and compelling moments as well. One poignant moment happened when one of our female participants began to cry when asked about communication within her relationship. Between sobs, she shared with the other women in the group that her husband has ignored her feelings and needs for twenty years. When she said something he didn't like, he simply shut her out and acted as if she wasn't even there—sometimes for days on end. I would like to stress a very important point: Ignoring and detaching emotionally from the person you say you love is a blatant form of emotional abuse. Certainly there are going to be times when you do not feel like dealing with a situation, but pouting, sulking, or giving someone the silent treatment do not make things better. In fact, they tend to get worse and escalate into other forms of control and manipulation within the relationship. It is crucial to be fair and to set aside time to discuss issues that may go unresolved. When that time comes, communicate calmly. Aggressive language is not fair, especially when you can be assertive in a positive way and still get your point across. Our focus group member told us that her husband called her names and concentrated his attention on her weaknesses. Helpless, she felt even more vulnerable to him when he finally began to talk to her again. I recognized this pattern of control immediately. After the focus group ended, I prescribed several counseling sessions for the woman in the hopes that she would be able to regain her own emotional strength.

When you are discussing issues with your mate, straying from the subject at hand is unproductive. Active listening is key to solving any problems and unless you reiterate to your partner what you are hearing them say, then you may misconstrue what they are trying to tell you.

One of the men in our focus groups admitted to the facilitator that he saved up his hurts and hostilities as ammunition and did not openly discuss them when they occurred. He honestly thought that it was important to "win" any arguments with his wife, so he kept a scorecard. Caring, kindness, and clarity played no part in communication with his mate. Not being able to admit he was wrong was a huge difficulty in his relationship because he felt that it would make him look weak and soft. His competitiveness kept him from seeing how much his mate really cared for him. In a constant state of struggle for control in the relationship, this man did not realize that the struggle was really within himself. Upon further investigation, we found that his wife was content with his handling things in their relationship and making all of the important decisions for both of them. She was very religious and felt as though she should stay silent and allow him to be in charge. Although she wanted very much to have a closer relationship, he made it very difficult and she settled for an absence of communication in the marriage out of tradition.

As you can see, it is crucial to accept your partner for who they are and assume they cannot and will not change just to make you feel good. Your partner is not in the relationship to take care of you, their job is to be responsive to your needs, and your job is to be responsive to theirs. They cannot make you "happy" and you cannot make them "happy." When you enter into a relationship, you join forces and make happiness possible for each other by being available emotionally and physically. Each person must take full responsibility for creating their own outcome.

Our focus groups revealed much about how African Americans communicate. Our results often revealed a pattern of indifference, but also reflected positive aspects indicating a foundation of communication could still be built. It is obvious that black males must become better communicators in relationships. Information about establishing better communication is generously provided so that black males and their mates can begin to overcome barriers within their relationships. Healthy discussion and problem solving through good communication are the hardest goals to reach within the black family unit. Recognizing that your mate is the most important person in your life is the key and realizing that they are your closest friends will serve to enhance the quality of black family life.

A Personal Bill of Rights is a list of reasonable and ordinary expectations for people to have for themselves

—Author Unknown

1. I have numerous choices in my life beyond mere survival.
2. I have a right to follow my own values and standards.
3. I have a right to dignity and respect.
4. I have the right to express myself as long as I am not abusive to others.
5. I have a right to all of my feelings.
6. I have a right to determine and honor my own priorities.
7. I have a right to say no when I feel I am not ready, it's unsafe, or violates my values.
8. I have a right to recognize and accept my own value system as appropriate.
9. I have the right to have my needs and wants respected by others.
10. I have the right to terminate conversations for any reason.
11. I have the right not to be responsible for others' behavior, actions, feelings, or problems.
12. I have a right to make mistakes and do not have to be perfect.
13. I have the right to improve my communication skills so that I may be understood.
14. I have a right to be uniquely me, without feeling I'm not good enough.
15. I have a right to feel scared and to say, "I'm afraid."
16. I have the right to experience and then let go of fear, guilt, and shame.
17. I have a right to make decisions based on my feelings and my judgment for any reason.
18. I have a right to change my mind at any time.
19. I have a right to set down roots, nest, and feel secure.
20. I have the right to my personal space and time needs.
21. I have the right to be flexible and be comfortable with doing so.
22. I have a right to make friends and be comfortable around people.
23. I have a right to be in a safe nonabusive environment.
24. I have the right to forgive others and to forgive myself.
25. I have the right to give and to receive unconditional love.
26. I have a right to enjoy being sexual and to celebrate my sexuality.
27. I have a right to my own spiritual beliefs and to celebrate them.
28. I have a right to be creative in voice, body, and spirit.
29. I have a right to feel free in my body, i.e., to sing, dance, jump, skip, etc.
30. I have the right to express any of the above as long as I am not abusive to others.
31. I have a right to grieve over what I didn't get and needed, and what I got that I didn't need or want.
32. I have a right to say "not yet" when I feel I am not ready, it's unsafe, or violates my values.
33. I have the right to joyfully receive without feeling guilt, shame, or over-responsibility.

34. I have the right and accept the responsibility to honor the rights of others regarding all of the above.
35. I have a right to be loving and giving.
36. I have a right to healthy relationships of my choice.
37. I have a right to discover and know my inner child.
38. I have a right to be angry with someone I love.
39. I can be healthier than those around me.
40. I can take care of myself, no matter what.
41. I have the right to trust others who earn my trust.
42. There is no need to smile when I want to cry.
43. It is OK to be relaxed, playful, and frivolous.
44. I have a right to expect honesty from others.
45. I have the right to change and grow.
46. I have the right to be happy.

Note: Clear, compassionate, and timely communication is an obligation attached to personal rights.

Chapter 10

SEXUAL ABUSE ISSUES

People who treat other people as less than human must not be surprised when the bread they have cast on the waters comes floating back to them, poisoned.

—James Baldwin

Sitting in the corner of the room, I couldn't help but look up when the rotund, neatly coifed, religious woman proclaimed loudly, "What a beautiful dress! You look so special!" to one of my sisters. This expressive woman's name was Auntie Mabel. In a voice that could jolt anyone awake, and in one sentence, she voiced her opinion of my sister, as on previous occasions, with a sense of appreciation affirming a unique admiration for her. Certainly, her praise for my sister was genuine; however, it backfired on me in a negative way so subtle that no one noticed. Except me.

My mother used to take all of us to dinner every Sunday after church. The gatherings were always held at one of her church friends' houses, and one day in particular we went to Auntie Mabel's house. It was extremely neat—everything had a proper place—yet it was warm, comfortable, and inviting. Even though our families were not related, my mother's friend insisted that we call her "Auntie Mabel," saying that we were much like her own children and trying to treat us as such.

My three sisters really enjoyed socializing at Auntie Mabel's house because she inevitably showered them with special gifts and constant praise. Being insecure, as most young kids are, my sisters and I competed for her personal attention and were especially vulnerable to her special approval and compliments. My sister's egos were set aglow by the continued compliments from this nice lady, but I sat in the corner twiddling my thumbs, feeling left out and alone. Auntie Mabel and my mother always seemed to fuss over the girls and to pay a great deal of attention to them. I was often the last one in the room to be recognized and when Auntie Mabel finally noticed me she simply said, "And you boy, with your nappy hair, you staying out of trouble?" Comments such as this tickled my sisters and mother, who giggled at her remarks. All this made me feel even worse than when I was being ignored.

Looking back, I know now that Auntie Mabel meant no harm by the way she interacted with me. In fact, it was her way of showing affection for me and perhaps she thought that speaking "strong" to me was the way it was supposed to be. I can only surmise that since I was a boy, she felt that I didn't need the same type of nurturing and being made to feel special that was bestowed upon my sisters.

Unfortunately, these were not rare occurrences and seemed to happen whenever our family would go out. Adults, especially women, paid more attention to my sisters. I concluded then, and do today, that mothers seem to nurture their daughters and care more for their safety, while black boys are often thought to be able to fend for themselves.

Perhaps this custom of caring and nurturing the needs of the female child evolved from African culture. Perhaps this showing of affection and providing for a young girl's safety is more important than it is for boys. Although these conclusions are difficult to make, what is true is that all children need to be emotionally and physically nurtured and cared for equally.

It is true that males and females manifest obvious societal differences, but do the differences lie in gender? Or do they lie in society's perception of what either gender is supposed to need? Societal perceptions appear to play the stronger role in the development of our children. Young black males who grow up engulfed in negative criticism become men with emotional scars. They are additionally harmed if they grow up without hugs and positive praise, never experiencing the deep emotional and unconditional love necessary to achieve a healthy sense of self. Erroneously, many adults feel that black boys are, by nature, self-reliant and thus not in need of cuddling and being held and kissed.

How many times have the phrases "If you kiss that boy, you'll make a sissy out of him" or "Boys don't cry" been uttered? These types of statements are damaging and make it quite difficult for black boys to properly develop their own sensitive natures. The argument that young black males can—and must—fend for themselves has placed some boys in precarious situations, resulting in physical, emotional, and sexual abuse.

When I was a child, my sisters would wake up in the mornings feeling apprehensive, anticipating our mother's morning ritual of combing their hair. Instead of seeing this as something I didn't have to go through, I construed it as yet another opportunity for my mother to pay more attention to them than to me. Being the male child, I was always expected to prepare myself for school, comb my own hair, and find my own clean clothes, despite having no one to show me how to do these things. These early morning encounters were not fun for the girls. They would scream and struggle as my mother yanked first a comb through their knotted hair, then a heated straightening iron back through it. Nevertheless to me, the ignored child, the torture they received at the hands of my mother seemed better than what I received.

At about ten years old, I finally began to attract a certain amount of attention as I began doing odd jobs to pay for my school lunches. Part of the money I made always went to my mother, who would then compliment me on being her "little man." I began to see being a provider as a good thing and, if I wanted the females in the family to like me, I would have to be the "little man" and not a young boy with emotional needs. Sometimes these part-time jobs took me into very dangerous places. For example, once while I delivered newspapers a pack of dogs chased me. Another time a group of teenage boys beat me up and took the money I had worked all day to make.

While the early 1960s were less perilous than today, when children are increasingly reported as murder victims, my youthful experiences nonetheless struck me with fear. The fear became a personal feeling I did not feel that I, the strong "little man," could share with my family. I could not tolerate any of them perceiving me as a fearful little child. There are a great number of young black men who as children, like me, fended for themselves in an often hostile world. As young men they find themselves poorly equipped with the mental and emotional foundation necessary to withstand a blitz of social pitfalls.

Considering all the people who inhabit the earth, young black men are perhaps the least understood. Many times we fail in our responsibility to address the needs of young black men and their safety. We fall short in our attempts to assist young blacks to develop healthy behaviors, attitudes, and beliefs so they can grow into healthy black adults. As a culture, we fail as a society because we simply assume that black boys are not children but "little men" who will someday become social pariahs.

During a discussion with a group of black men in one of my focus groups, one man suggested that maybe women harbor a resentment so deeply rooted in their psyche they believe that black boys will hopelessly grow into unproductive nuisances anyway. He submitted that they probably turn their attention instead to teaching young girls to defend themselves against the macho aggression of boys. Not surprisingly, he wasn't the only black man in the discussion group embracing this theory. Whether it is custom or simply apathy for the welfare and safety for young black men, the speculation holds some truth. Why else would so many black men conclude the same things?

How black men feel about themselves is the sum total of all they have been surrounded by as well as how their environment and experiences that have affected them internally. *Sexuality* is the sum total of how black men feel about themselves; therefore, it would stand to reason that anything negative in the life of a young boy would predictably reap dire consequences in his adult life. Boys who are sexually abused or, for that matter, abused in any way are prone to negative behaviors as an adult and often become abusive to others. This pattern offers a probable explanation of why some men experience faulty interpersonal relationships and why mental illness and drug and alcohol abuse within the black male population are on the rise.

It is because of the lack of social nurturing that young black men become victims of violence, particularly of physical and sexual abuse.

The frequency with which black men reveal to me that they were sexually abused as children astounds me. In fact, during the research for this book I heard it more times than I can recount.

Exploring the data of sexual abuse among black male children and adolescents, I realized two important facts: It is a problem defined by some researchers as a hidden epidemic, but it does indeed exist. And parents, doctors, and blacks in general must wake up to this problem which affects the black man's sense of self and the subsequent ways he expresses his sexuality.

Interestingly, some men are not aware that they were abused as children. To one survey question a man responded that he had had sex with an adult when he was only ten years old. The sex act occurred with a prostitute who had been provided by the boy's father as a birthday present. In our group discussion, he reported the event as "cool" in an attempt to impress others. But no matter how "cool" the story of sex and seduction was made to sound, the conclusion remained that a prostitute having sex with a ten-year-old child is *never* healthy. It is blatant abuse. Moreover, his boyhood experience had a profound influence on how this man felt about women and his own sexuality.

The group member eventually shared with us how the prostitute had been aggressive with him and how he had felt inadequate during the whole encounter. As a young child, he had not been mature enough to handle the emotional impact of a sexual encounter. As an adult, he experiences a strong need to show women how adequate he performs sexually. In turn, he has been unable to sustain any long-term intimate relationship with a woman because of his need to constantly prove himself sexually. One can never know how deeply the scars remain from his first sexual encounter at the age of ten.

In a 1998 article titled "Sexual Abuse of Boys," William C. Holmes and Gail B. Slap report that poor black boys raised in homes without a father are at high risk for sexual abuse. Published in the *Journal of the American Medical Association*, the authors conclude that a high percentage of men who commit crimes such as rape and other sexual offenses were themselves sexually abused as children. The recidivism rate is further aggravated, Holmes and Slap argue, by the fact that young boys are not inclined to talk about their abuse because they are afraid they will be blamed for bringing it on themselves or that they will be viewed as unmasculine and thereby subject themselves to ridicule and rejection.

In some cases, homosexual tendencies are fostered during this early abuse. Because of the biases that many blacks harbor toward boys with qualities considered feminine, those boys often refuse to discuss these qualities openly, and tend to act out only behind closed doors. Often, they seek understanding and advice from older men, making them susceptible to sexual abuse. Sometimes these boys mentally redefine the sexual abuse as a normal act. They project trustworthiness onto an older man, and if they are taken advantage of sexually, the boys conclude that the act must reflect true affection. Subsequently, a large portion of these effeminate boys grow up to live active homosexual lifestyles.

For a multitude of reasons, then, parents and other adults should pay as much attention to sons as to daughters. Sexual, emotional, and physical abuse can occur right under parents' noses, as seen in some of the following scenarios. For all men who read these stories, those who are honest with themselves will recognize the relevance of accounts in shaping their own sexual selves.

Mr. R shared this first story with me two weeks after I told him about my book in progress about black male sexuality. Approaching me about something he had seen as a young child, I assured him that I would protect the confidential nature of whatever he desired to share. I wish to thank him for this contribution, as it is both poignant and affecting, and represents the abuse and its smoldering effects on a young child.

Mr R: "When I was younger, instead of studying right after school, I would join a group of boys and go to the beach for some fun. It was hot during the summer so this was our favorite activity. Most of us were around ten years of age but usually there were older boys and girls who were well into their teens swimming and running around. I noticed some of them touching each other in ways that I found arousing. My friends and I knew very little about sex but, out of curiosity, we went to the beach to see what we could see. I recall one afternoon when a girl from my class was being accosted by a group of the older boys a short distance from where we were sitting. We had heard that the girl, who was eleven, was already having sex with older boys and she was well developed for her age. Of course, we didn't know this to be true, as it was just the 'talk.' But in class she paid very little attention to my friends and me and it made us mad. Like many kids our age, we wanted to be liked and she ignored us.

"Anyway, late on this hot afternoon, there she was, running from the older boys in a skimpy bathing suit and laughing as she ran. Suddenly the high-spirited fun changed and, looking back on this incident, it had the quality of a rape in progress. The boys had picked up the girl and carried her to a secluded area just under the boardwalk. We ran toward the direction of her screams, not to aid her, I'm ashamed to say, but to again see what we could see. At the time, I didn't even know what the word 'rape' meant.

"As we approached, we looked through the small crowd of boys who encircled her and held her down on her back with her legs spread so all could see her privates. It was the first time I had ever seen a girl naked. One boy roughly stuck his penis into her and I saw white fluid leak from her vagina. I was mesmerized by what I saw. Her screams and the fact that these boys were raping her meant little to me at ten years old. I felt scared but very curious.

"An adult from above on the boardwalk heard the young girl's cries for help and called aloud for the police and my group and I scattered along with the assailants. I did not know what happened after that afternoon, but someone said they had seen the girl in the principal's office the next day and she was all swollen and had many bruises on her face. She was transferred to another school and the boys who raped her were expelled. I saw the girl a few years later on the playground and immediately recalled that event in my mind. At that time, I had no pity for her and in fact became sexually aroused, and believe it or not, I even tried to hit on her for some of the same action that I witnessed under the boardwalk. When she turned me down, I maliciously told her that she had gotten what she had deserved. I was thirteen at the time."

It is not surprising that Mr. R was a child who grew into a man with his share of difficulties with women. He also confided that he had problems respecting women and being able to express himself without actually having sexual intercourse. He had had no father in

the home to advise him of proper and healthier ways to better oc-
cupy himself, and it had therefore been exceedingly difficult for Mr.
R to develop a healthy sexual self.

The next story is about a man, Mr. K, who shared childhood experiences similar to my own. He, too, was taught that boys were "little
men" who did not show their feelings or fears. When beaten by his
parent he was forbidden to cry or to show any form of weakness.
This mild-mannered professional man was very candid about his past
during our interview, telling a most intriguing story, one truly typical
of black men who may question their masculinity.

Mr. K told me that he came from a big family of mostly girls. He
didn't know his father, but he was close to his mother. He termed
theirs a "special relationship." Since there was no adult male in the
house, his mother depended on him to do most of the chores. He
told me that his mother loved his sense of responsibility and self-
sufficiency. He cannot recall her holding him, telling him how much
she loved him, or teaching him how to be a man once he left the
house: "I was a man while in the house but when I left it I was
treated like a child." Mostly he felt that he was either ignored by
most adults or hated, especially by the white people he encountered.

Mr. K felt the only acceptance he found was with a group of thugs
he called "friends." Most of those friends shared the same unfortunate family history. They were boys not quite in their teens and they
made their own rules. For fun they "would beat on smaller kids and
take their lunches." When breaking windows and flattening car tires
got boring, they began to exercise their sexuality toward the opposite
sex. He recalled that he felt like a man when he grabbed a breast or
pulled up a dress.

One especially exciting activity was when he and his group would
go around and peek in the windows of unsuspecting people. At
night, he and his friends would sneak over to the houses of girls they
knew from class. The group made a pact never to tell anyone of their
voyeurism. As they sat quietly at the windows, they became aroused
as the girls undressed, and they would all masturbate together. They
coined the phrase "circle-jerk" to describe their collective sexual act.

"When we began to ejaculate, we really felt like men. We had not
begun to have intercourse with girls and that was as close as we could
get." He went on to tell me that this type of aberrant behavior oc-

curred for several years until one day one of the boys in the group put a new slant on things.

Mr. K said that they had physically matured and felt a strong sense of empowerment with regard to their sexuality. Some had begun to have sex, so when one of the guys in the group suggested that they should all go downtown to have a look into the windows of a house that homosexuals were known to frequent, it sounded appealing.

"What men did to one another for some reason inflamed our sexual curiosity. I was fourteen when I made my first trip to the house. We were not disappointed in what we saw. Men were having oral and anal sex with each other." In some instances they saw people they knew, older boys they thought were "all man, at least that was the way they profiled themselves on the streets. One night we even saw a friend's father receiving oral sex from one of the men."

During this period, Mr. K admitted that "emotionally I was confused about this new activity, basically because of the way we ridiculed homosexuals, and there we were, excited by spying upon them." It was at this point that he became concerned and began to question his own sexuality. He could never have disclosed this to his family because they would have rejected him.

"A pal of mine ran away from home when his mother caught him and another boy playing with their penises in his room instead of studying. The mother was enraged and called him a 'faggot' for several months and even told his relatives and friends what had happened." At the time, Mr. K kept all of this to himself.

Even with all of his self-doubt and emotional turmoil, Mr. K said that he would still go along with the window peeping and masturbating so that his friends would like him. Then a life-altering event occurred.

"One day I went to the house alone. I am not sure why I did this, but something happened to me that day that changed everything. While I was crouched on one knee at a window looking in a dark room I suddenly heard a noise behind me. As I turned, I saw three men who quickly grabbed me and pulled me into the house. One of the guys said, 'So you want to peek? Why not join us?'

"Another man I didn't recognize showed up once we got into the room. They held me down and performed oral and anal sex on me. I was helpless to fight those men off and felt totally degraded. I was threatened that if I told anyone what had happened, they would go to the police and say that they had seen me peeking in their window."

Because of their threats, Mr. K never told anyone then, but one of the boys he had hung around with in his old neighborhood had seen him leaving the house. He stated that he had lied and vehemently denied that anything had happened and the matter was finally dropped. However, he confessed, the residual pain of that day emotionally scarred him for life. To this day, he will not associate with anyone known to be gay and has been accused of being totally homophobic as an adult.

Mr. K entered therapy after his third wife left him for another man. He confided that during the therapeutic process he had found that, due to his early childhood experience of sexual abuse, he had been overcompensating by being macho, insensitive, and aggressive with people, and with women in particular. He wanted to feel like a real man, and "that experience as a child has had a lot to do with the way I feel about myself today."

While the unfortunate fact exists that some with biases toward gay people will allow their negative feelings to be reinforced by reading about Mr. K's experiences, most black people will recognize the true tragedy of his story. What happened to Mr. K as a child should never happen to anyone. It is important to understand that most sexual abuse occurs outside the home, as reported in many of the cases interviewed. Also, the abusers of younger boys are usually family members, while it is typically strangers who abuse older boys, particularly when the abuse is sexual, as in Mr. K's case.

It is critical to protect our very young children, and to continue this protection once the child is old enough to leave the house alone. Perpetrators of sexual abuse toward black boys are not always men; women abuse three out of every ten black boys, using psychological and verbal pressure instead of physical force.

For example, one man reported that he was raped at age nine by a friend of the family. The woman would fondle him when no one was around. She told him that if he did not do what she wanted, she would tell everyone that he was a girl and not a boy. The abuse became so overwhelming that he began to fear women in general, as well as his own penis, believing it was something "evil." Only later did he realize that this alcoholic woman had been abusing him, since he was too young at the time to understand. This man is now happily married, but it took years of therapy and much involvement in his church to overcome the feelings of guilt he had carried for many years.

In each of the preceding stories, the same issues influenced how each black man felt about accepting his own behavior. Many of the men demonstrated feelings of shame, hostility, anger, resentment, fear, rage, and even acceptance. I encountered many who were very comfortable with being openly homosexual and who had experienced early childhood sexual abuse at the hands of older men. Black male children must not be exposed to the hidden epidemic of sexual abuse by sexual predators, but rather given the opportunity to form a healthy understanding about sex and to develop their own sexual identities as they grow into adulthood.

Countless studies have generalized findings or made suggestions for helping homosexuals to cope with biases of heterosexual society and where blacks are not typically respesented. However, Pamela M. Wilson, author of "Black Culture and Sexuality," suggests that there is an identifiable set of social factors, as well as background experiences which shape African American sexuality, such as "a man should be a man and a strong provider for his family" and "a woman should be a woman and caretaker of the home and children." These ideas are sterotypical and outdated. as well as background experiences which shape African American sexuality. These experiences affect the sexual attitudes and behavior of blacks in general. As we enter the third millennium, developing sound moral values and harmony in the black community is a worthy and potentially rewarding goal. Emphasizing political, economic, and social advancement, while eliminating the abuse of our children, paves the way for healthy and fruitful lives.

During the preparation for this book I came to realize that many of the black men who shared their secrets did so because they could trust me, their doctor. As the professional many black men turn to first for an often uncomfortable discussion about their sexuality, the physician must be sensitive to and nonjudgmental of various sexual lifestyles. If any reader has had an experience that seems consistent with sexual abuse, please find someone to talk to about it so that it does not fester and cause problems in relationships with others. The men in these stories needed a lot of help to sort out what happened to them in their early lives, and were successful in doing so. Blacks who have been abused should understand that they are victims, just as the man who was raped was a victim, and his experience does not make him less of a man.

Protect our children, both boys and girls, from sexual abuse by paying close attention to what they are doing, who they are with, and where they are going. Keep in mind that it could happen in your family. It is a hidden epidemic that affects more black males than realized, and probably has directed how survivors have both identified themselves as men and how they have related to women in relationships. Remember, black boys can form bad habits when they are unsupervised and away from home. Black boys feel that their masculinity is important and sexuality is a part of being masculine. They define their masculinity always in sexual terms first, unless they have been taught otherwise from a very early age that not simply their penis, but affection, hugging, loving, and true intimacy are at the core of who they are and who can hope to become.

Chapter 11

CREATING POSITIVE SEXUAL ROLE MODELS

I have a dream that my four little children will one day live in a nation where they will not be judged by the color of their skin but by the content of their character.

—Martin Luther King, Jr.

Dr. King gave voice to the dreams of every African American when he spoke these historic words on August 28, 1963. They were the dreams of equality, respect, and opportunity for everyone, regardless of their heritage. Although we have come a long way in the quarter century that has passed, the job is not yet finished. We still carry the psychological scars of oppression and, until we heal, the stereotypes that bind us will continue to proliferate. Future generations are dependent upon what we do today, and in order for black men to dispel the negative myths that define us, we must provide positive role models to younger black men in order to help them develop healthy sexual identities. Sexual identity is not simply the physical sexual self. It also includes how we perceive ourselves and project that perception outwardly to others.

I once spoke at a conference sponsored by a national organization for boys. There were about 250 young men between the ages of eight and fourteen in the audience; most were black. I shared with them my personal story: my father and family, athletic career, education, and work. When I was finished, I asked how many of them wanted to be doctors. Only two hands went up. I then asked how many wanted to be basketball or football players. Nearly every hand went up.

In the minds of these young boys, I was not cool enough to look up to. I was wearing a suit with a bow tie. I did not have gold chains around my neck or rings on my fingers. I spoke in proper English with no slang and as far as they were concerned, I was just corny, or perhaps a geek.

How could I have been so naïve to think that I could compete with the "cool" images that often negatively influence our kids? Athletes and rap stars are the primary role models for a vast majority of young black men. But are these the icons of success that black men should be emulating? Let's face it, hip role models are over-hyped creations of the media whose lives, lifestyles, and behavior are very far removed from the daily reality of black kids. Inspiration and the reinforcement of achievable dreams such as a good education, satisfying career, and family unity is the cornerstone of success, not the conjured fantasies of easy money, easy sex, and easy living.

As I left the boys' conference, a cloud of sadness began to engulf me. I wondered what I could have done differently, and questioned the effectiveness of my redefining success for them. What could I have done to convince them that being intelligent and educated was indeed "cool," and healthy goals to strive for? In addition, these kids had made it clear during an open discussion what they thought was important: SEX.

Young people learn about sexuality by observing the adults in their lives. I pondered whether it was a good thing for children to learn from adult rappers, or even to pattern their behaviors after elite athletes who often feel that social laws do not necessarily apply to them.

Parents should never underestimate the impact that the love, affection, and security they provide have on their children. Affection within the family such as hugs, kisses, touching, and compliments makes children feel safe and secure. They form a genuinely positive respect for themselves, and their attitude toward sexuality becomes so much more than simply physical conquest. Positive family affection encourages a child to continue that behavior in their daily lives and further into adulthood.

Life can be difficult for blacks in general. In particular, raising black male children is often extremely tough due to a number of reasons, but one of the most important ones is overcoming our own style of interacting with them. It's easy to fall into the same pattern of talking to black male children that has been duplicated for years. That is, assuming that young black males should learn to fend for themselves and and that they require less affection and attention or a "firmer hand" than females. When single black women raise male children, strong male role models become especially important. Youth groups, mentoring programs, and athletic organizations are all places to find older black men who are realistic role models, not like those on television or the radio. As I said before, the Boys' Club that I joined early in my life played a key role in helping me to develop a sense of identity.

As all parents know, our children will someday repeat every word that we say. It is the same with behavior. Fostering healthy sexual development requires an understanding of ourselves and a dedication to communicating about the expansive nature of sex and sexuality with our young people.

After that fateful day with those youths, I decided to explore ways in which African American men could serve as models for the next generation, helping them learn about healthy sex, relationships, and family.

Two transformations must occur in order for black men to become good role models: changing negative attitudes into positive ones and changing unhealthy behavior. Changing attitudes is not as simple as it may sound. Much has occurred historically to contribute to why black men feel and think the way they do. A person who is stressed out and fears for his own survival feels bad about who he is as a person, so he is unable to project a positive image to others, let alone be a role model to young blacks. Anger, resentment, and aggression many times replace love as reactive emotions working alongside negative attitudes, which only compounds the black man's inability to be a role model for his children. Sexual gratification is often used as an outlet and is substituted for love or the temporary release of negative attitudes when the black man is under the gun of social oppression. Sexual gratification is often used as an outlet or escape valve for the release of negative emotions such as anger, aggression and stress. In some instances it can even be a substitute for the emotion of love.

For the most part, the attitudes of black males have hardened over the years. Because of increasing social burdens, men see themselves as less than perfect and subsequently sacrifice their families' needs in order to satisfy their own need to become more complete. People who feel that their dignity has been stripped away and their means to make a living reduced may regress to a more primitive state of behavior, acting on their emotions rather than looking for a positive solution to their situation. Negativity breeds negativity and since children are often viewed as an added economic burden instead of an added joy, they often face the wrath of an unhappy and socially challenged father. Having a positive attitude toward life instead of dwelling on the negative creates an atmosphere in which a loving husband and healthy role model can flourish.

This current negative trend is contrary to our past history when black fathers, many of whom were tenant workers, would have their sons accompany them to work. Not only did this aid the family in making more money, it afforded the father time with his son and the opportunity to be a good role model. These black fathers reinforced self-respect and proper work ethics. Without a father who is emotionally available and positively interacts with his children, how could the black family survive? Who will be the role models for our children if we do not consider the role of being a father positively?

In addition to suffering economically, black men many times find themselves at an educational disadvantage. An inadequate education can be an impairment in societal adult roles, and can also become a source of guilt, or more subtly, poor self-esteem. Due to a limited source of information, black men avoid dealing with their sons because they do not feel adequate. This negativity for oneself, in turn, reflects negatively toward the child.

A man wants to feel like a man in the eyes of his son, and when he does not, he may retreat and give up his role as a father.

The second transformation that must occur in order for a black man to be a role model is a change in behavior: he must act the way he wishes his son to act. How he interacts with others will both directly and indirectly affect his ability to be an effective role model. A man with a temperamental nature may act violently; this must cease and be replaced by love and calm. Primitive lustful behavior in the black man's relationship with women must be discarded and replaced with intimacy and healthier ways of exercising sexuality.

Studies show that black men lag behind other ethnic groups in achieving their socially economic potential due to limited educational preparation. Human beings naturally want to be perceived as smart and informed. For example, I was once amazed at how a stranger reveled in giving me directions to my destination when I was lost in a city, even though he did not know the directions either. Because he did not want to appear uninformed, he gave me false information and behaved oddly. Of course, I eventually found my way, but why did this stranger behave this way in the first place? Perhaps because he was unprepared for the question.

I also recall early in life that when I asked my father a question to which he did not know the answer, he became angry, as if to say, "Look, I don't know the answer to your question and because of that I should kick your ass!" Of course, I realized this almost immediately and I stopped looking to my father for answers. Perhaps if he had taken the time to say to me, "Son, I don't know the answer to that, let's look it up together and find out," I would have had more respect for the man who called himself my father.

Likewise, I have found myself in a similar situation with patients. When they ask me a question that I have difficulty answering immediately, for a split second I tend to feel inadequate. I have a tendency, like others, to overcompensate by aggressively showing what I do know. Recognizing this pattern has allowed me to disregard this primitive impulse and simply say "I don't know." Patients accept the response and all is well. I can honestly say that I have never had a patient stamp out the door because I could not answer his or her every question.

Black men who have a limited information base should not feel pressured, nor should they project their insecurities onto others. Limited knowledge can cause a person to fear what is unknown to them, and that fear can lead to anger. Children have such limited knowledge of the world around them that we must educate ourselves and become role models.

Anger as an outward extension of an inner fear is demonstrated in the biases and racist attitudes of a group of people when they have limited information about another group who may not share the same character traits. The group harboring the anger and hostility blames others for their differences and they are the ones who, in fact, possess the fear. Their fear can be attributed to ignorance, which is defined as a lack of knowledge. Fear is also felt by those who are the subject of racism. For example, many black men fear for their safety or feel that they may not meet the "social standards" of the racist majority. These fears can be translated into individual feeling of inadequacy or the fear of not feeling worthy enough to be a role model for a young black child. Role modeling cannot occur when there exists a veil of fear from within. It is necessary for black men to understand their fears and not hide them under a cloak of aggression, anger and self-doubt.

When I accepted the fact that I was inept when it came to maintaining a healthy relationship, the healing began to take place within me. When I began choosing not to hide behind my anger and machismo, I truly embarked on a more wholesome journey toward manhood. I even began to feel better about myself and it is now easier for me to be a positive role model for others.

How can black men begin to feel better about themselves? The answer is simple and was insightfully and succinctly stated by the famous actor-director-writer Spike Lee: "Do the right thing." Yes, black men should just start doing the right thing. Well-being can result from doing that which is good. The next time you feel gloomy, do something good for someone else. You can begin role modeling by doing very simple things that are unselfish. It doesn't have to be a major deed: simply give a dollar to a beggar in need of a meal and see how good you feel afterward. Unless a man is truly devoid of a conscience, there is a part of his self that always wants to do the right thing. If black men would commit to good and not evil during each waking moment, their lives would change dramatically, and undoubtedly, so would public opinion and stereotypes.

In order to be a role model, we have to project love inward and positively view ourselves as imperfectly human. No one is perfect and as black men, we must remember that our young children come into this world loving us unconditionally, with no expectations. It is through our own negative attitudes that we let our children down by not projecting ourselves outwardly to them. Young people need to know that no one is perfect in the world. When they know this, they are more equipped to cope with the obstacles that life places in their path. Once we accept and love ourselves, we can unselfishly extend this love to others.

Unselfish love creates a sense of brotherhood that spills over onto our young black children. They learn that a black man's actions should be exercised to benefit those around him and not to harm others. This is when the black man truly becomes a role model that exemplifies dignity, trustworthiness, and optimism for future generations. By definition, this is truly what brotherhood means; a concept that is gravely needed for African Americans to survive.

Brotherhood is not a new word in the culture of black men. If I may allude to a medical idiom for a moment, the concept of brotherhood is like a malarial fever that comes and goes and affects the person who has it profoundly. Like the fever, brotherhood has boldly surfaced and resurfaced in the history of African Americans, inciting enthusiasm that was followed by a period of apathy by many black men. Most notably, early accounts of the power of brotherhood can be traced to the late 1700s when a young black man named Prince Hall created a society of black men dedicated to the pride, dignity, and the education of black men; thus Black Freemasonry was started. They became the first truly organized brotherhood of role models for future generations. In the twentieth century, the Black Muslim and Black Power movements have encouraged black men to follow a positive path and to ensure the survival of black men and their families in America. The Million Man March moved black men to be more for their families, even though the enthusiasm generated in the black community from that march waned. Unfortunately, it seems as though nothing can capture the attention of every black man and convince him to be a role model; and nothing yet has compelled the majority of black men to love each other and to "Do the right thing."

THE "RIGHT THINGS" THAT ROLE MODELS DO

A role model is a person who exhibits behavior that one would want to emulate. The behavior is based on proper manners and good intentions and reflects many virtues like honesty, trust, and, most important, love. It has been said that a person should surround themselves with people that they wish to be like and this couldn't be more true. This is what we must teach our sons.

Since the purpose of this chapter is to discuss black males as positive sexual role models it is important to mention that up to now much has been said about the negative aspects of the black man's behavior, but they must be pointed out directly and not by metaphors. The truth must be told about what is really happening in the lives of black men.

Keep in mind that this is not a discussion about black adult males who teach their young sons how to better perform the act of sexual intercourse. That is not what sexuality is; if it were, I would be calling this chapter "Role Models for Sexual Intercourse" and that is not the purpose of this book at all. As a reminder from previous chapters, sexuality is the composite of the emotional, spiritual, and the physical makeup of the black man. It involves the way in which he sees himself as a man and how he relates to others. A healthy sexual image does *not* reflect the size of one's penis, but the size of one's ego. Sexuality in its most healthy state is self-less not self-ish.

Black males can do more to become better fathers, role models, husbands, and yes, even lovers by expressing their sexuality in improved ways. Perhaps the best way to explain healthy behavior with respect to sexuality is by sharing real life situations in which black men have demonstrated their sexuality as healthy, both upon initiating a relationship and through its developmental stages. These stories are true and somewhat provocative.

First and foremost, I changed the names to insure anonymity and by doing so I was able to conduct no-holds-barred discussions with those involved. Many of the black men opened up in ways that made even me flushed with emotion. Habitual and stereotypical behavior was revealed. In some cases, the interpsychic struggle of the black man to be unlike the sexual animal that society often perceives him to be came through loud and clear. Many resisted their inner inclination to be a "stud" and therefore can be considered positive sexual role models.

Some people may ask, "How on earth did you get a group of black men to open up in such a candid and sensitive manner?" My only reply is that I shared my own story with them, was nonthreatening, and, indeed, lucky. Being a black man also helped; however, the truth is that I used every professional skill I had to promote an open discussion with members of an ethnic group that is normally reticent about what goes on in their heads and I sincerely thank those who shared themselves with me.

I include four stories and each corresponds to the four phases of a relationship outlined in Chapter 3, "The Black Man in Relationships." The phases are: (1) attraction, (2) sex and infatuation, (3) barrier of control, and (4) the merging of selves. Each of the men, in my view, offered the best demonstration of positive role model potential because of the choices they made in exhibiting their sexuality.

STORY ONE: ATTRACTION— THE STORY OF MR. G

Mr. G is a thirty-five-year-old African American lawyer who is married and has two beautiful children. This story happened on his first day of law school and it is being told from his point of view and in many of his own words:

"I arrived to class early and sat in the last seat of the last row of the large amphitheater. I did this because it afforded me the opportunity to look down on the professor and the other students as they filled the large lecture hall. I also thought that being in the back was safe, because it was common knowledge that those who sat up front were subject to be called on to answer questions. I had struggled to get into law school and felt very insecure." As the steady stream of freshman students began to fill the seats, "she came in! Man! My heart didn't just skip a beat, it seemed to stop. This sister was fine like wine! She had that '60s look. You know, with the long dress and bedraggled hair?" However, her body was "kickin'" and it overshadowed the "Annie Hall" look she had about her. "As she paused to look around the lecture hall at the top of the stairs, just a few feet away from me, our eyes met. I have to tell you, I literally wiped the drool from my mouth and smiled. She was cool as ice and she returned my stare with what I thought looked like a cross between a smirk and frown, like she was thinking 'You ain't gettin' none of this, Bro!' "

She walked down the stairs towards the front of the class and "I thought that showed extreme confidence, but my focus was on her *ass*. "Her curvaceous, S-shaped back made her butt rise up and it looked like two large watermelons that alternated up and down as she walked carefully down the stairs. A warm glow developed in my groin and I realized that I had a hard-on.

"I suddenly began to recall how I had acted as a teenager and later in college. I had been a 'dog.' Anything in a skirt was subject to my sexual overtures, and anything *pretty* in a skirt, I had to have sex with. To tell the truth, that macho behavior didn't get me anywhere. I developed venereal diseases on more than one occasion and impregnated several girls. They had all undergone abortions, which I was not proud of.

"In my junior year of college, I had a spiritual awakening. After almost failing out of school, I met with a professor who was sort of a mentor to me. He said point blank to me 'Brother, what the hell are you doing to yourself? If you want to die, then go and jump off a bridge.' This man went on to say to me that I should be thankful for just being in college because other black men were stuck in the ghettos wishing for such an opportunity. He also said, 'Look at the way you're treating your sisters [other women], don't you realize that they *expect* black men to be 'dogs?'' An epiphany occurred; I cried openly and it was then that I vowed to change my ways. It was also around this time that I decided to go to law school. I stopped partying and began to show respect to those around me, especially black women.

"Embarrassingly, there I was, several years later and sitting in my law school class with a hard penis, disrespecting a sister—again! We didn't speak that first day and as time passed, I made a conscious effort to greet her with the utmost respect. I wasn't about to surrender to my old demons and fulfill the stereotype that my undergrad mentor pointed out. Whenever our paths crossed, I made it a point to look her directly in the eye and listen carefully to what she had to say. She was very smart, a fact that I later found comforting. She held her own in legal debates and excelled in class. I noticed her body less and less, and was quite frankly transfixed by her wonderful mind.

"We eventually became study partners, and to my surprise, I did not feel intimidated by her superior intelligence. I was proud of her! She made me feel great about being black and a man. Not once was I preoccupied with lustful thoughts while we studied. She seemed to enjoy the way I treated her and confided to me that I wasn't like the other guys who just wanted to 'jump her bones.' I started to see all women in a different light and found myself focusing on their minds, not their bodies, when I was in their company. I fell in love with my law school study partner and she with me. We married a day after we graduated and now are in law practice together. We have been together for ten years and have two lovely children, a boy and a girl. Every chance I get to teach the importance of respecting women to my eight-year-old son, I do. My wife and I talk to our children about looking at people in their totality and to treat others as they would want to be treated. By the way, in those quiet moments my wife and I have together when the kids are asleep, she nudges me in the side and says to me "Remember that first day we saw each other in class and you gave me that look? What were you thinking?" It is then that I hold her the closest and with a grin tell her, "I was thinking how very much I loved you."

STORY TWO: SEX AND INFATUATION— THE STORY OF MR. S

Mr. S is a fifty-one-year-old African American nightclub owner who is currently involved in a long-term relationship. He has four children from a former marriage and two grandchildren. This is how he told me the story, and with his permission I have reprinted it here:

"I've owned a nightclub for almost twenty years. My first wife divorced me after three years of marriage. I think she just could not adjust to the night-life scene. You know how that is. You know what is so ironic? We met in my club, so she know what I was all about. She always complained about the late hours I spent at the club. I guess that it didn't help that I came home drunk and with lipstick on my shirt [he shakes his head]. They called me 'King Gee' and I was the MAN!! Yeah, the babes all wanted a piece a me. I'd walk into the club and all eyes were on me. I coulda had any woman I wanted. Sure, I was hurt when she left me, but hey, life goes on. Anyway, after a lot of years living like that I began to slow my roll [slow down]. I even was in two rehabs for alcoholism and one of those babes' boyfriends got jealous and shot me! That's when I realized that I was livin' too fast. After I slowed down and relaxed, I was just concerned about running a good business. You gotta stay sober and away from the women to do that, y'know?

"I can remember the night I met the woman that I'm with now as if it were yesterday. I was in my office at the club doin' some paper work when I glanced through the two-way mirror onto the dance floor. That's when I first saw her. She was there socializing with a group of girls but she really stood out. She had this glow about her and was graceful and beautiful, but what I noticed the most was that she looked so confident. I left the office and went over to her with the intention of not only meeting her but of having her as my woman. I was really taken in by her seductive smile and after talking awhile with her, realized that she was focused and very smart. I was, y'know, intimidated at first, because I found out she was in college and I barely finished high school. She didn't even seem impressed when I told her that I owned the club. After beggin' her for weeks, she finally agreed to go out with me. We had sex and I found out she was a 'freak'. She had my 'nose' [attention] after a month and I had to have more. I didn't ever get into any deep conversations because I felt insecure. But in bed, yeah, I was "the man"! I thought that was enough, boy was I wrong. I didn't think she'd ever leave cuz I was "the man." I felt dominant and started to get real possessive. When she did not show up at the club, I'd call her. When she didn't answer, I'd show up lookin' for her at her job or school. I was out of control. . . . Sheesh, she even called the cops once and said I was stalking her. My friends said I was pussy-whipped and since my dick got hard every time I thought of her, then I probably was.

"I never even told anyone how I really felt during this period in my life. When I was with her, I felt so important. Here I was, a mid-dle-aged man with a young, smart babe who gave me good sex. Since she kept havin' sex with me, I thought I had her under my control. This was the good times I thought. I had a bad feelin' though. I thought that if I didn't control her that she would pack up and leave. I was scared, and without the sex I didn't think she would love me.

"I didn't see her for weeks because she was avoiding me. But she called one night out of the blue and invited me to supper. When I got to her house, she looked different. She looked so proper, like a teacher, and had her hair rolled back . . . even had those granny glasses. She had traded her sexy clothes for the schoolteacher look. She hesitantly smiled when I sat on the couch. I didn't want to mess this up. Then she said to me, 'You know G, why is it that I make you feel so insecure when we are together?' I couldn't say anything, I just looked down at the floor. She said, too, that my fear of losing her had made me a crazy man and she couldn't deal with that. 'The fact is, I do love you for who you really are, not this monster that you don't try to be, but seem to become when you feel insecure. G, you have a lot more to give then just . . . sex.'

"We talked for several hours that night and for the first time I began to see her as a woman instead of focusing on her in a sexual way first. She was sensitive and very patient with me because she loved me. I actually talked about how I really felt and listened to what she said. I wasn't threatened anymore, and suddenly, she became less of a sex object and more of a love interest. That was ten years ago. We're still together and are going to get married next month. Oh yeah, and I went to college, too. She encouraged me and I'll be graduating in a year. Hey Doc, I want you to be there."

STORY THREE: THE BARRIER OF CONTROL— THE STORY OF MR. T

Mr. T is forty-five years old and now in a healthy relationship. However, before his marriage, an incident occurred that changed his life. He told me the following story, which is paraphrased and quoted directly from our conversation.

"When I first met this girl, I was a successful CEO, thirty-nine years old, and she was my receptionist and twenty-one." In the beginning he was very attracted to her beauty but later he found her

clerical skills to be even more appealing. "She was young and inno-
cent, and was obviously socially naïve, particularly when it came to
men." Her skills helped her to move up in his company, and soon she
became his personal assistant. "Up until then, I had always tried to
keep my personal life separate from business, but after one year I invited her to a Christmas party. She drank a lot until she became tipsy
and on the way home she leaned over and gave me a wet kiss that
sent chills through me from head to toe." He walked her to the door
and she invited him into her apartment. At first he was somewhat reluctant to go in because he didn't want her to think he was taking advantage of her. "We made love that night. It was snowing and I
remember clearly what she said to me: 'This is the first time that I
have been with an older man.'" She shared this with him during intense lovemaking that lasted into the morning. "As I penetrated her
deeply she moaned and called me 'daddy,' and this increased my excitement of being in control. She cried in my arms and told me she
loved me. Ironically, I later chuckled, and to be truthful, I was more
moved by my feelings of power over her than her words of love for
me."

He made her promise to never divulge their little secret, and of
course she agreed because she wanted to be with him. "I told her it
was bad for business and that it may even jeopardize her position at
the company." Using this threat, he managed to manipulate her into
thinking that her job would be in jeopardy and that her silence was
merely a part of her job. He went on to say, "I was surprised that
things were going so smoothly. No one even knew that I was sleeping
with my assistant. The fact that I could have her when I wanted to
made me feel even more powerful. Everything was on my terms. I
just ignored her feelings completely."

When she would go into his office, he would put his hand on her
butt or feel her breast if the mood hit him. "I really didn't care if she
liked it or not, and she was powerless to object. One day while she
was bent over the fax machine sending out documents, I came up
behind her and slid my hand up her dress. Startled, she stood up and
turned toward me, looked me straight in the face and with tears in
her eyes, and said, 'I've had enough of your bullshit . . . I quit.'

"I was shocked and even angry when she walked out the door and
told me that she would be suing me for sexual harassment." He

thought that he had everything under control and was sure that their "secret" and the threat of losing her job would keep her quiet. Also, he was convinced that she would never go through with her threats. "I was so wrong, and found myself in court defending my actions.

"My only defense was that we were lovers, and that the behavior I displayed was just playfulness and was harmless." During the suit, she told the judge that since she had allowed him to make love to her he thought it gave him the right to do whatever he wanted. She felt that he no longer respected her as a human being. She went on to say that all he wanted to do was have sex with her. "She said that my control over her made her emotionally unstable and that she feared me. She had even begun to see a therapist." This enraged the judge who later found him guilty and sentenced him to serve ninety days in jail, ordered him to pay a hefty fine, and awarded her several thousand dollars in the suit. "In his closing statement, the judge said something to me that I'll never forget. He said, 'It saddens me greatly to have you before me, an intelligent and professional black man and certainly not the norm for this court. You should be ashamed, some role model you are. You, sir, are spiritually inept and disrespectful; don't you think it's hard enough trying to get people to respect you? The label "sexual predator" is not something that you should be proud of. How dare you take sexual liberties with this woman.' I was embarrassed that in a courtroom full of people, a white judge would say that to me. You know something? He was right.

"While I was incarcerated for what seemed like forever, I prayed and pleaded for God to forgive me. I can't say exactly what happened, but I finally achieved atonement. Although it was too late, when all was said and done, I did feel love for the woman who put me in jail, but was unable to show these feelings to her. I had disappointed others and myself, and was now suffering the consequences. I wrote her a remorseful letter and asked her to forgive me. I wasn't surprised when she never answered the letter."

That experience changed this man forever. He subscribes to being a moral and sensitive man and sought help to assist him in changing. "It was hard to learn why I behaved like that, but to this day, I have not tried to control another women, much less another human being."

STORY FOUR: THE MERGING OF SELF—
THE STORY OF MR. O

Mr. O is a twenty-seven-year-old man who has been in a relationship for five years. He is a chemist for a large pharmaceutical company and has two children from a former marriage. This story is true and told from his own experience.

"To get in shape I enrolled in an aerobics class and she was the instructor. Right away I wanted to meet this girl. I have to tell you, she wasn't the best-looking woman that I had ever been with but she seemed pretty confident, had a great body, and that turned me on. I've always been told that I am pretty attractive and have never had problems with getting a woman; however, keeping them was another story.

"You know, I was a charmer but really pretty self-centered. I think the reason was probably because I felt intellectually superior to most of the women I dated, and even tried to intimidate them by talking to them about things they knew nothing about. Looking back, women always seemed to leave me because they felt insecure about this and I'd always found myself alone. In fact, the day that I met the aerobics instructor I had just come out of a relationship and had promised myself that I was finished with women. I was working on my dissertation and really didn't have the time to deal with nonsense anyway. I made my studies a top priority.

"Anyway, this woman was really exceptional and had all the right stuff. It was rumored that she was a 'freak,' just shy of promiscuity and relationship indiscretion that could have scarred her reputation at the club, but I chalked these innuendoes up as frivolous 'jock talk' that men do at these clubs when they see a fine, independent woman with a great body. When we met she came across as assertive and focused, a posture that made me nervous. Since I did not have the control, but since my intentions were only for friendship, the feeling of powerlessness didn't bother me much.

"She had just come off a bad relationship too, one in which her kindness and love had been taken for granted. The rumors about her spread by people who did not know her appeared to bother her less than they did me. When I would question her of the authenticity of this talk from other men she would neither confirm nor deny it. She would say that she did what she did to emotionally survive and didn't give a damn what anyone said or thought about her. 'And as for those men at the club,' she retorted, 'they can kiss my nice, round, muscular butt.' I had never seen this kind of arrogance in a woman and found myself very attracted to her, but thought being romantically involved with her was undoubtedly another real challenge to my macho ego, and quite frankly I was not sure if I could cut the mustard. Was it possible for two strong willed individuals to make it together? I wondered.

"We began to see each other and seemed to get along very well. I was able to intellectualize without her feeling intimidated and she asserted herself both in conversation and behavior in a way that made me admire her even more. Our once-a-week encounters blossomed into our seeing each other every day and finally we made the decision to move in together.

"As the relationship grew I noticed that after a year we had both changed. I had begun to shed that masculine facade that hid my inner fears and begun to trust her. She then began to show me a more loving and softer side of her personality that I initially thought was not present because of the cavalier "Joan of Arc" attitude and image she projected to everyone else. We became one, and as our love grew so did we. It was as if we could read each other's thoughts. As a result of this harmony we accomplished a great deal, more than I had in any past relationship. Our chores and tasks of the union were not role-dominated and because of the respect and love we felt for each other we eagerly did what we could to ensure each other's happiness. Because of my relationship with her I was able to breeze through my studies to finish the dissertation. We were married after she completed her first year of medical school. That was five years ago."

Each of these stories illustrates how black men have become good role models, particularly in their relationships where sexuality and perception of a sense of self were tested. The four men confronted their own conscious assessment of what a healthy man should be and how a woman should be treated. Each confronted his respective demons and resisted a seemingly inherited ugly nature to overcome the negative stereotype of the black man. Once they decided to do the right thing each made a conscious effort to change his behavior and attitudes, and most important, they forcibly challenged public expectations of them to be sexual predators. Mr. G, the law student, realized that being attracted to a woman need not be rooted in lust. Mr. S, the night club owner, found out that he had to loosen his tight grip on love in order to flourish in his relationship. Once he came to terms with his own insecurities he began establishing a healthier relationship. Mr. T, a successful businessman, had to go to jail before he could conduct himself as a healthly male; fortunately he learned the lesson that power and control in a relationship only fuel negative myths about black men. Finally, Mr. O surrendered his fears of love and was able to receive the best gift of a relationship: the merging of oneself with another human being.

Chapter 12

THE SURVEY RESULTS AND SUMMARIES

Life has been your art. You have set yourself to music. Your days are your sonnets.

—Oscar Wilde

This chapter contains the results of a survey that was administered in an inner-city Harlem neighborhood (New York City) and also in an inner-city section of Philadelphia. The implementation of the survey to black men was no small task. Not all of them agreed to participate and a large portion who answered the survey did so reluctantly and with much skepticism. A convenience sampling of black men was utilized in both cities and several paid workers ventured out into their communities to ask black men specific questions about sex. In order to qualify for the survey, the men had to fit a predetermined profile. More than 500 black men were surveyed and fewer than 400 were suitable for discussion. Those surveys that were not included for interpretation contained incomplete answers, unintelligible responses, or were age-inappropriate.

My initial intention was to create a sex study unlike any that has been done before. A study that would be complete in its inclusion of only black males, a group that has heretofore been either impregnable or virtually ignored by social scientists. Even Kinsey and Hite barely skimmed the surface of the deeper recesses of the black man's psyche.

My original intention of conducting a nationally representative survey of black men was thwarted because of the money and time that was necessary for such an undertaking. Remarkably, major industrial and educational foundations were reluctant to participate, not because it wasn't a worthwhile project, but because they had never done extensive personal research in the black male population. Some even deemed it "politically incorrect."

Nonetheless, many wonderful people collaborated with me on this project. They are professionals and dear friends of mine who supported my efforts wholeheartedly and whose moral and spiritual support added to the breadth and depth of the final results. They often guided me through the maze and minefield of incendiary content matter and insisted that I focus on what was best and most appropriate for you, the reader. I feel that not to mention them now would be just short of an insult including even perhaps a slap in the face of my higher power.

First and foremost, I must mention my life companion, Brenda A. Ford-Smith. As my personal research assistant, she was invaluable in the preparation of not only the survey instrument, but also the entire book. Her efforts of coordinating the focus groups, supervising survey administration between New York and Philadelphia, managing the surveyors, creating a database, and compiling research for the book's publication was nothing short of sensational. In addition to her overall supervision and support of me, she also worked as an editor for the project and is my biggest fan. Brenda and I are wonderfully committed to one another and I love her with all of myself.

Second, I must mention my good friend and colleague, Mark De-Haven, Ph.D. His never-ending enthusiasm and insight during our collaborations, not to mention his linear thinking, has been wonderful. Dr. DeHaven assisted with the inception of the survey instrument and provided the descriptive analysis of the results. I met Dr. Mark DeHaven when he was a professor at the University of Florida. While I was finishing a residency in family medicine, he befriended and aided me in becoming a researcher and, also perhaps, a better clinician. His expertise is that of a true researcher and epidemiologist and his current appointment is Vice Chairman and Professor of the Department of Family and Community Medicine at the University of Texas, in Dallas. Also included in this project was Mr. James Wadley, Director of Sexual Studies at the University of Pennsylvania. Mr. Wadley helped to establish the survey and provided a clear-sighted analysis of the results. He is a gifted young man who has completed all of his course work for his Ph.D. His interpretation of questionnaire responses added circumspection and a unique difference of perspectives.

THE SURVEY

Sexuality research presents numerous obstacles to survey researchers and there is no consensus regarding how best to undertake projects that focus on sensitive topics. Ideally, it is desirable to use probability sampling techniques to gather survey data whenever possible. These techniques ensure that the sample of respondents from the data that are gathered are representative of the larger population from which they are drawn. However, so little is known about the attitudes of black men in the area of sexuality that it is possible to consider the survey to be exploratory. As an exploratory study, the survey of black men can reasonably employ a nonprobability technique, since its objective is to begin describing these attitudes rather than to present definitive information about all African American men.

In the area of survey research, the idea of using nonprobability techniques to gather data on sexually explicit matters is not without precedent. The landmark study of sexuality of American women conducted by Kinsey et al. (1953) was not representative and the data were obtained through personal contacts, volunteers in organizations, and other nonscientific means. Similarly, magazines and personal contacts provided the information for the Redbook Report on Female Sexuality (1977) and the Hite Report (1981). As in the preceding studies, the data reported here were gathered from a convenience sample of African American men. Although this approach limits a generalization of the findings, it nonetheless provides tremendous insight into an area where practically no information currently exists.

Characteristics of the Black Men Who Were Surveyed

Complete information was gathered on a total 329 respondents. The average respondent was relatively young, with about 62 percent being under the age of thirty-five and 93 percent between the ages of sixteen and sixty-four. More than half of about 54 percent—responded that they had never been married, while almost 29 percent were married at the time of the survey. More than three-fourths of the sample were heterosexual (78 percent) and about 18 percent considered themselves to be either homosexual or bisexual. Additionally, the group was mostly educated, with about 46.2 percent responding that they had a high school education and about 43 percent having some college or beyond. Almost three-quarters of the respondents reported a having personal income in the last year of below $30,000.

A Description of Their Attitudes and Behaviors

Respondents were asked numerous questions related to sex and sexuality, women and love, and relationships and family. Many of the questions asked respondents to indicate the amount of agreement with the statement being read by the interviewer using a 5-point Likert scale. Although there were minor variations on some of the questions, in most cases the response categories were 1 (strongly disagree), 2 (disagree somewhat), 3 (neither disagree nor agree), 4 (agree somewhat), or 5 (strongly agree). In some of the following discussion the mean response is reported, and is calculated as the arithmetic average of all of the respondents combined on a given question. Thus, the higher the mean score the more the group tended to agree with the statement. Conversely, items with a relatively low mean score indicate general disagreement with the statement. Finally, a mean score of 3 would indicate that the sample of respondents was relatively ambivalent about the statement and had no strong feeling one way or the other.

Main Survey Concepts

Family

The survey asked two questions related to family life, specifically parenting. One asked respondents whether being or becoming a parent was important to them. The mean for this item was 4.3, indicating that on average respondents agreed pretty emphatically with the statement. For a related statement, that both sexes could take care of children equally well, the mean was 4.2, reflecting the general belief that men and women are capable of sharing child-rearing responsibilities.

Relationships

The questions dealing with relationships focused on marriage and fidelity, and the responses suggest a degree of tolerance for extramarital sexual relationships among the sample. About 37 percent of the sample disagreed strongly with the assertion that having sex outside the marriage enhanced their relationship at home; an additional 14 percent disagreed somewhat. However, the remaining respondents were either ambivalent (20 percent) or tended to agree with the statement (29 percent). Similarly, only 53 percent of the sample felt that a married person having sex with someone other than their spouse was always wrong. Some thought that it was almost always wrong (16 percent), but almost a third of the sample were either ambivalent or disagreed with the statement.

Were you unfaithful in past relationships?

When reading the responses to the black male survey, it was interesting to see just how the black men answered this question; I'm certain a few eyes will open wide. There is a joke, "When little boys and girls were in grammar school, the girls went to health classes and the boys went to acting class so that they could learn how to lie and deceive the opposite sex." This, by no means funny, actually occurs in real life to some degree.

Love

Generally speaking, respondents tended to feel that love was something worth experiencing. When asked whether it is better to love and be hurt than not to know love at all, 63 percent either strongly agreed or agreed somewhat, and the mean score for the group was 3.8.

The value that the respondents placed on love was also reflected in responses to the question about whether love made you feel weak or inferior. Only about one in five respondents (20 percent) felt that love was an indication of weakness.

Women

When it came to their relationships with women, most of the men in the sample felt that they treated women appropriately, either most of the time (48 percent) or all of the time (34 percent). The mean score for this item was 4.1. Regarding sexual relations with women, although the mean score was 3.0, about 40 percent agreed that a woman had an obligation to have sex with her partner. Almost identically, 42 percent of the sample believed that men have greater sexual needs than women, although the mean score on the item was only 3.1.

Sex

More than half of the respondents (54 percent) agreed strongly or somewhat strongly that sex and intimacy are two different things. Almost six out of ten respondents (58 percent) felt that sex included both pain and pleasure. The greatest level of agreement related to sexual activity was on the issue of what is acceptable between consenting adults. The vast majority of respondents (79 percent) agreed strongly or somewhat agreed that any kind of activity is acceptable as long as both persons participate freely. The mean score on this item was 4.2.

The second area that exhibited a high level of agreement was related to ensuring that one's sexual partner had an orgasm. The mean score on the item was 4.1, and 75 percent agreed strongly or somewhat agreed that they always try to make sure that their partner has an orgasm during sex.

A final area addressed by the survey was that of autoerotism. When asked about how often they masturbate, the largest response category was some of the time (45 percent), followed by none of the time (40 percent) and frequently (15 percent).

Sexual Development

When asked how old they were when they had sex for the first time, the ages given ranged from two to forty-seven years. On average, men in the sample had sex for the first time when they were about fifteen years old. In order to learn more about development, questions were asked in three broad areas related to how respondents learned about sex, and why and with whom they had sex for the first time. The men were asked to select from a list of responses all of the ways in which they had learned about sex. The three most popular responses were from peers (67 percent), from family (42 percent), and from the media (37 percent).

Respondents also were asked the main reason why they chose to have sex for the first time. Among the categories listed, the one most chose was that of being curious and ready for sex (41 percent). This was followed by the category of having affection for the partner with whom they had sex (19 percent) and peer pressure (13 percent). The survey also asked about their relationship to the person with whom they had sex for the first time. The largest percentage of respondents (35 percent) had sex for the first time with someone they were in love with but not married to or someone they had just met (11 percent). Approximately 5 percent of those surveyed had sex with their spouse after the wedding.

Sexuality

The survey also asked respondents who they were mostly attracted to; men, women, or both. The vast majority indicated that they were sexually attracted to only women (74 percent) or mostly women (8 percent). However, a sizable percentage indicated being attracted to both women and men (11 percent), and 7 percent admitted being attracted mostly or only to men. When asked whether they had ever had a homosexual experience, 28 percent admitted that they had. The top three reasons given for having had sex with another man were being curious or ready for sex (26 percent), having affection for the sex partner (24 percent), and being under the influence of drugs and alcohol (13 percent).

Anger or Abuse

A series of questions was asked intended to gauge the types and relative prevalence of abusive behavior engaged in by those in the sample. Less than 20 percent of the respondents engaged in abusive behavior involving ridiculing or insulting women, criticizing their mate, intentionally humiliating their mate, or behaving violently around or toward their mate. The abusive behavior admitted to by the largest percentage (53 percent) was that of ignoring their partner's feelings. About 27 percent of the respondents also admitted harassing their mate about suspected sexual affairs.

Impotence and Sexual Dysfunction

The group generally reported good health, with about 8 percent indicating having been treated for impotence at some point in their lives. To varying degrees, respondents had experienced different forms of sexual dysfunction. About 53 percent had experienced coming to climax too quickly at some time during their lives, and about 40 percent had felt anxious about their ability to perform just before having sex. Additionally, about 27 percent had experienced a lack of interest in having sex and an equivalent number had experienced trouble achieving or maintaining an erection. Fewer than one in five had ever been unable to come to a climax.

The Relationship between Age, Attitudes, and Behavior

The way in which respondents answered some of the survey items appears to be related to their age. Thus, it is possible to speculate that among African American men, attitudes toward sex may be affected by maturation. Subgroup analyses were conducted comparing the attitudes of men twenty-four years of age or younger (41 percent of the sample), with those who were older than twenty-four (59 percent of the sample). The mean score on the survey items was calculated for both age groups, respectively, and a statistical test was performed to determine whether the mean scores of the two different groups were significantly different. Significantly different in this context refers to a statistically meaningful difference.

Although there was very strong agreement overall with the statement that becoming a parent was important, the older men scored significantly higher on this question (mean score: older, 4.4; younger 4.0). Indeed, close to 70 percent of the older men agreed strongly with this statement compared to only about 54 percent among younger men. A similar difference was detected in the question dealing with caring for children, but the difference was in the other direction. When asked whether both sexes could take care of children equally well, the older men's mean score of 4.0 was significantly lower than the 4.4 score of the younger group.

The two groups were also significantly different in their attitudes toward relationships with women. For example, only 11 percent of the older men agreed strongly with the need to earn more money than their partner compared to 26 percent of the younger men (mean score: older, 2.4; younger, 3.1). The younger men also tended to think that men have greater sexual needs than women. Almost 50 percent of the younger men agreed strongly or somewhat agreed with this statement compared to about 38 percent of the older men (mean score: older, 2.9; younger, 3.4). Finally, regarding whether men should initiate sex, about 34 percent of younger men either agreed strongly or somewhat agreed compared to about only 18 percent of those in the older group (mean score: older, 2.3; younger, 3.0).

The younger men also tended to have become sexually active at a younger age. Their average age when they first had sex was 14.0

years compared to an average age of 15.1 years for the older men. And finally, although the difference was not large in absolute terms, younger men tended to endorse more strongly the idea that any kind of sexual activity between adults is acceptable as long as participation is consensual. Their mean on this question was 4.3 compared to 4.1 for the men in the older group.

The following are some of the questions that were asked in the survey. If you would like a copy of the survey instrument in its entirety, please see the author's contact information.

Some insight into the survey analysis and some of the questions that were included in the survey:

1. How old were you when you had sex for the first time?

The responses of the black males in our survey seem to reflect most current reports indicating that adolescents are having sex at an earlier age than in past generations. Our survey results show that the younger males had their initial sexual encounter earlier than the older respondents. In general, a major percentage of people begin to form intimate relationships and to explore what they like and don't like in a sexual partner before or during adolescence. By the time men and women reach their senior year in high school, many have experienced some form of sexual contact. There is no clear explanation why this trend has occurred, but societal influences should accept some of the blame; media hype and sexual exposure have influenced the younger culture profoundly. Today's adolescents begin to form intimate ties with potential partners, tending to act out society's "script" for dating, which tells us how to act when we are with someone. For example, a man and woman meet; they exchange phone numbers; they talk on the phone; they decide to go out; and at the end of the date, they may kiss. The next time they go out, they caress and touch one another, and eventually have sex. I am sure in the inner city where most of our survey was conducted, the script is not that simple. Complex social scripts are sustained by boundary lines for personal space in the inner cities. It can be argued that some of the men who responded to our survey perhaps had no script and were victims of sexual abuse spawned out of spontaneous impulses and emotions. This assertion is based on the fact that more than a few of the men reported having their first sexual experience at or before the age of seven, prior to emotional maturity. Perhaps the questions concerning anger can shed some light on the subject of early negative emotional episodes. Many of the men checked more than four of the items that showed anger to be a presenting factor in their relationship. A few shared that their first sexual experience was given to them as a birthday present from their father.

Perhaps it may have been interesting if the respondents were asked, "What do you think sex is?" People interpret the word sex in so many different ways that it seems difficult to determine what exactly the respondents may have meant. The males who responded that their first sexual encounter was before the age of ten probably experienced inappropriate touching. Nevertheless, what they construed in their minds to mean sex has little bearing on the overall profound impact that whatever happened is still remembered—even today.

2. *What was the main reason you chose to have sex for the first time?*

People have sex for all kinds of reasons: to show affection, to earn money, to relieve boredom, and to assuage curiosity. Many of our respondents, particularly those who indicated that their first sexual encounter occurred between the ages of nine and twenty-one, said they were curious and ready to have sex. As boys become men and learn more about themselves and others, they naturally develop a curiosity to explore their sexual feelings by forming intimate relationships. Sex is advertised on billboards, television, the radio, in magazines, books, and discussed in barbershops—it's "all over the place." So the media and peer groups seem to be the primary source of information about what an intimate relationship should be.

With the apparent omnipresence of sex and sexuality in our lives, why are so many people ashamed to discuss the matter with their children? Knowing the facts may squelch their curiosity. Many schools teach the basic concepts of reproduction, and even sex education, but teachers may not talk enough about values, decision-making, contraception, and pregnancy, or they may be reluctant to discuss other issues related to negative behavior rooted in the curiosity of just having sex. Some schools even hand out condoms, and certainly this could be considered a good thing; however, it does not mean those students receiving the condoms are getting a proper education about safe sex.

When sexuality is not discussed at home or in school, it seems mysterious and people become intrigued about what all the hoopla is about—especially when they see sexy images everywhere.

3. *The first time you had sex, what was your relationship to that person?*

Not too long ago sex outside of marriage was always looked down upon. Today, with the sexual revolution, the easy availability of contraception, the women's rights movement, and even the *Roe v. Wade* decision, individual attitudes toward sex have changed drastically. Sex is now viewed as an activity to be enjoyed by single as well as married people, yet responsibility for this enjoyment has yet to evolve. This appears particularly true with many of the young black males who do not consider the consequences of teenage pregnancies or the dangers of sexually transmitted diseases. Almost 60 percent of the black men surveyed said that they were not married and did not know their partner well when they had their first sexual encounter. These findings indicate that there is an increasing acceptance of sex outside the context of marriage and that some men were willing to have sex with someone whom they did not know all that well. Young black men should get to know their partners more completely before they place themselves at risk. Take time to talk with your partner about your sexual histories before hopping in the sack with them.

4. *My sex partner must be an excellent lover or I will leave for another partner.*

Sometimes I am approached by people who say that they plan to leave their partner because they "don't know what to do in bed," or "don't know how to work it." I am saddened to hear these comments. When I ask these people if they told their partner what pleases them sexually, they respond "I don't have time to teach anyone anything," or that "she should just know." About one-third of the respondents in the survey indicated that they would leave and look for another partner if theirs was not an excellent lover. What these men fail to realize is that for each new relationship, they must be willing to teach their partner about what they find pleasing because their current partner may be different from their previous love. Communication is key. You have to talk with your partner and tell them what turns you on or off because they can not read your mind.

It is also important to be patient with your partner. Not everyone is as skilled or proficient in their lovemaking. I believe that good lovers know how to bring out the best in their partners. In fact, there may not be such a thing as a bad lover, only people who don't know each other's needs. It seems that approximately 45 percent of the black men in our survey have similar feelings to mine, since they reported that they would not leave their present partner to look for another lover.

Of these same respondents who would not leave, I am sure that many of them may consider sex to be a smaller part of the relationship compared to those who would leave because of "bad" sex. The males who seem to value the relationship over the sex may have a larger concept of intimacy, and how to incorporate sex into intimacy.

5. *Any kind of sexual activity between adults is okay as long as it is consensual.*

It may not be surprising that the younger males in our survey agreed with this question. Perhaps the traditional standards for what is right or wrong have loosened over the years. Nonetheless, most of our sample did agree with this statement. Healthy relationships are those in which both people are allowed to express themselves sexually without the fear of being judged or rejected. Sometimes when our partner asks to do something differently or to break the routine, we quickly reject their creativity, their imagination, and their individual sexual expression. These suggestions should at least be considered; however, it is also important to know your limits and to be able to convey your expectations to your partner so that you can continue to feel comfortable with them. Couples need to set up rules and boundaries for sex as well as be open to new and exciting things that you and your partner may come up with.

6. *I am a better lover after a drink or two.*

Because alcohol is a depressant, it relaxes people and helps them feel at ease. About 25 percent of our respondents support the notion that they are better lovers after a drink or two. Some males may enter sexual encounters feeling anxious or worried about many different things. Perhaps the need to fulfill the black-man-as-stud image occupies their thoughts and after getting high they find themselves more at ease and ready to enjoy an intimate moment.

The fact remains that black men would be much better off if they refrained from anything that alters their consciousness. Drinking alcohol impairs judgment. Those who drink and use drugs are less likely to wear condoms or to talk about the consequences of sex, and sometimes do things they can't recall, like not getting consent or committing rape. Alcohol and sex do not mix.

7. *How often do you masturbate?*

Someone once said that 99 percent of all people masturbate and the other 1 percent lie about it. According to this statement, it appears that 40 percent of the black men surveyed lie about it. However, some people clearly chose not to masturbate, either because they have been told that it is sinful, nasty, and disgusting or because they are simply not interested. Others believe masturbation causes nightmares and delirium, or have been told that it makes "hair grow on their palms." There are all sorts of beliefs and notions about masturbation and they all play in how we view ourselves as sexual beings and also how others perceive us.

From a cultural perspective, black men are inclined to believe that masturbation should not be substituted for having sex with a partner. Frequent masturbation is even viewed as one's inability to find a sexual partner and is considered to be only for the weak. This misconception of what it means to be a man prevents one from feeling positive about his body and learning how to please it. Masturbation is a way to explore the body and to learn about what does or does not feel good, which is helpful in educating potential partners. And by the way, I have never heard that masturbation ever resulted in pregnancy or "hairy-palm syndrome."

8. *I always try to make sure my partner has an orgasm when we have sex.*

Almost 75 percent of the black males in our survey indicated that they try to make sure that their partner reaches orgasm during sex. It would have been interesting to ask these same males how they do so, and how they can tell that their partner is actually having an orgasm and not faking. Perhaps the greatest blow to a man's ego is being told by his lover that he does not know how to please them sexually. The flip side to this is that some people get so caught up in pleasing their partner that they forget to convey to their partner how they can be pleased. Of course, this may not be the case with most black men, since women sometimes refer to them as "selfish lovers." Talking with your partner about what you like or dislike before sex and then teaching your partner what to do is essential for a healthy sexual relationship.

9. *Pain and pleasure go together in sex.*

Fifty-eight percent of the black males who participated in the survey indicated that pain and pleasure go together in sex. Does this mean that black men enjoy S&M? Does this explain why they are prone to violence? Or does causing another human being pain make one a "MAN?" Certainly, there are varying degrees of what is deemed "pain." A light spanking or tugging of the hair could be construed as pain by some, and as stimulating by others. Since everyone views pain differently, there is no real way to measure this outcome. However, it can said that since many black men statistically tend to be the aggressors, then they may often incorporate some level of pain into sexual encounters.

10. *Sex and intimacy are two different things.*

Fifty-four percent of the black males surveyed said that these two terms have different meanings. It would be interesting to follow these men to determine just how successful their relationships are. Perhaps they don't understand that sex may be a part of intimacy and intimacy can be a part of sex. The two terms are seemingly intertwined in that a man can feel a need to be intimate by lighting some candles, burning incense, turning on soft music, giving his partner a bath, then an oil massage, and having passionate sex because of the intimate setting that was created.

Twenty-seven percent of the males feel that sex and intimacy are the same. One could speculate that these men may be better lovers and more proficient at maintaining their relationships since they view intimacy as being necessary for good sex. They may be more creative while making love, more willing to communicate, and less likely to have sex without being intimately involved with their partner.

What's interesting about sex and intimacy is that when two people meet, they typically go to great lengths to be romantic and to show their potential partner that they are really interested in getting to know them. People work hard to create intimacy in their relationships. But as time goes on, people often lose interest and their motivation to create intimate moments with their partner. They begin to take each other for granted. Ideally, as hard as people work to establish a relationship, they should work equally hard to maintain it. Keeping the intimacy in sex and the sex in intimacy is necessary for relationships to flourish. More important, people have to be willing to work as hard as they did when their relationships were new.

11. *Has stress or pressure in your life interfered with your sexual activities?*

Over two-thirds of the black males who participated in the survey indicated that stress and/or pressure has interfered in their sex life at some time or other. They were also asked if just before having sex they felt anxious about their ability to perform. Over 40 percent responded that they did feel anxious before being with their partner sexually.

Black males carry a lot of baggage into new relationships. They can be dealing with unemployment, racism, and trying to provide for a family. In addition, they must live in the wake of sexual stereotypes: Some feel that they must have a big penis or be able to have intercourse all night. These stereotypes place restrictions on black men as individuals and keep them from expressing themselves as individuals. If black men are thought of as sexual predators and studs, then their intellect and passion to achieve economically, educationally, and socially are minimized.

12. *Have you ever come to a climax too quickly?*

Fifty percent of the black men in our survey responded that at one point or another in their lives, they reached orgasm too quickly. The problem is knowing how these black men define "too quickly." For example, did they consider twenty seconds, twenty minutes, or two hours as being too quick? These results could relate to the stereotypes and myths that many black males subscribe to. If they are unable to "go all night long," they may believe they are inferior sexual partners.

A little less than half the black males indicated that they have never climaxed too quickly. However, 70 percent of these men also responded that they never had trouble achieving or maintaining an erection. How could this be when in the preceding question, half of the same sample said that they did in fact have sexual dysfunction at one time or another. Whatever the reason for their sexual dysfunction black men must realize that help is available. If they can learn to divorce themselves from negative stereotypes that can prevent them from asking for help, they can overcome sexual problems and still be a "MAN."

13. *Do you find sex pleasurable?*

While the majority of the men said that they found sex pleasurable, one-third of our sample indicated that they did not. It would be interesting to ask the group that did not find sex pleasurable what they considered to be a "pleasurable" sexual encounter and whether or not they informed their partner that they felt unsatisfied.

14. *Have you ever had a homosexual experience?*

Surprisingly, over 25 percent of our males indicated that they had had a homosexual experience. What is interesting about this finding is that homophobia and heterosexuality are so enmeshed and entrenched in the black community that one would never expect that this many of the men have had a homosexual experience. Author Lynn Harris has written several books about the struggles of African American men to be truthful with themselves and their community about their sexual orientation. Harris captures the difficulty and the social barriers that exist within the black community because there are social stigmas for being anything other than heterosexual. Many men may fear that if they are perceived as being gay, they will lose the support networks they need to survive in American society.

15. *Both parents/both sexes can take care of children equally well.*

Although, the younger males answered this question slightly differently from the older men in our sample, 75 percent of all the males indicated that it was somewhat important for both parents to be equally involved in raising children. This is surprising because many people think that black men show little responsibility for their children by abandoning them, neglecting them, and just simply being "trifling." In addition, 77 percent of the black men in the study indicated that both sexes can take care of children equally well. Sure, there were some black men (3.4 percent in our survey) who believe that being or becoming a parent is not important, but the majority of men welcome parenthood and all of its responsibilities. It would be interesting to ask these men about the perceived barriers or stressors that may discourage some black men from taking care of their children. Also, it may have been helpful if we asked them what skills are needed to rear a child successfully.

16. *Men should always initiate sex / I must earn more money than my partner / Women are obliged to have sex with their partner.*

As I indicated in the survey review, these questions resulted in the younger males answering differently from the older ones. Since the equal rights' movements of the sixties and the push for more "egalitarian" attitudes, women have made great strides socially, economically, and politically. In addition, women have also made tremendous gains sexually: it has become more acceptable for women to ask men out on dates, initiate sex, and be sexually creative with their partners. When asked about their attitudes toward women, the black men who participated in the study reported some interesting things. Over 70 percent indicated that they did not believe that women should stay at home while a man earns the money. Similarly, 50 percent of the men disagreed with the statement that men should always initiate sex. About 34 percent of the respondents asserted that they must make more money than their partner, while 38 percent of the men reported that they did not. Also, when asked whether or not women have an obligation to have sex with her husband or boyfriend, 42 percent of the male respondents indicated that women are supposed to be ready upon the wish or command of her partner. On the other hand, 40 percent of the black male participants disagreed with this statement. These findings may be reflective of a growing acceptance of women as equals. Even though a large number of men still believe that men should always initiate sex, or that they should make more money than their female counterparts, our findings point toward an erosion of sexist attitudes.

17. *Extramarital affairs enhance my relationship at home.*

Some men assert that having relationships outside of their primary relationship gives them variety, spice, and adventure. In addition, there are a few women who may condone extramarital affairs because of the "shortage" of "good black men." Of course, doing so usually leaves them vulnerable and left emotionally shortchanged by not having their partner there when they need them. Men may believe in the double standard: it is okay for them to engage in extramarital affairs but they would never tolerate their women doing the same. Many black people have been involved in abusive relationships, infidelity, and overall neglect of their mates, which has resulted in the 67 percent rate of divorce. The loss of intimacy, poor social conditions, and erosion of individual creativity has left many black couples struggling to find answers to hold their relationships together.

When asked about extramarital affairs, slightly less than 30 percent of our surveyed males reported that they enhanced their relationship at home. I wonder if their mates knew of these other affairs. In addition, it may have also been helpful to find out *how* these other relationships enhanced their relationship at home. I present this question because when we asked the same black males what they thought about people who have sex with someone other than their spouse, 70 percent considered the people wrong. Finally, it should not go without mention that approximately 50 percent of the black males indicated that they disagreed with the extramarital affairs enhancing their relationships.

During the many focus groups, I talked about communication to help people practice the way in which they talk to each other about sensitive issues. This is still a very difficult area in my own life. I tend to close up when I feel pressured or pain about something. In addition, some people lack confidence in their partner's ability to understand what is really going on in their minds. We tend to underestimate the strength of our relationships and do not give our partner credit for the help they can offer or the benefit of the doubt. Also, some people lack the skills it takes to negotiate what they want out of relationships. They unwillingly yield to one another in hopes that things may get better or that doing what their partner wants will eventually allow them to do what they want. It is my hope that this survey will provide some insight into what black men are really thinking and feeling.

TERMINUS

Here I am, at the completion of a project that took nearly four years to write. Indeed, it has been quite a journey. In the beginning I knew that there was a story to be told, but I often wondered if it could be presented just as poignantly as it deserved. There were many hurdles that I had to personally overcome in order for these pages to be filled with these sentences of my life, as well as the lives of others. Perhaps the biggest daily obstacle to the book's success was the constant wondering if anyone would read it—and I thank you for the time you took to do so.

Having escaped the perils of inner-city living as a child and going to medical school in my late thirties, I found writing a book about the sexuality of black men to be an equal challenge.

The question I often asked myself was, "Should I be like the fly on the wall and only observe and record my findings about black men?" Certainly an objective study of other black men would be insightful and perhaps even beneficial, adding to a more complete understanding of the African American male psyche. This is mainly because most studies have tended to either exclude or generalize us in their respective sex studies. But I knew that it would not be enough. In order to make this book show reality as it truly is, I had to place myself in the middle—as one of those black men who had issues.

As a professional, I wasn't certain that I could do this, as I tend to want to keep my private life just that . . . private. I wondered if I could be open and honest as I was telling my story. Being a seasoned black man, I've had my share of bad relationships that included an inability to communicate intimately with the opposite sex. I struggled with revealing myself to the world, but I knew that if I did, many truths about black men could be told. Brenda, my partner in life, said to me one day, "If you are going to write a book about the difficulty that black men have in relationships and include yourself as an example of one of those men, I would want to read it because it's the way life really happens. In fact, if anyone has a story to tell, it would be you."

Brenda was right. What better example could I have than myself? Not too many years ago I was in the throes of nonsense in relating to women and now, after expecting more of myself, simply being a better person and companion, and having some success, perhaps I did have a story to tell. God only knows that now in my recovering life when I hear the complaints of women I meet both personally and professionally, there is not much that I hear that I cannot identify with. It is because of this that I have included myself in the book, so that perhaps I can help those men who still struggle in their relationships and offer insight to the women in their lives. By making a bold step in my life to become a better person for both myself and others was the key to a truly fulfilling life with another person. The truth of the matter is that writing this book assisted me personally as well. It afforded me the time to gain introspection and realize where I've been and just how far I had to go to achieve quality in my own relationship today. There were times during interviews with different black men when I had to pat myself on the back and say "What a job well done," or tell myself, "Whew! I'm glad that I'm not there anymore." Other times during the process of listening to the heartfelt stories of some men who were in failing relationships, I saw that I, too, was still making some of the same mistakes and had to stop and take a personal inventory.

All in all, the whole process was very cathartic and rewarding for me. I understand better the myths that affect us and the subconscious or subliminal way in which they propel black men to behave the way they do.

I know black women will read this book, but it is my hope that black men will read it as well, because it will only assist them in seeing their relationships clearly. Hopefully it will be as helpful to them as it was for me to write. Black men have suffered enough and hopefully this book can assist in the healing. Perhaps by reading this book black men can become better fathers, husbands, and lovers and black women can receive insight into the mind of the black man.

I would like to thank those individuals who assisted me along the

Current time: 10/29/2014,16:42
Pickup library: CHAVEZ
User name: MOORE, CELESTE MONAE L

way, especially the interviewers who worked to bring the book to fruition. And last, but definitely not least, to the couples, women, and black men who shared their private stories with me over the many years of my personal and professional life and allowed them to be told.

References

Akbar, Na'Im. "Paradigms of African American Research." In R. Jones, ed. *Black Psychology*. Berkeley, Calif.: Cobb & Henry Press, 1991.

Bagarozzi, Dennis A. "Family Therapy and the Black Middle Class: a Neglected Area of Study." *Journal of Marital and Family Therapy*, April (1960): 159–165.

Blassinggame, John W. *The Slave Community*. New York: Oxford University Press, 1979.

Butts, J. "Adolescent Sexuality and Teenage Pregnancy from a Black Perspective." In *Teenage Pregnancy in a Family Context*. Philadelphia: Temple University Press, 1981.

Cross, William E. *Shades of Black*. Philadelphia: Temple University Press, 1992.

Davis, G.L., and Cross, H.J. "Sexual Stereotyping of Black Males in Interracial Sex." *Archives of Sexual Behavior*, 8 (1979):269–279.

DeMarco, J. "Gay Racism." In M. J. Smith, ed. *Black Men-White Men: A Gay Anthology*. San Francisco: Gay Sunshine Press, 1983, 109–118.

Fenichel, Otto. *The Psychoanalytic Theory of Neurosis*. New York: W.W. Norton, 1995.

Gatewood, Willard B. "Aristocrat of Color: The Black Elite." *Journal of Southern History* 54 (1998):3–19.

Gutman, Herbert G. *The Black Family in Slavery and Freedom, 1750–1925*. New York: Random House, 1977.

Harris, E. Lynn. *Invisible Life*. New York: Anchor Books, 1994.

Hemphill, Esset (ed.) Beam, Joe (Contributor). *Brother to Brother: New Writings by Black Gay Men*. Boston: Alyson Publications, 1991.

Herek, Gregory M., and Capitanio, J.P. "Black Heterosexuals' Attitudes Toward Lesbian and Gay Men in the United States." *Journal of Sex Research* 32(1995): 95–105.

Hernton, Calvin C. *Sex and Racism in America*. New York: Anchor Books, 1992.

Holmes, William C. and Gail B. Slap. "Sexual Abuse of Boys: Definition, Prevalence, Correlates, Sequelae, and Management." *Journal of the American Medical Association* 280 (1998):1855–1862.

Hunter, Mic. *Abused Boys: The Neglected Victims of Sexual Abuse*. New York: Fawcett, 1991.

Johnson, Leanor B. "Blacks." In H.L and J.S. Gochros, eds. *The Sexually Oppressed*. New York: Association Press, 1997, 179–189.

Jones, Reginald L. *Black Psychology*. Berkeley, Calif.: Cobb & Henry Press, 1991.

Joseph, Gloria J. *Common Differences: Conflicts in Black and White Feminist Perspectives*. New York: Anchor Press, 1991.

July, William, II. *Brothers, Lust and Love*. North Carolina: Main Street Books, 1998.

Lourde, Audra. *Sister Outsider*. Trumansburg, N.Y.: Crossing, 1984.

"The More the Merrier: It's Going to Take Hard Work by All to Make the Greek Picnic Safe, Enjoyable and Profitable." (Editorial). *Philadelphia Inquirer*, August 28, 1998, p. A26.

Neal, A.M. and Wilson, M.L. "The Role of Skin Color and Features in the Black Community: Implications for Black Women and Therapy." *Clinical Psychology Review* 9 (1989):323–333.

Nobles, Wade W. (1980). "African Philosophy: Foundations in Black Psychology." In R. Jones, ed. *Black Psychology*. New York: Harper & Row, 1980.

Ramseur, H. "Psychologically Healthy Black Adults." In R. Jones, ed. *Black Psychology*. Berkeley, Calif.: Cobb & Henry Press, 1991.

Salzman, Shuster, West. (1996). *Encyclopedia of African-American Culture & History*. Simon & Schuster and Prentice Hall, Intl., 1996, 5:2419.

Schreier, Barbara A. "Moving Beyond Tolerance: A New Paradigm for Programming About Homophobia/Biphobia and Heterosexism." *Journal of College Student Development* 1 (1995):19–26.

Silverstein, Barry and Krate, R. *Children of the Dark* Ghetto: *A Developmental Psychology*. New York: 1976.

Staples, Robert "The Myth of Black Sexual Superiority: A Reexamination." *The Black Scholar* 9 (1978):16–22.

——*The Black Woman in America*. Chicago: Nelson Hall, 1973.

——"The Sexuality of Black Women." *Sexual Behavior* 2 (1972):4–15.

Tajfel, Henri. *Social Identity and Intergroup Relations*. Cambridge: Cambridge University Press, 1982.

Tajfel, Henri and Turner, J. "An Integrative Theory of Intergroup Conflict." In W.G. Austin and Worchel, S., eds. *The Social Psychology of Intergroup Relations*. Monterey, Calif.: Brooks/Cole, 1979, 33–47.

Troupe, Quincy. "Poem for My Father." In Boyd and Allen, eds. *Brotherman: The Odyssey of Black Men in America*. New York: Ballantine, 1996.

United States Bureau of the Census. *Household and Family Characteristics: March 1990 and 1989*. Washington, D.C., 1990, 6.

Weinberg, Martin S. and Williams, C.J. "Black Sexuality: A Test of Two Theories." *The Journal of Sex Research* 2 (1988):197–218.

Werner, Emmy E. and Smith, Ruth S. *Vulnerable But Invincible: A Longitudinal Study of Resilient Children and Youth*. Adams Bannister Cox Publishers, 1989.

White, Joseph L. and Thomas A. Parham. *The Psychology of Blacks: An Afro-American Perspective*. Upper Saddle River, NJ: Prentice Hall, College Division, 1984.

Wideman, John E. *Fatheralong: A Meditation on Fathers and Sons, Race and Society*. New York: Vintage, 1995, 4–5.

Wilson, Pamela M. "Black Culture and Sexuality." *Sexuality, Ethnoculture and Social Work*. 1 (1986): 29–46.

Wright, Richard. "Black Boy." In Boyd and Allen, eds. *Brotherman: The Odyssey of Black Men in America*. New York: Ballantine, 1996.

INDEX

whirling, 33–34
White, Joseph L., 5
Wideman, John Edgar, 165
Wilde, Oscar, 203
Williams, Serena and Venus, 121, 122
Wilson, Pamela M., 183
women, black
    black male anger and women's health is-
      sues, 108
    Black Power movement and treatment
      of, 17
    the black woman's perspective, 69–86
    communication and sexuality, 149–72
    coping with black male anger and abuse,
      115
    correlation between absentee fathers and
      black female disease rates, 96
    educated, 49
    as femme fatale, 53
    historical stereotyping of, 18, 36–37
    history and its role in determining how
      black men relate with, 50

    image of, 37–38
    raising black male children, 186–87
    religion and its influence on how black
      males treat, 48–49
    role models, 37
    role in raising fatherless children and
      keeping families together, 95,
      96–97
    STDs and sexually active women, 142,
      143, 144
    survey questions on, 208
    as target of black males unhealthy ap-
      proach toward relationships,
      12–13
women, white, black males and, 2, 19, 20–21
women's obligation to have sex with their
    partner, survey questions on, 221
Woods, Tiger, 121–22
work ethic, 116
Wright, Richard, 20